FOUNDING SOCIOLOGY?
Talcott Parsons and the Idea of General Theory

FOUNDING SOCIOLOGY?

TALCOTT PARSONS AND THE IDEA OF GENERAL THEORY

John Holmwood

LONGMAN
London and New York

Longman Group Limited
Edinburgh Gate, Harlow
Essex CM20 2JE, England
and Associated Companies throughout the world.

*Published in the United States of America
by Longman Publishing, New York*

First published 1996

ISBN 0 582 29165 8 PPR

British Library Cataloguing-in-Publication Data

A catalogue record for this book is
available from the British Library

Library of Congress Cataloging-in-Publication Data

Holmwood, John, 1950
   Founding Sociology? : Talcott Parsons and the idea of general
theory / John Holmwood
      p.   cm.
   Includes bibliographical references and index.
   ISBN 0-582-29165-8
   1. Parsons, Talcott, 1902-   .   2. Sociologists--United States.
   3. Sociology--United States.   I. Title.
   HM22.U6P36   1996
   301'.092--dc20   95-40206
                                                                    CIP

set in Times 10/12
Produced by 7

Produced through Longman Malaysia, LWP

CONTENTS

ACKNOWLEDGEMENTS

I should like to thank the following friends and colleagues whose encouragement and helpful comments on earlier versions of the book both improved it and kept me to the task: Bob Blackburn, Wendy Bottero, Sarah Caro, Dave Campbell, David Garland, Sarah Irwin, Desmond King, Greg McLellan, Rolland Munro, Martin Kusch, Ken Prandy, John Scott, Adam Seligman, and Janet Siltanen. I owe a special debt of gratitude and friendship to Sandy Stewart with whom I have collaborated for many years and with whom most of the ideas expressed in this book were developed.

INTRODUCTION

Talcott Parsons is one of the most important and most controversial sociologists of the century. Born in 1902, his first publications in sociology were in 1928 and he maintained a prolific output until his death in 1979. His work continues to generate passionate responses, but, as I shall suggest, these are often based upon a fundamental misunderstanding of what he was arguing. In particular, during the 1960s, his work was subjected to extensive criticism, most of it misleading, after which his work was dismissed and frequently used in a ritualistic manner as the summation of all that was deficient in a mainstream, 'positivist' sociology that had been superseded. Recently, however, there has been a revival of interest in his work by some of his erstwhile severest critics. Habermas, for example, argues that, "any theoretical work in sociology today that failed to take account of Talcott Parsons could not be taken seriously".[1] Turner goes further, suggesting that previous criticisms of Parsons have turned out to be superficial, representing "shifts in theoretical dialect rather than fundamental changes in discourse. Parsonian sociology is the dominant *episteme* and . . . the promise of a new domain of concepts has yet to be realised".[2] There has even been an explicit revival of Parsonsian sociology. Alexander, for example, has energetically promoted Parsons's work such that neo-Parsonsianism (or neo-functionalism) stands alongside, neo-Marxism and neo-Weberianism as a distinct position in contemporary sociological theory.[3]

If Parsons has returned to be a central figure in current debates, his work continues to be much misunderstood. It is something of an indictment of the discipline of sociology that the arguments of one of its major figures in the twentieth century remain obscure not just to the practitioners of other disciplines, but also to its own. I hope to remedy this situation in this book. The main reason for writing the book, however, is the intellectual challenge of presenting a new appreciation of Parsons's work and, in the process, contributing to contemporary theoretical arguments.

Part of my purpose will be to set out and evaluate Parsons's ambition to provide a general framework of theory which would serve as a secure foundation for social scientific inquiry. This scheme, he argued, must recognize the importance of human agency and the role of structure. With this framework Parsons sought to synthesize hitherto opposed approaches and, thereby, overcome the tendency of social scientific inquiries to polarize around the mutually opposed claims of 'structure' and 'action'. Taken together, he argued, these different, one-sided approaches seemed to imply a crisis in social scientific reason, with the field characterized by fragmentation and a consequent relativism. In contrast, it was Parsons's belief that the positive contribution of each of the different approaches could be incorporated in a single, coherent theoretical scheme.

Although most social theorists since Parsons have outlined their own undertakings in opposition to that of Parsons, I shall argue that many of his critics share his conception of the foundational role of general theory. My basic contention is that Parsons's general theory is fundamentally flawed and, indeed, that the very programme of general theory in sociology is mistaken. Although general theory is argued by Parsons (and others) to be necessary in order to ground empirical inquiry, it is evident from the fate of Parsons's scheme (and, indeed, the schemes of the current proponents of general theory) that it soon takes on a life of its own and becomes the object of seemingly endless elaborations separated from any programme of social scientific research. A division of theory and research was not what Parsons had intended, nor is it what those who follow the same route intend, but it is, I shall argue, a necessary consequence of the project of general theory. Indeed, for many, the current revival of interest in Parsons will have created considerable misgivings. It will be viewed as confirming the turn of sociological theory away from substantive, located problems of explanation and research, toward issues of 'meta-theory', or theory about theory. I share these misgivings. Certainly, these are the terms in which Habermas or Giddens address Parsons's work and, it is precisely as a 'meta-theoretician' that Alexander defends and promotes his contribution to current sociological theory. Given the broad acceptance of such a programme – or 'dominant episteme', as Turner calls it – the detailed criticism of Parsons's particular version serves a wider, and ultimately more important, purpose; namely, the criticism of the 'dominant episteme', itself, which has had such a hold over the sociological imagination.

Before I begin my detailed treatment of Parsons's theoretical scheme, I shall first set out the broad contours of theoretical debates in sociology over the last half century. My purpose will be to show a theoretical impasse where attempts at theoretical reconstruction have reproduced the very problems which gave rise to the perceived need for reconstruction. Fragmentation calls forth an attempt at synthesis, but each attempt at synthesis breaks down and is argued to contribute to fragmentation which, once more, is the occasion for others to claim the need for a synthesis. So, Parsons proposed a synthesis of 'structure' and 'action', but is argued by others to have contributed to their unsatisfactory division in which 'action' is displaced. This is the occasion for others to claim that a synthesis is necessary and the unproductive cycle begins again, but with less certainty that a solution might be achieved.

These are difficult times in which sociology increasingly appears to be beset by a crisis of confidence. There are major doubts expressed both about the meta-theoretical character of much sociological theory and its interest to anyone outside the confines of the academy. This crisis of confidence is bound up with the unsatisfactory nature of developments in sociology in the 1960s and since. Essentially, the extensive criticisms to which Parsons's work was subjected in this period gave rise not to a reconstruction of the sociological undertaking but to its further fragmentation and dissolution, of which postmodernism is the ultimate, deeply unsatisfactory, expression.

The hopeful optimism of Parsons's own attempted reconstruction of social theory is not reproduced in contemporary debates. In part, this is a consequence of the different circumstances in which he wrote. As I shall show in Chapter 1, for a brief period the audience for sociological argument appeared unified, such that the idea of a professional consensus around basic categories must have seemed plausible. Now, not only have sociological approaches fragmented, but their audience seems to have fragmented too, such that any claimed professional consensus now appears to be exclusive, rather than inclusive. In these circumstances, the relativism of postmodernism appears realistic and the foundational ambitions of general theorists seems, at best, unrealistic and, at worse, the totalitarian and exclusive undertaking that postmodern theorists criticize.[4]

Although the pretensions of general theory have recently been criticized by postmodern theorists, I do not believe that they offer any solution to our current problems because postmodernism entails a denial of any coherent explanatory undertaking in sociology. Ultimately, as I shall seek to show, it is no more coherent to attempt to ground different sociological undertakings in particular identities, than it is to seek a single coherence. What I propose in this book is a way through this impasse. While I shall offer an essentially negative judgement about Parsons's contribution to sociological argument, my concerns are entirely positive. As I shall show, the evident flaws of general theory do not render social explanation impossible, as postmodern theorists might suppose. Coherent explanatory undertakings, I shall argue, do not require a consensus upon pre-given categories which are foundational and beyond reconstruction. The self-evident failures of foundational general theory need not lead us to postmodern conclusions. My aim in this book, then, is to suggest, not only a new interpretation of Parsons, but a way of 'doing' sociology beyond the impasse of contemporary sociology.

If the current task facing social theory is to renew sociological argument and its contribution to public life, it is a task whose realization requires a detailed address to the issues that have formed contemporary theory and its problems. If no adequate solution to our current problems can be found in Parsons's work (or in the kind of theoretical undertaking with which he is associated), it remains the case that, as Habermas argues, his work is central to any proper understanding of *what our problems are*. For better or worse, there are few modern sociologists with a stronger claim than Parsons to have defined these issues for us.

NOTES

1. See J. Habermas, 'Talcott Parsons: problems of theory construction', *Sociological Inquiry*, 51(3), 1981, p. 173.
2. B.S. Turner, 'Parsons and his critics: on the ubiquity of functionalism', in R.J. Holton and B.S. Turner, *Talcott Parsons on Economy and Society* (London, Routledge and Kegan Paul, 1976), p. 200.
3. See especially his four-volume, *Theoretical Logic in Sociology*. J.C. Alexander, *Theoretical Logic in Sociology, Volume I: Positivism, Presuppositions and Current Controversies* (London, Routledge and Kegan Paul, 1982); *Theoretical Logic in Sociology, Volume II: The Antinomies of Classical Thought: Marx and Durkheim* (London, Routledge and Kegan Paul, 1982); *Theoretical Logic in Sociology, Volume III: The Classical Attempt at Synthesis: Max Weber* (London, Routledge and Kegan Paul, 1983); *Theoretical Logic in Sociology, Volume IV: The Modern Reconstruction of Classical Thought: Talcott Parsons* (London, Routledge and Kegan Paul, 1984).
4. See, for example, J-F. Lyotard, *The Postmodern Condition: A Report on Knowledge* (Minneapolos, University of Minnesota Press, 1984).

1

THE AGE OF SOCIOLOGY?

The work of Talcott Parsons has been subjected to sustained critical attack over the last few decades of sociological argument. These attacks were not directed at his work alone and, in the broader criticisms of professional social science, Parsons's view of sociology came to be assimilated to a position which he had initially opposed. In consequence, throughout the period, Parsons's theories have frequently been misrepresented and misunderstood. Yet, despite the almost universal hostility directed at his work, the current revival of interest in his theories is no mystery. The conditions in which he proclaimed his view of the role of sociology were similar to those currently associated with postmodernism. However, where these conditions, for many, seem now to presage the end of sociology, for Parsons they heralded a new 'age of sociology'.[1] In these circumstances, it is perhaps not so strange after all that those who are uneasy with the fragmentation (and nihilistic relativism) associated with postmodernism, should turn again to Parsons, or (where theorists retain their hostility to his approach) to positions which are not as far removed from his as they might suppose.

THE CURRENT CRISIS

A sense of crisis is pervasive throughout current theoretical discussions in sociology. On the face of it, this is nothing new. Crisis-claims have been a perennial feature of sociological debates and, arguably, crisis is a necessary condition of sociology as an undertaking. After all, sociology is an activity in the societies of which sociologists are themselves members. Such an activity could only make sense where social relationships lack transparency and that lack of transparency constitutes a problem for people in the conduct of their lives. Nisbet makes the point well. According to him, historically, sociology is a

1

product of the social dislocations that brought about the modern social order.[2] Sociology, he argues, emerged in response to the collapse of old political regimes in Europe at the end of the eighteenth century in the face of the rise of industrialism and demands for democratic political representation. In these circumstances, when traditional relationships were being transformed, sociology gave meaning to new social arrangements, discovering the 'order' that underlay what, from a 'traditional' perspective, appeared to be mere 'disorder'. Following Nisbet, Habermas argues that sociology has a special relation to crisis. "Sociology," he writes, "became the science of crisis par excellence; it concerned itself above all with the anomic aspects of the dissolution of traditional social systems and the development of modern ones".[3]

Invariably, talk of crisis was accompanied by claims for reconstruction and renewal, both socially and theoretically. Current discussions of crisis differ. Nowadays it appears that sociological theory has exhausted its potential for further insight and development. Seidman, for example, in a recent commentary on the state of sociological theory, writes that it, "has gone astray . . . unconnected to current research programs, divorced from current social movements and political struggles, and either ignorant of major political and moral public debates or unable to address them in ways that are compelling or even understandable by nontheorists."[4]

Seidman's judgements are not idiosyncratic. There does seem to be something particularly acute and distinctive about the current crisis in sociology. We do not lack social problems with which to engage. Turner and Wardell, for example, compare our current situation, where many Western societies are experiencing a crisis of the welfare state, with the problems of legitimacy exhibited by liberal states at the turn of the century.[5] They suggest that our social crisis should have had the same motivating significance for us that the problem of solidarity in a liberal republic presented to Durkheim, for example, but they conclude that, patently, it has not. Like Seidman, they complain that, "the core of sociological thought is failing in its relations with audiences that are outside the walls of disciplinary sociology."[6] Current social problems, various commentators imply, are urgent and pressing, but, apparently, they are beyond sociological reconstruction, at least as sociology is currently constituted.

Yet only recently it had all seemed so different and promised so much more. If Seidman's, or Turner and Wardell's, comments seem despairing it is because the substance of their criticisms was first made several decades ago as a prelude to a transformation of social theory which would address the very flaws they are now identifying and, in the process, would contribute to social renewal. Indeed, Nisbet's own interpretation of the historical conditions of sociology was itself part of that re-evaluation. It was indicative of a change in the way in which social theory was being addressed and it contributed to a more general sense that a shift in the substance of sociological theory, parallel to that earlier shift that Nisbet had analysed, was underway. The 1960s had seemed to mark a watershed in sociological theory where dominant paradigms of social science – what

Atkinson called the 'orthodox consensus' – were being challenged by 'radical alternatives'.[7] We are now coming to the end of several decades of critical self-reflection which began in the 1960s and which have culminated in our current sense of an impasse.

Where social theorists had initially looked forward both to a new theoretical order and to a new social order, it seems that the current despair is a reflection of the *failure* of the promised transformation(s). In these circumstances, any current crisis is *within* and *of* sociology. *Our crisis is our irrelevance to the current crisis of society*, reflecting, perhaps, a change in the very nature of society and social problems. Indeed, it is the claim of many theorists of 'postmodernity' that modern society has changed and that its substance is beyond the categories of sociology.[8] On this perspective, 'social integration' appears to be a sociological fiction and anomie a routine feature of postmodern social life. Ultimately, then, postmodernism offers the possibility that sociology is merely the discourse of modernity and with postmodernity comes not the continued requirement of sociology, but its displacement.[9]

SOCIOLOGY AS A PROFESSION

Prior to the radical shift in sociological sensibilities that took place in the 1960s, the dominant perception was that Western societies had entered a period characterized by an 'end of ideology'.[10] The defining ideological conflicts of early capitalism – essentially, between a bougeois ideology of 'radical individualism' and a socialist ideology of 'collectivism' – had, it was argued, lost their relevance in the 'mixed' and affluent economies and pluralistic political systems of modern industrial societies. As one of the foremost commentators on these developments, Daniel Bell, argued, "in the Western world . . . there is a rough consensus among intellectuals on political issues: the acceptance of a Welfare State; the desirability of decentralised power; a system of mixed economy and of political pluralism. In that sense . . . the ideological age has ended."[11] For some commentators – though not, it must be stressed, for Bell himself – it seemed that, with the end of the ideological age, political discourse could be reduced to issues of technical and professional expertise and the determination of public opinion through mass media and advertising. This was convenient because a growing demand for social scientific expertise had, as part of the political policy process, sustained the growth and professionalization of social science (especially in the USA).

These conditions favoured a conception of sociology in terms of value-neutral technical competence, in contrast to the ideologically engaged inquiries of classical sociology. Sociologists, it seemed, need not (indeed, should not) articulate a public position, nor claim their significance in relation to any particular values. The knowledge produced by social inquiries, it was argued, was independent and value-free, objectively warranted and available as 'expertise' to whomsoever had a use for it. Thus, associated with the end of the

3

'ideological age', was the view that 'ideology' would be replaced by 'science' and that a scientific sociology could bring an accumulating knowledge of the social world. Sociology should be 'post-classical'; like the natural sciences, it had progressed (or should have progressed) and left the 'classics' and their 'ideological' definition of issues behind.

According to this 'positivistic' view, the conceptual confusions and ideological controversies in which sociology was founded as a discipline would be dissolved. Like scientific knowledge in general, sociological knowledge can be left to accumulate. There was no place for a general theoretical undertaking, only piecemeal and gradual additions to knowledge through empirical research. On this understanding, then, there is a sharp distinction to be made between the history of sociology and its current task – between what Merton calls the 'history' and 'systematics' of sociological theory.[12] If later additions to knowledge look less dramatic than any earlier contribution, it is only because they have become more specialized and dependent upon 'institutional' settings, rather than 'personal' creativity. Individually, we are less than our forebears, but collectively we are considerably more. Even great figures are left behind, dwarfed by the scope and scale of sociology's progress.

Parsons did not share the positivistic definition of the sociological task with other 'end of ideology' theorists, and, in fact, his misgivings pointed to deficiencies in the project which were to dominate later discussions of social theory. Nevertheless, he did share their commitment to the professional status of sociology and he articulated a sophisticated justification of that status. In Parsons's version of the 'end of ideology' thesis, for example, the professions, in general, play a crucial role in the resolution of the 'individualism-socialism' dilemma that had characterized the earlier phase of capitalist development.[13] Despite their apparent monopoly of expertise, Parsons held that the corporate form of professional organization provided an ethical self-regulation of relations with clients such that any apparent monopoly operated in the general, public interest, rather than in the private interest of professionals themselves. In this way, he argued, the professions introduce an element of 'disinterestedness' into the organization of social activities against an earlier, predominantly commercial ethos of self-interest. These developments enabled a different understanding of the 'utilitarian', or self-interested, element itself, not as a *basic human motive*, but as a consequence of a particular type of *social structure*. Moreover, the social structure had changed to displace self-interest, without at the same time over-emphasizing the public activities of the state. The professions, then, were crucial in their role mediating the 'individualism–socialism' dilemma and had contributed significantly to the end of the 'ideological' age.

According to Parsons, the professions distinguished themselves from mere trades by virtue of the fact that their knowledge was based upon general university learning. The profession of learning was at the core of the professional complex and sociology, itself, had come of age into a new professional role. Parsons's claims represent a heady mix. For him, the 'end of ideology' presaged the 'age of sociology'.[14] Disciplines such as economics and psychology had reached maturity during the period of early and developing capitalism, brought forth by the requirement on the part of public authorities to understand the nature of the new forms of economic activity and their human costs which had been unleashed by capitalism.[15] With the transition to mature capitalism, Parsons argued, so problems of 'scarcity' recede to be replaced by the problems of 'affluence'. Indeed, as with postmodern theorists now, the decline of 'scarcity' was associated by Parsons with the identification of 'culture' as a peculiarly significant dimension of mature modernity. For Parsons, this is the era of sociology which, while it overlaps with the 'psychological' and 'economic' era, involves the recognition that the complexities of large-scale, or 'mass', society require an analysis that goes beyond individual behaviour and, therefore, beyond the individualistic assumptions of economics and psychology. Unlike Nisbet and Habermas, then, it was Parsons's claim that sociology derived its true force from the maturing of modern industrial society, rather than from the period of its birth (a claim which is implicit, for example, in the very status which Parsons attributed to the 1890–1920 generation of social theorists in his first major book, *The Structure of Social Action* (New York, Free Press 1937)).

Parsons was aware of tensions as the discipline of sociology confronted this new challenge of public relevance. The 'European' tradition in sociology had retained strong links with humanist social philosophy. However, this also meant that, implicitly, it was tied to a different, and less relevant, set of ideological issues than those that were emerging with mature, modern society. On the other hand, the 'American' tradition of sociology was tied to a pragmatic orientation to social problems, hostile to 'over-intellectualized' theory. The 'technical' sophistication of the discipline that had grown around this orientation, together with the hostility to theory, meant that it had distanced itself from any new public role. It was in this 'gap' between the 'European' and 'American' traditions that Parsons sought to define his own role, unifying them within the categories of a general theory which would thus provide a secure consensual basis for the discipline in its coming of age.

The security of this new basis proved short-lived. By the 1960s the dominant positivistic perspective on social issues had been shaken and displaced, but not by a new professional consensus. The post-war settlement had given way to division and new ideological conflicts. Indeed, almost simultaneously with the declaration of the 'end of ideology', other, more dissident, theorists were identifying the underlying contradictions of that 'post-ideological' order where new forms of 'exclusion' were producing the threat of a growing 'underclass'.[16] By the end of the decade, a 'new left' was ascendant, accompanied by new forms of social and political militancy, perhaps, most importantly, that of a student movement within the academy itself. Waiting in the wings was the feminist movement, which in the 1970s emerged to identify issues of social exclusion and segregation on the basis of gender and their neglect within sociology.

5

The heyday of 'positivist' social science in the nineteenth century had coincided with the socially elite position of social scientists and their implicit acceptance of the 'modernizing' role of the state. As the professional basis of the social sciences expanded, it seemed, at least initially, that nothing would disturb the dominant image of scientific activity. The greater inclusiveness of the modern democratic state would merely imply a wider acceptance of social scientific activity and participation in its benefits. Merton for example, writing in the 1940s with no sense of what was to come, described the ethos of science in straightforward terms of its norms of universalism, disinterestedness, organized scepticism and communism (where the findings of science were viewed as the product of social collaboration and assigned to the community).[17]

Against Merton's expectations, what ensued was a fundamental change in the nature of the audience for sociological theory. According to Barnes, for example, the post-war period marks a fundamental shift in the balance of power and interests among the different parties – social scientists and citizens, sponsors and gatekeepers – to sociological research.[18] The consequence is that there is no longer an unitary audience for sociological argument. On the one hand, the development and expansion of modern citizenship has created new relationships between social scientists and those regarded as the 'objects' of their research. The claims of the latter to special consideration now have more obvious weight against the claims of the former to be pursuing 'disinterested' inquiries. Secondly, 'sponsors' of research have their own research agendas, and access to research situations is guarded by different, organized groups whose 'interests' must be negotiated. These changes in the social context of research which are continuous with the rise of professional social science have altered the way in which that social science is perceived. As Barnes puts it, there has been "a movement away from positivism towards a hermeneutic view of knowledge and from an evaluation of knowledge as a source of enlightenment to an evaluation in terms of power and property".[19] In contrast to a 'positivistic' approach to social problems, *who* defines *what* behaviours as socially problematic, and the *resources* they have for making their definitions stick, become the central issues.

To its critics, positivist (or 'empiricist' – the terms were frequently used interchangeably) sociology seemed obsessed with trivial issues when compared with those that motivated 'classical' social theory. Moreover, Parsons's structural–functional theory of society offered no real alternative (and, indeed, came to be designated as a form of positivism, itself). It was the major social theory of the time with pretensions to grasp large-scale social processes, yet it, too, seemed fundamentally flawed. With its emphasis upon social integration and common values, it seemed too much a part of what had given way, too determined by the assumptions of an 'end of ideology' and, therefore, ill-equipped to give insight into the social conflict and disorder which increasingly seemed so evident. From either perspective – the theoretically detached particularities of 'abstract empiricism' or the theoretical abstractions of Parsonsian 'grand theory'[20] – the sociological imagination appeared diminished.

6

Faced with the task of explaining new developments, sociology was found wanting and new perspectives emerged to take up the challenge – perspectives which emphasized conflict and the 'complexities' of everyday life against the 'simplifications' of 'positivistic' theories of social structure. Compared with the concerns of classical sociology, sociology was now argued to have lost its bearings, too dependent upon an out-moded model of disinterested science and removed from any requirement to justify itself by the concerns of day-to-day living. The humanist counter-tradition came increasingly to the fore and, with it, the claim that the positivist project of a science of society had been a mistake.[21] In place of an emphasis upon law-like regularities of social behaviour, advocates of the humanist position argued that the true task of inquiry was to understand the different moral dilemmas that are posed for human beings by the exigencies of life in all its concrete, historical particularity. In this way, actors and their 'internal' motives for acting came to be placed at the centre of inquiry, in contrast to positivistic social science's apparent preference for the 'external' determinants of behaviour; that is, for explanations given in terms of the systems in which actors were located. This latter characteristic was a central feature of Parsons's theoretical scheme, and was precisely what gave rise to its characterization as a variant of positivism.

As a consequence of these radical critiques, sociology began to enter a crisis of self-confidence, where its current offerings – even when gathered collectively – hardly seemed to fulfil the promise of progress and, indeed, looked insignificant when placed against those of its founding period. While all sociologists could (and probably still can) recite Whitehead's dictum that, "a science which hesitates to forget its founders is lost",[22] amnesia no longer appeared to be a positive condition. Whitehead goes on to suggest that early science is "ambitiously profound in its aims and trivial in its handling of details", with the implication that any subsequent progress of science is associated with a decline in profundity and a corresponding rigorous attention to detail. For many, the proponents of modern positivistic social science, far from dwarfing the achievements of the founding giants, had, it seems, subverted their undertakings and trivialized their concerns. As Wardell and Turner put it, "the 'advantages of the division of labour' of which Weber so casually speaks in 'Science as a vocation' gradually have evolved into a cage of iron".[23]

More telling yet is that the narrowing of purposes is now perceived to have failed to produce a compensating progressive development. The detailed division of labour in modern sociology does not appear to have brought about the same results that have characterized the natural sciences. For many sociologists writing in the 1960s and since, judged by the standards of the natural sciences, *sociology has failed*.[24] It seems that however much earlier generations of sociologists have believed in the project of positivistic social science and had set themselves the task of bringing it to fruition, the current judgement is that it failed morally *and* practically. This is not simply the partial judgement of hostile critics. One of the most influential contemporary advocates of positivistic social science, Jonathan Turner, asks the question: 'can sociology be a cumulative science?' To pose the question at all as a possible *future* for sociology betrays the implicit judgement that it has not been realized in the present.[25]

With the criticism of positivism, came an attack upon the professional claims of sociologists. Rather than being the embodiment of neutral inquiry, or the disinterested mediation of competing public claims, professional sociology was increasingly seen as the embodiment of particular interests. Gouldner's *Coming Crisis of Western Sociology* was, perhaps, both the culmination of the criticisms and their definitive statement.[26] Sociologists, he argued, had 'swallowed' – indeed, had helped to form – the 'ideology' by which the professions promote their own private interests at the cost of the interests of their clients or a wider public. Yet, as Parsons had observed, sociologists themselves were professionals, espousing the cognitive claims of science, objectivity and social utility. What is sauce for the goose is sauce for the gander. At best, the disinterested inquiries of 'professional sociological positivism' seemed irrelevant to the pressing social and political issues at hand, but Gouldner's criticism was yet more severe. Professional sociology was partisan and not just in the sense of implicitly supporting the status quo. It was, Gouldner argued, part of the modern 'military-industrial-welfare complex', sponsored by Government agencies, including the military, on an increasingly large scale.[27] Sociology had become absorbed into the management of the advanced state, and this had become part of the apparatus of social control. If the 'powers-that-be' pay the piper, they can call the tune.

According to Gouldner, there is no neutral position. Neutrality was the mask behind which those with interests in the maintenance of social hierarchies disguised the partiality of their positions. This is an argument which has assumed even greater resonance as its implications have been taken up and extended by feminist theorists who argue that the concepts of positivist social science are not merely those which suit a hierarchical ruling apparatus, but a patriarchal ruling apparatus, in particular.[28] According to Gouldner, a more adequate sociology – that is a 'reflexive' sociology which applied its understandings to itself – must recognize that, "every social system is bent upon crippling the very sociology to which it gives birth".[29] Instead of hiding behind the mask of neutrality, sociologists had to ask whose side they were on and the answer, from the point of view of a properly radical and reflexive sociology, was the 'oppressed' and 'excluded'.[30] A sociology which identifies with 'outsiders' must itself be 'outside', or, at least, maintain its distance from the patronage of those who operate the prevailing system.

AFTER RADICAL SOCIOLOGY

Gouldner's attack upon Western sociology, and in particular its expression in the writings of Parsons, identified sociology as part of a social liberal establishment, confident in the applicability of its knowledge to the solution and amelioration of social problems within the framework of the advanced welfare state and its professional practitioners. Yet, he believed, Parsons and the other 'sunshine sociologists' were to be in for a rude awakening. Their technocratic appraisal of society was threatened by new social problems and burgeoning social movements which challenged the existing social order. The contradictions of welfare capitalism, he argued, were becoming increasingly apparent. The flavour of the times is well captured in the preface to Gouldner's book, where he evokes the image of Hegel in his study in Jena, writing with the sound of battle in his ears as the troops of the 'French Revolution' approached. Gouldner writes, "social theorists today work within a crumbling social matrix of paralyzed urban centers and battered campuses. Some may put cotton in their ears, but their bodies still feel the shock waves. It is no exaggeration to say that we theorize today within the sound of guns. The old order has the picks of a hundred rebellions thrust into its hide".[31]

A lot of water has flown under the bridge since Gouldner wrote; little of it confirms his sense of the historical currents. Barely two decades after he wrote, the situation looks quite different. Changes in the social and political agendas of modern societies have, indeed, been rapid: the spectacle of Paris 1968 and the perceived instability of capitalist regimes has given way to the drama of Prague and Berlin 1989 and the demise of communist regimes. The 'social liberal' political establishment in the USA has collapsed, but, for the most part, it has been the 'new right' radicals and 'moral majority' conservatives that have filled the space. Elsewhere, the 'left' is in crisis, even if the rise of the 'right' to the centre of politics has been less prominent. Everywhere, it would seem, social and political opposition has subsided and fragmented, rather than coalesced. Of the social and theoretical movements which challenged the old orthodoxies only feminism has lasted the course, but it, too, has been shaken by the collapse of the other movements − especially, Marxism − to which it was allied. Feminist theory is not merely one of the fragments, but is, itself, subject to fragmentation.[32]

The rapid and spectacular demise of former communist regimes has also had an impact upon the perception of the relative merits of sociology and economics as academic and practically relevant disciplines. There is a parallel between the fate of 'social democracy' in Eastern Europe (and elsewhere) and the fate of sociology. Where, on the face of it, social democracy might have been thought the prime candidate to inherit from the collapse of communism, the discrediting of the latter has, at least in the short term, discredited the former as well. The 'market' has come to the fore and with it the discipline, economics, that enshrines its claims. Every sociologist in Britain can recite Margaret Thatcher's comment that, "there is no such thing as society, only individuals and their families". If there is no such thing as society, there is no object of a distinct sociological inquiry. An 'economics of society' is, thus, in tune with current political sensibilities and, indeed, 'rational-choice' theory, with its assumptions of egoistic, rational calculating actors is currently enjoying a revival as the basis of a hoped-for unified social science.[33]

9

Certainly, whatever the 'contradictions' of the welfare state, it is not the 'new left' of radically reflexive sociology which has taken the platform. Neo-liberal theory, individualistic in its orientation and hostile to the welfare state (and, by extension, hostile to the discipline of sociology whose professional interests the welfare state had once seemed to embody), holds the centre of political debate.[34] Indeed, one of the ironies of our current situation is the way in which 'new left' criticisms of 'welfare capitalism' were adopted by 'new right' theorists. Having criticized welfare arrangements as mechanisms of social control which failed to address the real, underlying issues of inequality and exploitation and having challenged the extent to which political action within capitalism could, therefore, produce an authentic amelioration of social problems, the 'new left' critics of the welfare state were unprepared for a political mobilization by those who embraced capitalism, but shared their views on welfare arrangements.

There has been little re-assessment of the social and political assumptions of 'reflexive' sociology, little reflexivity, or self-criticism, in the light of recent experience. However, one of the major figures in the 'radical' critique of the professions, Randall Collins, has reflected upon the consequences of that 'radicalism' for the professions more generally. He writes that, "the professions are beginning to be undercut at their ritual core. This does not mean that the professions are prepared to abolish themselves (although some sociological radicals, including myself, have sometimes made suggestions in this direction). After all, it is on the basis of the academic enclave, the core of professional self-generation ... that these critiques have been mounted. Sophisticated professionals nowadays may talk self-critically, but they do so not as part of their professional activities. They undercut themselves only in terms of confidence and subjective legitimacy, not in their salaries and autonomous conditions of work."[35] On Collins's own arguments, where the professions are self-interested monopolies seeking to maximize their own advantages, it is highly unlikely that any general 'undercutting' of the professions would have taken place. Rather, as he observes, it would seem to be a phenomenon peculiar to the professions of the 'ritual core', or the professions of the 'academic enclave'. The sociological attack upon 'professional standards' has been most debilitating in academic social science, undercutting both confidence and subjective legitimacy (perhaps, here, having some consequence for salaries and autonomous conditions of work!).

The wider political and social radicalism of the 1960s contributed to the demise of old orthodoxies, just as it is the general collapse of this radicalism which has undermined confidence in the theoretical alternatives. The most obvious intellectual victim of these changes has been Marxist sociology. Until quite recently, it had been possible to declare, as did Wallerstein in 1982, that, "someday soon, it may be that we will discover that Marxism had suddenly become the universal *Weltanschauung* of the late capitalist era and its successor system".[36] Scarcely a decade later and Marxism is being laid to rest because, as Alexander and Giesen put it, "most radical movements have faded away, and in the eyes of many intellectuals Marxism has been morally delegitimated."[37] This judgement about the moral de-legitimation of Marxism is precisely what 'end of ideology' theorists had claimed in the 1950s.

In the process, these ideological transformations have modified earlier criticisms of the political stance of sociology. For Gouldner and others writing in the 1960s and 1970s, Parsons was the archetypal apologist for US capitalism. Then the commitment to social amelioration and inclusive citizenship was tainted by its association with the reproduction of welfare capitalism. Now, when that welfare project itself is threatened, it is suggested that Parsons was, in truth, a 'social democrat' or 'left humanist', not recognized as such because of the lack of a social democratic political tradition in the USA.[38] Now, it seems, Parsons's help might be enlisted to bolster a critical undertaking in sociology which otherwise appears to be fading. It is, indeed, a nice irony that recent research in the Parsons archive reveals that his activities in student politics in the 1920s had earned him that 'badge' of student radicalism in the 1960s, an FBI file.[39]

Parsons's own intellectual history certainly does mean that his work is bound up with issues in our own times, but as part of our problems, rather than the means of solving them. For example, his early work was concerned to establish the independent role of sociological categories against any one-sided emphasis upon the standard assumptions of economic theory and their application to all social issues (such as is now being claimed by rational-choice theorists).[40] At the same time, he wrote when the 'institutional economists' were challenging the assumptions of laissez-faire as irrelevant to the social structures of an advanced industrial society and he was broadly sympathetic to their practical aims of establishing principles for government intervention and the regulation of markets. These questions of the nature, role and consequences of market exchanges, of the subordination of broader questions of the purposes of work and employment to the interests of 'consumers', remain pressing issues for us and are central to those public debates which, Seidman argues, sociologists have failed to address.[41] If Parsons's own brand of 'sociological economics' has failed, there are important lessons to be learned from that failure, because, with the exception of Marxism (which has also failed), it represents virtually the only systematic address to the standard categories of economics within sociology.[42] Now, once more, we confront the claim that what from a sociological perspective requires to be explained – 'self-interest' as a defining motive in human activities – is to be placed beyond explanation as a methodologically necessary assumption of social inquiry. The 'age of sociology' has not materialized (or, at least, was soon over) and the disciplines of psychology and economics appear to have retained their place at the centre of mainstream social science.

The current situation is gloomy. It is a situation of abstract generalities, theoretically disconnected and contradictory particularities, disillusioned professionals and chastened activists. If 'scientific sociology' has failed to deliver the goods, and has abdicated an address to the moral issues of our time, 'radical' approaches seem equally confounded. It seems that after several decades of criticism, the only thing that radical sociologists have subverted is the sociological undertaking itself. Moral discourse is not advanced by the acceptance that there are only partial and mutually exclusive viewpoints. As I shall argue in the next chapter, 'local injustices' are no easier to define than 'global injustices', once the criteria of inclusive theory are abandoned. But, it is no longer credible that we shall find an answer to our problems by re-asserting the claims of a foundational, general theory as the basis of a renewed professional consensus. That project may once have seemed credible. For example, when Parsons and Merton wrote, modern democratic conditions seemed to secure a unified audience for sociological argument (or at least, for them, the threat of 'totalitarianism' was posed by fascism and Stalinism, not by inclusive social theory). We shall not return to similar conditions, but that does not mean that we must give way to a relativism in which anything goes. What I shall try to demonstrate is a way around the debilitating relativism which has been the culmination of the hyper-criticism of the last decades of sociological argument, without invoking the false hopes of foundational theory.

NOTES

1. The term is used by Parsons in his essay, 'Some problems confronting sociology as a profession', *American Sociological Review*, 24(4), 1959, pp. 547–59.
2. R. Nisbet, *The Sociological Tradition* (New York, Basic Books, 1966).
3. J. Habermas, *The Theory of Communicative Action, Volume 1: Reason and the Rationalization of Society* (London, Heinemann, 1984), p. 4.
4. S.A. Seidman, 'Postmodern social theory as narrative with a moral intent', in S.A. Seidman and D.G. Wagner, *Postmodernism and Social Theory* (Oxford, Basil Blackwell, 1992), p. 47.
5. S.P. Turner and M.L. Wardell, 'Epilog', in M.L. Wardell and S.P. Turner (eds), *Sociological Theory in Transition* (London, Allen and Unwin, 1986).
6. Ibid., p. 163.
7. R. Atkinson, *Orthodox Consensus and Radical Alternative* (London, Heinemann, 1972).
8. See, for example, J. Baudrillard, *In the Shadow of the Silent Majorities Or, The End of the Social and Other Essays* (New York, Semiotext[e], 1983); J-F. Lyotard, *The Postmodern Condition: A Report on Knowledge* (Minneapolis, University of Minnesota Press, 1984).
9. See J. Baudrillard, *In the Shadow of the Silent Majorities or, the End of the Social and Other Essays*. Among recent commentators on this theme, Lemert suggests that, "history may be moving against sociology". See C. Lemert, 'Sociological metatheory and its cultured despisers', in G. Ritzer (ed.), *Metatheorizing* (London, Sage, 1992), p. 132. For their part, Crook and his colleagues comment that, "the continued salience of sociology is far from assured". See S. Crook, J. Pakulski and M. Waters, *Postmodernization: Change in Advanced Society* (London, Sage, 1992), p. 237.

10. See, for example, D. Bell, *The End of Ideology: The Exhaustion of Political Ideas in the Fifties* (New York, Free Press, 1960). As the sub-title to Bell's book indicates, he, at least, anticipated that the 'end of ideology' was a temporary phase, a vacuum waiting to be filled.

11. Ibid., pp. 402–3.

12. See R.K. Merton, *Social Theory and Social Structure* (Free Press, New York, 1968).

13. See especially, T. Parsons, 'The professions and the social structure', in *Essays in Sociological Theory* (New York, Free Press, 1954).

14. See Parsons, 'Some problems confronting sociology as a profession' in *Essays*.

15. As Parsons puts it, "while the economic era of ideology was related to the *fact* of industrialization, the psychological era has been related to industrialization's *consequences*". Ibid., p. 553.

16. See, for example, G. Myrdal, *The Challenge to Affluence* (London, Victor Gollancz, 1962), A. Gouldner, *The Coming Crisis of Western Sociology* (London, Heinemann, 1970). In fact, 'end of ideology' theorists such as Bell, made similar arguments. See, for example, D. Bell, *The Coming of Post-Industrial Society: A Venture in Social Forecasting* (London, Heinemann, 1974).

17. R.K. Merton, 'Science and democratic social structure', in *Social Theory and Social Structure* (New York, Free Press, 1968).

18. See J.A. Barnes, *Who Should Know What? Social Science, Privacy and Ethics* (Harmondsworth, Penguin Books, 1979).

19. Ibid. p. 22.

20. The terms are those of C. Wright Mills, whose attack upon sociological orthodoxies was the most important and widely cited indication of the new theoretical sensibility. See C.W. Mills, *The Sociological Imagination* (Oxford, Oxford University Press, 1961). See also D. Willer and J. Willer, *Systematic Empiricism: Critique of a Pseudo-Science* (Englewood Cliffs, Prentice-Hall, 1973).

21. Perhaps the most important work in the Anglo-American debate was P. Winch, *The Idea of a Social Science* (London, Routledge and Kegan Paul, 1958). See also A.R. Louch, *Explanation and Human Action* (Oxford, Basil Blackwell, 1966).

22. A.N. Whitehead, *The Organisation of Thought, Educational and Scientific* (Westport, Greenwood Press, 1974).

23. M. Wardell and S.P. Turner 'Introduction: dissolution of the classical project', in Wardell and Turner (eds), *Sociological Theory in Transition*, p. 16.

24. This dual judgement – of the *success* of natural science and the *failure* of social science – is graphically expressed by Giddens in his comment upon the 'positivistic' approach to social science, which aimed to, "reproduce in the study of human social life, the same kind of sensational illumination and explanatory power yielded up by the sciences of nature. By this token, social science must surely be reckoned a failure." See A. Giddens, *New Rules of Sociological Method* (London, Hutchinson, 1976), p. 13.

25. J.H. Turner, 'Introduction: can sociology be a cumulative science?', in J.H. Turner (ed.) *Theory Building in Sociology: Assessing Theoretical Cumulation* (Newbury Park, Sage, 1989). Nor is Turner very optimistic for the future. Like Turner and Wardell, he believes that the 'division of academic labour' has become an iron cage, albeit one which militates against the positivist project. Sociology, he argues, has institutionalized an unhelpful division of specialisms, "professional sociology is now structured in ways that divide theory and methods, while partitioning the field into a

large number of substantive specialities. The result is that substantive researchers ignore theory and each other, and that substantive researchers, theorists, and methodologists operate in considerable ignorance of, and unconcern about, each others' work." Ibid., p. 16.

26. See A. Gouldner, *The Coming Crisis of Western Sociology* (London, Heinemann, 1970).

27. Of particular symbolic significance was the publicity surrounding 'Project Camelot', an US army funded project on counter-insurgency in Latin America. See I.L. Horowitz, (ed.), *The Rise and Fall of Project Camelot* (Cambridge, MIT Press, 1967).

28. See, for example, S. Harding, *The Science Question in Feminism* (Milton Keynes, Open University Press, 1986); D. Smith, 'Sociological theory: methods of writing patriarchy', in R.A. Wallace (ed.), *Feminism and Sociological Theory* (London, Sage, 1989).

29. Gouldner, *The Coming Crisis*, p. 498. Gouldner also has in mind the fate of Marx's theory in communist societies which drew their legitimacy from it.

30. In fact, Gouldner merely offers a radical inversion of Parsons's own definition of the role of 'professionals'. According to Parsons, one aspect of the mediating role of the profession is between the 'collectivity' interests embodied in 'systems' and the 'individual' interests reflected by 'deviants'. Where Parsons ultimately accepts the standpoint of the 'collectivity', Gouldner is suggesting that sociologists should adopt the standpoint of what Parsons would identify as 'deviants'. See Parsons, 'The professions in the social structure', *Essays*.

31. Gouldner, *The Coming Crisis*, p. vii.

32. Hawkesworth, for example, expresses the fear that a crisis in 'malestream' social theory is being reproduced within feminism in its apparent embrace of mutually exclusive epistemological claims. See M.E. Hawkesworth, 'Knower, knowing, known: feminist theory and claims of truth', *Signs: Journal of Women in Culture and Society*, 14(3), 1989, pp. 533–57.

33. Margaret Thatcher's claim is echoed in rational-choice theory. Elster, for example, writes, "there are no societies, only individuals who interact with each other". See J. Elster, *The Cement of Society: a Study of Social Order* (Cambridge, Cambridge University Press, 1989), p. 248.

34. In fact, 'new left' and 'new right' criticisms of welfare states are very similar. Each stresses the 'bureaucratic' nature of the modern state and each argues that welfare is a form of 'social control'. See J. Holmwood, 'Welfare and citizenship', in R.A. Bellamy (ed.), *Theories and Concepts of Politics* (Manchester, Manchester University Press, 1993).

35. R. Collins, 'Market closure and the conflict theory of the professions', in M. Burrage and R. Torstendahl (eds), *Professions in Theory and History* (London, Sage, 1990), p. 41. Somewhat inconsistently, Collins showed no taste for the 'debunking' of sociology as a profession, except latterly when he has engaged in the 'debunking' of those radicals who would seek to undercut the 'ritual core' of scientific sociology! See R. Collins, 'The confusion in the models of sociology', in Seidman and Wagner (eds), *Postmodernism and Social Theory*.

36. I. Wallerstein, *Unthinking Social Science: the Limits of Nineteenth Century Paradigms* (Cambridge, Polity, 1991), p. 200. Wallerstein's claim has similar qualities of hubris to Davis's claim that sociologists were 'all functionalists' shortly

before the major theoretical onslaught upon functional analysis in sociology. See K. Davis, 'The myth of functionalism as a special method in sociology and anthropology', *American Sociological Review*, 24(5), 1959, pp. 752–72.

37. J.C. Alexander and B. Giesen, 'From reduction to linkage: the long view of the micro-macro link', in J.C. Alexander, *Action and its Environments: Towards a New Synthesis* (London, University of California Press, 1987), p. 288. This judgement is not restricted to critics of Marxism. For example, Paul Hirst's obituary to the leading Marxist theorist of the period, Louis Althusser, is an obituary to Marxism, written, moreover, by one who was at the forefront of the challenge to 'bourgeois' social science in Britain in the 1970s. Althusser's "pushing of Marxist philosophy to the limit", he writes, "showed finally and irrevocably that Marxism could not be built anew on defensible foundations." P. Hirst, 'Obituary for Louis Althusser', *The Guardian*, 24 October 1990, p. 39.

38. For the standard criticisms of Parsons's political stance, see Gouldner, *The Coming Crisis*; A. Hacker, 'Sociology and ideology' in M. Black (ed), *The Social Theories of Talcott Parsons: A Critical Examination* (Englewood Cliffs: Prentice-Hall, 1961); W.H. Buxton, *Talcott Parsons and the Capitalist Nation State* (Toronto, University of Toronto Press, 1985). On Parsons, the social democrat, see J.K. Nielsen, 'The political orientation of Talcott Parsons: the second world war and its aftermath', in R. Robertson and B.S. Turner (eds), *Talcott Parsons: Theorist of Modernity* (London, Sage, 1991).

39. See C. Camic, 'Introduction: Talcott Parsons before *The Structure of Social Action*', in C. Camic (ed.), *Talcott Parsons: The Early Essays* (Chicago, University of Chicago Press, 1991), p. xiv.

40. For a discussion of this aspect of Parsons's intellectual background, see C. Camic 'The making of a method: a historical re-interpretation of the early Parsons', *American Sociological Review*, 52(4), 1987. For a collection of essays on the debate between Parsons and his main 'radical individualist' critic, Homans, see H. Turk and R.L. Simpson (eds), *Institutions and Exchange: The Sociologies of Talcott Parsons and George Caspar Homans* (New York, Bobbs-Merrill, 1971), pp. 421–39.

41. Block, for example, in an argument which parallels that of Seidman, writes of our present times as a 'strange period' because, "people lack a shared understanding of the society in which they live. For generations, the United States was understood as an industrial society, but that definition of reality is no longer compelling. Yet no convincing alternative has emerged in its absence . . . Contemporary social theorists tell us remarkably little about the kind of historical era in which we live. Social theorists have become pre-occupied with meta-theory." F. Block, *Post-Industrial Possibilities: a Critique of Economic Discourse* (Berkeley, University of California Press, 1990), p. 11. Indeed, where issues of post-industrialism have been addressed the current, fashionable consensus in sociology seems to be to assert the authenticity of 'consumption' against an earlier critique of its 'inauthenticity'. On the former position, see M. Featherstone, *Consumer Culture and Postmodernism* (London, Sage, 1991), and on the latter, see H. Marcuse, *One-Dimensional Man* (Boston, Beacon Press, 1964). In this context, it is difficult to see how sociologists can critically address the role of the category of the 'consumer' in economic and political discourse.

42. The recent responses to the promotion of 'rational-choice' theory in sociology have simply repeated Parsons's criticisms without any appreciation of how the validity of

those criticisms might be affected by the deficiencies of Parsons's own approach. See, for example, B. Hindess, *Choice, Rationality and Social Theory* (London, Allen and Unwin, 1988).

2

THE THEORETICAL IMPASSE

The last decades have seen the fragmentation of sociological theory around mutually exclusive approaches with associated divergent epistemological claims. Among the approaches which emerged in the 1960s and after were those that took a rigorously structural, anti-humanist stance, as well as those that, with equal vehemence, took an anti-structural, humanist line.[1] There were anti-positivist forms of naturalism which stressed the possibility of a scientific sociology outside the strictures of positivist methodology, as well as anti-naturalist forms of humanist or interpretive sociology which denied the possibility of any form of 'science' of human action.[2] Increasingly, sociology appeared to be beset by irreconcilable differences. Yet, at least initially, each position presented itself as the way forward immune from the (false) criticisms implicit in any apparently alternative position.

SYNTHESIS AND FRAGMENTATION

The idea that a major transformation of categories and concepts was part and parcel of progressive development within any rigorously pursued undertaking had been reinforced by Kuhn's account of the history of the natural sciences as a process of dramatic change.[3] According to Kuhn, natural science did not develop in the way described by the standard positivist account of the gradual accumulation of knowledge, but, rather, through a series of revolutionary disjunctions in theoretical schemes, or 'paradigms'. In the terminology made popular by Kuhn, it seemed that in the 1960s sociology had entered a period of crisis in the dominant paradigm. The problem, however, was that no new paradigm seemed to emerge in sociology to take the place of the once-dominant scheme. Although Kuhn had emphasized the revolutionary character of paradigm change, he also characterized the intervening periods as periods of 'normal

17

science', which were defined by the hegemony of a single paradigm and routine work within its terms. The only exception to this situation was that of an early, immature period when a number of different schemes competed, before one eventually achieved dominance. From this perspective, it appeared that sociology was a 'multi-paradigm' science, which must mean either that it was an immature, pre-paradigmatic undertaking, awaiting the emergence of a dominant new paradigm, or that, in some way, it was defined by the irreconcilable differences that the various approaches embodied.

There can be little doubt that for most of the advocates of any one of the competing paradigms, the first of these possibilities best describes what motivated their activities. Each sought a major transformation of the sociological undertaking in its own image. Taken together, however, they seemed to signify the dissolution of sociology and a first step towards a resigned acceptance that unresolvable contradictions might lie at the heart of the discipline. This is very evident in the dramatic shift in the sociological sensibility over the last two decades. The transformation of the sociological *conscience collective* from optimism in the face of a new social and theoretical order, to despair and fatigue has been rapid. In 1974, when the first issue of the journal *Theory and Society* was published, Gouldner had written in the editorial statement how the old paradigms, such as positivism, structural-functionalism and rational-choice theory (or 'exchange theory' as it was then termed), were "losing their ability to convince, let alone enthuse" and new paradigms – "critical theory, ethno-methodology, neo-Marxisms, linguistically sensitive sociology, structuralism, and neo-Weberianism" – were replacing them.[4] Two decades later and the new paradigms seem to have fared no better than their predecessors. Alexander, for example, writes of *their* increasingly 'enervated' and 'debilitated' character.[5] The vital and creative phase of the 'new' paradigms has come to an unexpectedly premature end; they, too, have lost their ability to convince or enthuse. Their problems, according to Alexander, have been created precisely by their exaggerated claims for renewal, "by the flood of well-intended but too often grossly misleading critiques, by the false promise of imminent transformation".[6] At the same time, these critiques have even failed to dispatch the positivism which was their common enemy. Sociology, for Alexander, also continues to be undermined, "by the trivializing effect of the ever more powerful urge for 'scientization' ".[7] Sociology, it seems, is being pulled apart by competing and irreconcilable tendencies.

Despite this, Alexander remains optimistic. He believes that the crisis years are now over and that the current mood is one of eager anticipation.[8] What is anticipated, apparently, is a new systematic framework of theory which will re-integrate the profession of sociology and keep at bay the enervating consequences of the relativism implicit in a sociological undertaking *fragmented* among competing approaches. Calling for a 'new theoretical movement' which will *synthesize* the positive aspects of the different approaches in a single, consistent scheme of categories, Alexander sees encouraging signs in the writings of his contemporaries (in particular, in those of Giddens and Habermas). "Where even 10 years ago," he writes, "the air was filled with demands for radical and one-sided theoretical programs, in the contemporary period one can only hear urgent calls for theorizing of an entirely different sort . . . synthetic rather than polemic theorizing is now the order of the day".[9]

Alexander is altogether too sanguine. Once more in the recent history of sociological theory, apparently, 'imminent transformation' is promised, with little reflection upon how past promises have gone unfulfilled. After all, the positions which he now represents as partial and one-sided were initially offered as adequate and comprehensive; their apparent partiality is a consequence of their failure to establish their independence from the inadequate positions they sought to leave behind. At the same time, Alexander is, himself, a proponent of Parsonian 'neo-functionalism', one of the paradigms that Gouldner had judged to be a failure, morally and practically, and whose failure, for most, was held to lie in *its* one-sided emphasis upon processes of social order to the neglect of those of conflict and social change. At a minimum, we would require some account of how what was previously judged to have failed can be transmuted to success.

Alexander's project of a synthetic, general framework of sociological theory is offered as an exercise in metatheory, involving "theorizing without reference to particular empirical problems or distinctive domains".[10] This is not a characteristic peculiar to Alexander's work; it is precisely what Seidman describes as typical of much contemporary social theory, that it is disconnected from specific research programmes. It is a feature of the other attempts at general, synthetic theory – for example, those of Habermas and Giddens – which Alexander is drawing upon in support of his claim for a broadly-based new theoretical movement in sociology.[11] The various theorists of this 'new theoretical movement' are each concerned to construct general frames of reference without immediate substantive content. Once again, this is not new, but was precisely a feature of Parsons's general theory which some of the proponents of the 'new' paradigms, at least initially, had sought to redress. As Zeitlin, for example, had put it, "Parsons does not realise that most of the statements that can be made about *any* society are bound to be banal. One of the main reasons . . . for Parsons's ambiguities is that he defines his terms without any research purpose or problem in mind."[12]

In our current social and political circumstances, it is perhaps understandable that there are attempts to return to the 'old orthodoxies' which existed prior to the theoretical upheavals of the 1960s – for example, 'neo-functionalism', or 'rational-choice' theory. But even this theoretical recidivism is not new. A moment's reflection will be sufficient to recognize that the 'new' paradigms of the 1960s and after were, for the most part, themselves returns to even 'older' paradigms. Then we were offered neo-Marxism and neo-Weberianism (among others), to which Alexander now is proposing should be added, neo-Parsonsianism. In launching *Theory and Society*, Gouldner made the observation that it was a journal of its times, characterizing those times as a "moment when the institutional life of social theory and sociology seem exhausted and drifting . . . a time when sociology sees the road back more clearly than the way forward".[13] For quite some time, then, it has been the case that the 'way back' has been seen more clearly by social theorists than the 'way forward'. It is a depressing thought.

CYCLES OF CRITICISM AND RENEWAL

Many of the attempted reconstructions of sociological theory in the 1960s and 1970s made their claims for renewal via a new interpretation of classical social theory and its contemporary relevance. For most of the critics of sociological orthodoxy, Parsons was easily assimilated to what they were criticizing. His scheme was, at best, partial and at least a part of what he had neglected was to be found in those traditions of sociological thought he had sought to displace. Yet, Parsons, too, had set himself against one-sided approaches and had elaborated his own in terms of an address to the diversity of argument found among the 'classics' of the discipline. Indeed, Parsons's *The Structure of Social Action* (New York, Free Press, 1937) was the first in the genre of theoretical reconstruction through an examination of the 'classics' of the discipline and it would not be at all far-fetched to credit him with the invention of the 'classical project'; that is, the idea of a distinct mode of theorizing which could form the basis of contemporary practice as a sort of 'neo-classical' undertaking.

Parsons gave primacy to Durkheim and Weber, but relegated Marx to a subsidiary role. Parsons's claim was that the 1890–1920 generation of European theorists in economics and sociology[14] – Marshall, Pareto, Durkheim and Weber, in particular – marked both a culmination and a watershed in social theory in which the deficiencies of past traditions of thought were transcended and the elements of a satisfactory modern approach were laid down (albeit tentatively and in a not wholly satisfactory manner). In establishing this claim, Parsons attributed to Marx the status of an important, but essentially minor, figure whose insights had been absorbed and given more satisfactory statement by Weber. In fact, Parsons gave over little space to the discussion of Marx in *The Structure of Social Action*, but returned to discuss his work in a number of later essays, where he wrote, "Karl Marx was probably the greatest social theorist whose work fell entirely within the nineteenth century. His place in intellectual history is secure. As a theorist in the specifically scientific sense, however, he belongs to a phase of development which has been superseded."[15]

As Parsons's own work became the focus of criticism, so his treatment of the classics was criticized. His interpretations were argued to be as one-sided as the subsequent development of his own theory proved to be. I do not intend to go into these issues of interpretation in any detail; the claim that Parsons's interpretations are one-sided takes its force from the claim that his own scheme is one-sided, which, as I shall show in the following chapters, is difficult to

20

sustain in the manner in which it is usually proposed (that is, as a self-conscious commitment on Parsons's part). Nevertheless, that the deficiencies attributed to Parsons's developed theory should occur in areas in which Marx appeared to have answers seemed initially to confirm the Marxist view that modern sociology was an ideologically motivated reaction against Marx's theory, but one that had failed to displace it.[16] Increasingly, Marx's writings, sometimes in combination with Weber, were seen as the basis of an alternative approach.[17] Durkheim was firmly linked to Parsons, and with the slide in the latter's status, Durkheim's star also waned. Now the wheel has turned full circle. As Marxism appears to be in decline, so there has been a revival in the fortunes of Parsons, with Alexander's own return to the classics to reinstate the Parsonsian theoretical project (and, with it, that of Durkheim, too).[18]

These shifts in perspective could not be simply an issue of a changed socio-political context, important though those changes are for understanding the current situation of social theory. There is a deeper convergence upon theoretical categories. It might seem odd to claim that approaches which draw their inspiration from Marx are not that different from that of Parsons to which, on the face of it, they are implacably opposed. Certainly, the substance of Marx's theory of capitalism is quite different from the substance of Parsons's theory of modern society. However, those who were sympathetic to the sort of issues of power and conflict that are central to Marx's account of capitalism were seeking to draw out general issues for sociological theory, rather than to embrace Marx's specific explanations.[19] The problem to be addressed was that of social change, but the general insights on this topic that could be drawn from Marx's theories were not unambiguous. For example, from the perspective of a Marxist theory of capitalism, despite the emphasis upon contradiction, conflict and change, the problem must be how to explain an apparent stability of capitalism, or, at very least, the absence of the specific changes to which the theory lay claim. Despite setting out to address the factors producing change, then, theorists were brought to recognize the centrality in social life of those factors – for example, 'ideological incorporation' – serving stability, *precisely as a consequence of the exemplary status they attributed to Marxism.*

Moreover, as neo-Marxist class theorists grappled with the problem of how to use a theory of class polarization to account for the increasingly differentiated social circumstances of advanced capitalism, so their answers brought them to explanations not very far removed from those of Weberian theorists against whom, ostensibly, they were arguing. In accepting that 'intra-class' divisions were frequently more important than 'inter-class' divisions in defining interests and collective strategies, neo-Marxist writers adopted conceptual distinctions – for example, the control of 'marketable skill', or access to 'bureaucratic' position – which had initially been proposed by Weber in criticism of Marxist theories of class.[20]

It seems that Parsons might have been right all along, that the lasting sociological residue of Marx's approach was already contained in Weber's approach which had gone beyond it – and so, critics of Parsons moved closer to Weber as the source of an alternative sensibility. The most striking indication of this development is found in the work of Habermas. Where his earlier work drew heavily upon Marx and sought to apply and develop Marx's insights in criticism of subsequent developments of social theory, Habermas came to criticize Marxism for its failure adequately to account for normative structures.[21] Indeed, his recent statement of a 'foundational' theory of action makes little reference to Marx and the latter's role in Habermas's earlier writings is entirely taken over by Weber, who, as in Parsons's interpretation, provides pointers to an adequate approach, but failed fully to realize it in his own development of appropriate categories (this, perhaps, also explains Habermas's increasing sympathy for Parsons's theoretical undertaking).[22]

The cyclical nature of these attempts at re-formulation – and they have defined much theoretical activity in sociology over the last decades – is suggestive of a flaw at their heart. For each attempt, and however much their authors might resist any simple idea of linear theoretical progress, the re-statement of classical insights in a more adequate, 'neo-classical' framework should have achieved a systematic statement of sociological principles that rendered any subsequent return to the 'classics' unnecessary. Each return to the 'classics' in the face of the inadequacies of each particular, 'neo-classical' re-formulation makes it increasingly unlikely that such projects are the way forward, and, indeed, contributes to the sense of crisis in sociological theory, the sense that we might (or should) have come to the end of a particular kind of theoretical activity in sociology with no new way forward apparent.[23]

A POSTMODERN ALTERNATIVE?

Ultimately, Alexander's claims for a hegemonic 'new theoretical movement' are more prescriptive than descriptive. It may be that sociological theorists are now more circumspect and less radical in their social and political claims because they theorize in a 'cold climate'. It may also be the case that there is a general belief that the frequently bitter atmosphere in which previous theoretical disputes were conducted served to undermine the discipline, rather than to promote it. Any current uneasy truce, however, would belie underlying divisions. So, although the idea of a synthetic, general theoretical scheme or frame of reference is a significant feature of the contemporary scene, at least as important in defining the mood of our times is the postmodern perception of general theory as an impossible and perhaps even oppressive task.

For postmodern theorists, sociology is 'post-classical', but in a more radical sense than that implied by any positivist or neo-classical sociologist. For them, the evident fragmentation of social theory into a series of mutually inconsistent, partial accounts is something to be acceded to as the irremediable condition of social inquiry as modern societies enter a postmodern phase. According to Baudrillard, for example, postmodern 'social reality' is a 'chaotic constellation' which is 'unrepresentable', such that there is no such thing as 'the social' and, more radical than Margaret Thatcher, no such thing as the 'individual' either.[24] Accordingly, social theorists should give up any quest for generality and coherence, for the 'grand narrative' which will explain modern society. Those social theorists who seek a synthetic, general theory, argues Lyotard, betray their nostalgia for the 'whole and one', for certainty, in their reduction of the contradictory particularities of social experience into a singular narrative.[25] What is proposed is, "a war on totality", in which theorists should be, "witnesses to the unpresentable ... [and] activate the differences".[26] On this view, social theory cannot aim to represent social reality, but rather, it must, "invent allusions to the conceivable which cannot be presented".[27] Apparently, any sociological commitment to explanation must be discarded in the name of some exercise in the adumbration of 'fictions' or 'utopias'.

Postmodern theorists, too, are writing in the shadow of the failure of the social movements which a previous generation of social theorists had identified as the harbingers of social change. Thus, at least as important as the rejection of 'grand social theory' by postmodern theorists is their rejection of the embodiment of 'universalistic' claims in social movements. Indeed, the failures of putative social movements are apparent in Baudrillard's rhetorical proposal that conformity ('resistance to resistance') can be a subversive activity, a "form of refusal by over-acceptance ... [which] is the actual strategy of the masses".[28] What the masses are refusing and have refused, apparently, are previous generations of radical social theorists (including Baudrillard himself, in an earlier guise) and their claims for transcendence. In fact, postmodernism seems to reproduce the very substance of the 'end of ideology' thesis, that 'ideology' (or what postmodern theorists call 'narrative'), "which", as Bell put it, "once was a road to action has come to a dead end".[29]

In place of 'ideology', all that postmodernism seems to offer is particularistic, temporary resistance to any inclusive embrace that would reduce differences. As Seidman argues, "postmodernism carries no promise of liberation – of a society free of domination. Postmodernism gives up the modernist idol of emancipation in favour of deconstructing false closure, prying open present and future social possibilities, detecting fluidity and porousness in forms of life where hegemonic discourses posit closure and a frozen order. The hope of a great transformation is replaced by the more modest aspiration of a relentless defence of immediate, local pleasures and struggles for justice."[30] Since any resistance must be in the name of something which, on being achieved, will posit the possibility of 'closure' and new forms of 'frozen order', resistance to the 'falsity' of 'closure' must, indeed, be *relentless*. In opposing 'totalising' social theory with its requirement of 'closure', it seems that resistance is 'totalised'.

A number of feminist writers have seen a parallel, or 'elective affinity', between feminism – the one radical movement from the 1970s that has not 'faded away' – and postmodernism.[31] The 'universalism' of the claims of mainstream social theory, they argue, is confounded by the particularity of women's experience outside its supposedly general categories. The apparently gender-neutral character of the categories belies their patriarchal substance. This representation of basic epistemological and ontological assumptions of social theory as reflecting a male perspective is, quite obviously, one of the major reasons for the current unease concerning the claims of any reconstructive sociology. Where sociological categories claim to cover women's experience (or anyone else's, for that matter), but do not, the claims and the principles that they embody must be called into question. It would seem that feminist theory points to the need for the reconstruction of sociological approaches. The question is: What sort of reconstruction? Does the problem lie with 'coherence' as a condition of theoretical adequacy, or the falsity of the claim to have achieved it?

Those who have argued the former, are, implicitly or explicitly, on the terrain of postmodernism, where the condition of theoretical activity is the diversity and context-specific nature of experiences which is to be expressed in social theories which accept and embrace contradiction. Thus, Gross writes that the intellectual commitments of feminist theory are, "not to truth, objectivity and neutrality, but to theoretical positions openly acknowledged as observer and context-specific".[32] On this view, the 'social totality' cannot be grasped as a whole, but is made up of partial and mutually exclusive points of view. Feminist theory, therefore, should be concerned with the identification and elucidation of concrete, specific and located differences, denying the possibility of their inclusion within a coherent, and integrated scheme. From another perspective, however, it might seem the ultimate 'bad faith' that postmodern theory denies the possibility of an inclusive social theory or political practice just at the point that feminists have identified the specific ways in which women have been excluded from the structures of modern citizenship despite formal statements of their inclusion.[33] While a feminist argument must be that inclusion could not be a simple issue of the mere extension of existing forms of citizenship to women, but requires a transformation of those forms,[34] postmodernism seems to deny that there could be an inclusive citizenship, or inclusive social theory, at all.

Once again, the celebration of the impossibility of coherent social theory is not new. There are echoes of ethnomethodology, one of the new paradigms of the 1960s, in postmodern theory. Ethnomethodologists, such as Garfinkel and Sacks, for example, came to declare the impossibility of general theoretical sociology and, having done so, turned their back on any reconstruction of its categories, declaring themselves 'ethnomethodologically indifferent' to such concerns.[35] Much earlier, a similar hostility to general theory had emerged from within German idealism, against which both Weber and Parsons had argued. For example, Weber attacked the German 'historical school' for their acceptance of the 'unknowable' as peculiarly significant, claiming that their arguments were based on the mistaken idea that, "the dignity of a science or its object is due to those features of the object about which we can know nothing at all. In which case, the peculiar significance of human action lies in the fact that it is *inexplicable* and therefore *unintelligible*".[36]

It is easy to see why many commentators regard sociological theory as having lost its way. Given the current problems of sociological inquiry, it is, perhaps, not surprising that doubt over its possibility should give rise to the embrace of its impossibility. The general theoretical approaches of the last decades have been concerned with the elaboration of a categorial frame of reference – or 'new rules' – for sociological practice. Postmodern theorists, denying that there can be such an *a priori*, foundational framework, however, also deny the coherence and integration of theoretical categories and relations which would be conditions of adequacy in any positive, constructive sociology. Indeed, one of Parsons's severest critics in the 1960s, Dennis Wrong, has recently been moved to comment upon postmodern developments in sociological theory, "was it for *this* that we killed Parsons?"[37] The implication is that if only we had 'a-held on to nurse', we might have avoided the 'hungry lions' of postmodernism.[38] Returning to Nurse Parsons is hardly an attractive option. From either perspective – general, foundational theory, or postmodern fragmentation – sociological explanation is undermined.

There can be little doubt – Lyotard, Baudrillard, and others, notwithstanding – that the issues of sociological argument and modern society that we currently confront are also issues of explanation. The 'classics' managed to combine explanation and criticism, so it seems unlikely that now they are mutually exclusive or impossible undertakings. It is unlikely that 'reality' has changed so as to make sociology impossible, rather than simply in need of renewal. If current social developments and dilemmas of public life cannot be grasped in the categories of current social theories, it is more likely that the problem lies with the theories than that 'reality' itself has become intrinsically ungraspable. It is hard to resist the conclusion that the perception of the 'chaotic constellation' of modern social reality derives from the 'chaotic' nature of contemporary social theory. If this is so, the challenge is to *re*-construct its explanatory categories, not to *de*-construct the explanatory undertaking.

The problem, I shall suggest, is the way in which foundational, synthetic general theory has come to appear as the only possible alternative to the debilitating relativism of postmodernism. Neither position is adequate and, in fact, each feeds off the other. It will be part of my wider purpose to draw out the connections between the claims of general theory and the denial of those claims by postmodern theorists. It is the failure of general theory to achieve the synthesis it requires, a failure which is intrinsic to the very way in which the project is defined, which provides the categories and terms of postmodern theory, just as it is the fragmentation of approaches which seems to make a synthesis of their terms appear necessary. In critical examination of Parsons's theories it is my intention both to exemplify this argument and to return explanation to the centre of theoretical activity in sociology.

NOTES

1. On the former, associated with Marxism, see, for example, L. Althusser, *For Marx* (London, New Left Books, 1969). On the latter, see H. Garfinkel, *Studies in Ethnomethodology* (Englewood Cliffs, Prentice-Hall, 1967).
2. On the former, see, for example, D. Willer and J. Willer, *Systematic Empiricism: Critique of a Pseudo-Science* (Englewood Cliffs, Prentice-Hall, 1973), and on the latter, see P. Winch, *The Idea of a Social Science* (London, Routledge and Kegan Paul, 1958).
3. T.S. Kuhn, *The Structure of Scientific Revolutions* (Chicago, University of Chicago Press, 1962).
4. 'Editorial', *Theory and Society*, 1(1), 1974, p. i.
5. J.C. Alexander, 'The new theoretical movement', in N.J. Smelser (ed.), *Handbook of Sociology* (London, Sage, 1988), p. 77.
6. See J.C. Alexander, *Theoretical Logic in Sociology, Volume I: Positivism, Presuppositions and Current Controversies* (London, Routledge and Kegan Paul, 1982).
7. Ibid.
8. See J.C. Alexander, 'The new theoretical movement', p. 77. Even he had previously found the current state of sociological theory depressing. For example, he began his exercise in the reconstruction of theoretical sociology with the comment, "if sociology could speak it would say, 'I am tired'". See Alexander, *Theoretical Logic, Volume I*, p. xiii.
9. Alexander, 'The new theoretical movement', p. 77. See also, B.S. Turner, 'Parsons and his critics: on the ubiquity of functionalism', in R.J. Holton and B.S. Turner (eds), *Talcott Parsons on Economy and Society* (London, Routledge and Kegan Paul, 1986), p. 206. Like Alexander, Turner believes that most criticisms of Parsons are primarily moral and ideological objections to his view of American society.
10. Alexander, 'The new theoretical movement', p. 77. The significance of such an endeavour, according to Alexander, should be 'beyond dispute'. See also G. Ritzer (ed.), *Metatheorizing* (London, Sage, 1992) for an account of what he calls the 'coming of age' of metatheory.
11. See, for example, J. Habermas, *The Theory of Communicative Action, Volume I: Reason and the Rationalization of Society* (London, Heinemann, 1984); *The Theory of Communicative Action, Volume II: A Critique of Functionalist Reason* (Cambridge, Polity, 1987); A. Giddens, *New Rules of Sociological Method* (London, Hutchinson, 1976), *The Constitution of Society* (Cambridge, Polity, 1984).
12. See I.M. Zeitlin, *Rethinking Sociology: A Critique of Contemporary Theory* (Englewood Cliffs, Prentice-Hall, 1973), p. 24. Notwithstanding, Zeitlin's own book is an attempt to construct a general, synthetic theory much like anyone else's, in his case out of the writings of Mead, Freud and Marx (the latter moderated with Weber).
13. A. Gouldner, *The Coming Crisis of Western Sociology* (London, Heinemann, 1970).
14. For a broad discussion of the social and political context of this generation (including Freud, whom Parsons subsequently brought into his scheme), see H. Stuart Hughes, *Consciousness and Society: The Re-Orientation of European Thought, 1890–1930* (New York, Alfred A. Knopf, 1959).
15. See T. Parsons, 'Some comments on the sociology of Karl Marx', in *Sociological Theory and Modern Society* (New York, Free Press, 1967), p. 135. See also T. Parsons, 'Social classes and class conflict in the light of recent sociological theory', in *Essays in Sociological Theory* (New York, Free Press, 1954, revised edn).

26

16. See especially G. Therborn, *Science, Class and Society: On the Formation of Sociology and Historical Materialism* (London, New Left Books, 1970).

17. See, for example, A. Giddens, *Capitalism and Modern Social Theory: An Analysis of the Writings of Marx, Durkheim and Max Weber* (Cambridge, Cambridge University Press, 1971); *The Class Structure of the Advanced Societies* (London, Hutchinson, 1973). Habermas, for his part, addressed the philosophical background of German idealism and attempted to reconcile it with the claims of Marxism (see, for example, J. Habermas, *Knowledge and Human Interests*, (Boston, Beacon Press, 1971)), while in his more sociological writings he attempted to bring together Marx and Weber (see, for example, J. Habermas, 'Technology and science as ideology', in *Toward a Rational Society* (London, Heinemann, 1971)).

18. See, especially, his four-volume, *Theoretical Logic in Sociology*. J.C. Alexander, *Theoretical Logic in Sociology, Volume I: Positivism, Presuppositions and Current Controversies* (London, Routledge and Kegan Paul, 1982); *Theoretical Logic in Sociology, Volume II: The Antinomies of Classical Thought: Marx and Durkheim* (London, Routledge and Kegan Paul, 1982); *Theoretical Logic in Sociology, Volume III: The Classical Attempt at Synthesis: Max Weber* (London, Routledge and Kegan Paul, 1983); *Theoretical Logic in Sociology, Volume IV: The Modern Reconstruction of Classical Thought: Talcott Parsons* (London, Routledge and Kegan Paul, 1984). See also J.C. Alexander (ed.), *Durkheimian Sociology: Cultural Studies* (Cambridge, Cambridge University Press, 1988). See also R. Robertson and B.S. Turner (eds), *Talcott Parsons: Theorist of Modernity* (London, Sage, 1991).

19. For example, Althusser, to take a neo-Marxist writer whose work was highly influential in the period, was concerned to identify the principles of a materialist approach to history, distinguished from other, equally methodological, 'misreadings' of Marx. See Althusser, *For Marx*. Similarly, Lockwood, who was not interested in developing a specifically Marxist sociology, used Marx's theory of capitalism as an example of a type of approach different to that of Parsons, but without claiming that it was adequate as an explanation of capitalism. See D. Lockwood, 'System integration and social integration', in G. Zollschan and W. Hirsch (eds), *Explorations in Social Change* (London, Routledge and Kegan Paul, 1964).

20. See, for example, F. Parkin, *Marxism and Class Theory: A Bourgeois Critique* (London, Tavistock, 1979); J.M. Holmwood and A. Stewart, 'The role of contradictions in modern theories of social stratification', *Sociology* 17(2), 1983; D. Lockwood, 'The weakest link in the chain?', in D. Rose (ed.), *Social Stratification and Economic Change* (London, Hutchinson, 1988); V. Burris, 'The neo-Marxist synthesis of Marx and Weber on class', in N. Wiley (ed.), *The Marx-Weber Debate* (London, Sage, 1987).

21. See J. Habermas, 'On the reconstruction of historical materialism', in *Communication and the Evolution of Society* (London, Heinemann, 1979).

22. Now, Habermas sees the combination of Weber and Durkheim (and Parsons) as a more fertile basis for sociological development. See J. Habermas, *The Theory of Communicative Action, Volume I: Reason and the Rationalization of Society* (London, Heinemann, 1984); *The Theory of Communicative Action, Volume II: Lifeworld and System; a Critique of Functionalist Reason* (Cambridge, Polity, 1987). In a similar way, Lockwood has recently criticized Marxism for its failure adequately to address normative structures and he, too, sees an answer in Weber and Durkheim, indeed, in the categories Parsons initially outlined in *The Structure of Social Action*

27

See D. Lockwood, *Solidarity and Schism: 'The Problem of Disorder' in Durkheimian and Marxist Sociology* (Oxford, Clarendon Press, 1992). The response of some of those sympathetic to Marxism as the source of adequate categories is simply to argue that Marx was a precursor of Parsons's 'voluntaristic theory of action'. See, for example, M. Gould, 'Parsons versus Marx: "an earnest warning . . ." ', *Sociological Inquiry*, 51(3), 1981 pp. 197–218, and T. Benton, *The Rise and Fall of Structuralist Marxism* (London, Macmillan, 1984).

23. For example, few now have Parsons's self-confidence where he identified his own contribution with the terms, 'the state of general theory in sociology', or 'current scientific theory'. Parsons's claims for his own theory may be overweening, but what are we to make of current attempts to establish the 'foundations' of social theory which logically lay claim to everything, but timidly accept the reality of a plurality of perspectives." Ritzer, for example, proposes the necessity of 'synthesis', but qualifies his claim arguing that "while there is great interest in synthesis, there seems to be a recognition that earlier efforts to create a single, overarching synthetic theory were misguided . . . Rather, contemporary efforts at synthesis are more limited and circumscribed. Thus, we can think of the 'new syntheses' rather than a 'new synthesis'." G. Ritzer, 'The current status of sociological theory: the new syntheses', in G. Ritzer(ed.), *The Frontiers of Social Theory: The New Syntheses* (New York, Columbia University Press, 1990), p. 2.

24. Baudrillard writes, "this is, therefore, exactly the reverse of a 'sociological' understanding. Sociology can only depict the expansion of the social and its vicissitudes. It survives only on the positive and definitive hypothesis of the social. The reabsorption, the implosion of the social escapes it. The hypothesis of the death of the social is also that of its own death." J. Baudrillard, *In the Shadow of the Silent Majorities Or, The End of the Social and Other Essays* (New York, Semiotext[e], 1983), p. 4.

25. See J-F. Lyotard, *The Postmodern Condition: A Report on Knowledge* (Minneapolis, University of Minnesota Press, 1984), p. 81.

26. Ibid., p. 82.

27. Ibid., p. 81.

28. See J. Baudrillard, 'The masses: the implosion of the social in the media', in *Selected Writings* (Cambridge, Polity Press, 1988), p. 248.

29. See, D. Bell, *The End of Ideology: The Exhaustion of Political Ideas in the Fifties* (New York, Free Press, 1960), p. 393. Certainly, Bell is more circumspect and less inclined to embrace relativism than postmodern theorists, but his critique of 'ideology' contains the same themes. Thus, for Bell and postmodern theorists, alike, 'ideological' social movements are 'totalitarian' and oppressive in their attempt to transform people in line with their singular 'truths'. He, too, believes in smaller-scale and diverse 'Utopias' as the basis of meaning in an increasingly routinised world without the deleterious effects of 'ideological' social movements. For his part, Lyotard identifies the 'end of narrative' with the same post-war developments as Bell associates with the 'end of ideology'. Lyotard writes that the 'end of narrative' is, "an effect of the blossoming of techniques and technologies since the Second World War, which has shifted emphasis from the ends of action to its means; it can be seen as an effect of the redeployment of advanced liberal capitalism after its repeat under the protection of Keynesianism during the period 1930–60, a renewal that has eliminated the communist alternative and valorized

the individual enjoyment of goods." J-F. Lyotard, *The Postmodern Condition*, pp. 37–8.

30. S. Seidman, 'The end of sociological theory: the postmodern hope', *Sociological Theory* 9(2), 1991, p. 131.

31. See, for example, S. Hekman, *Gender and Knowledge* (Cambridge, Polity Press, 1991); E. Gross, 'What is feminist theory', in C. Pateman and E. Gross (eds), *Feminist Challenges: Social and Political Theory* (Sydney, Allen and Unwin, 1986); J. Flax, 'Gender as a problem in and for feminist theory', *American Studies* 1986, pp. 193–213; N. Fraser and L. Nicholson, 'Social criticism without philosophy: an encounter between feminism and postmodernism', *Theory, Culture and Society* 5(2), 1988, pp. 373–94.

32. Gross, 'What is feminist theory', p. 200.

33. Hawkesworth, for example, writes of the abandonment of 'reason' in postmodernism that, "at a moment when the preponderance of rational and moral argument sustains prescriptions for women's equality, it is a bit too cruel a conclusion and too reactionary a political agenda to accept that reason is impotent, that equality is impossible". See M.E. Hawkesworth, 'Knower, knowing, known', *Signs: Journal of Women in Culture and Society*, 14(3), 1989, p. 557. Similarly, Hartsock reflects upon the 'end of the individual' in postmodernism, that, "why is it that just at the moment when so many of us who have begun to be silenced begin to demand the right to name ourselves, to act as subjects rather than objects of history, that just then the concept of subjecthood becomes problematic?" See N. Hartsock, 'Foucault on power', in L. Nicholson (ed.), *Feminism/Postmodernism* (London, Routledge, 1990), p. 163.

34. See for example, J. Thompson, 'Women and political rationality', in C. Pateman and E. Gross (eds), *Feminist Challenges*; S. Benhabib and D. Cornell (eds), *Feminism as Critique* (Cambridge, Polity Press, 1987).

35. See H. Garfinkel and H. Sacks, 'On formal structures of practical actions', in J.C. McKinney and E. Tiryakian (eds), *Theoretical Sociology: Perspectives and Developments* (New York, Appleton-Century Crofts, 1970).

36. See M. Weber, *Roscher and Knies: The Logical Problems of Historical Economics* (New York, Free Press, 1975), p. 238.

37. D. Wrong, 'The present condition of American sociology', *Comparative Studies in Society and History*, 35(1), 1993, p. 188.

38. Hillaire Belloc offers the cautionary tale of Jim who ran away from his nurse and was eaten by a lion, with the moral 'always keep a-hold of Nurse for fear of finding something worse'. See, H. Belloc, *Selected Cautionary Verses* (Puffin Books, Harmondsworth, 1950).

3

THE IDEA OF GENERAL THEORY

In the previous chapter, I described an impasse in contemporary sociological theory where sociological theory appears irremediably fragmented, divided between competing and mutually hostile approaches with radically distinct ideas about the nature of social inquiry. Although the present crisis appears to be peculiarly deep and enervating, it is certainly not the first time that sociological argument has appeared to be beset by contradictory theoretical claims. Indeed, there has hardly been a commentary on sociological theory which does not adopt such dualisms as a device for explicating current theoretical arguments and their basis in a sociological tradition similarly characterized.[1] Moreover, in offering this diagnosis, commentators are merely echoing that made by Parsons in *The Structure of Social Action* (hereafter, *TSofSA*). In that work, Parsons described sociology as divided between the mutually exclusive claims of a 'positivist' tradition concerned with external constraints upon action and an 'idealist' tradition of inquiry concerned with subjective meanings of action. At the same time, in common with many theorists since, Parsons argued that each tradition contained important insights and the task was to find a general scheme of categories which would provide a systematic and consistent statement of those insights.

Giddens, for example, also identifies and criticizes what he sees as the dominant 'positivistic' approach to social inquiry in which, "there is no place for a conception of the actor as a reasoning agent, capable of using knowledge in a calculated fashion so as to achieve intended outcomes".[2] He contrasts 'positivism' with an alternative 'hermeneutic' conception, which he believes is also flawed, arguing that the opposition between the two positions has produced a series of unsatisfactory, contradictory 'dualisms' in social theory – 'dualisms' of 'subject' and 'object', 'individual' and 'society', 'voluntarism' and 'determinism'. In place of *dualisms*, Giddens proposes a *duality*, or mutal consistency, of the opposed categories. Habermas, for his part, characterizes the current theoretical dilemmas in terms of two, mutually exclusive, 'conceptual strategies', one a strategy of 'systems' which, "ties social scientific analysis to the external perspective of an observer", while the other strategy, "begins with the members' intuitive knowledge".[3] For Habermas, "the fundamental problem of social theory is how to connect in a satisfactory way the two conceptual strategies indicated by their respective notions of 'system' and 'lifeworld' ".[4] It is these claims for synthetic theory which Alexander believes constitute a 'new theoretical movement'.[5]

Sociology, it seems, has hardly moved on. If Giddens and Habermas are to be believed, the crisis of the last decades is to be solved by the very devices which gave rise to it. As early as 1935, Parsons had made the same distinctions and the same plea as Habermas, that, what he termed the 'objective' and the 'subjective', should be connected, but only after due recognition of what each separately contributed to sociological analysis, writing that, "the results of analysis of human behaviour from the objective point of view (that is, of an outside observer) and the subjective (that of the person thought of as acting himself) should correspond, but that fact is no reason why the two points of view should not be kept clearly distinct. Only on this basis is there any hope of arriving at a satisfactory solution of their relations to each other".[6] Indeed, TSofSA may be regarded as the systematic examination of the two views with the purpose of specifying their relations and, as such, one of the first detailed statements of a position which has become central to the self-understanding of contemporary social theory.

PARSONS AND HIS CRITICS: 'UNCRITICAL CRITICISM'

The idea of a synthetic, general framework takes its force from pre-existing divisions in the sociological undertaking. At the same time, all attempts at synthesis seem to reproduce the very divisions that its proponents are seeking to reconcile. So, just as a perception of a problematic and divided enterprise preceded Parsons's efforts at theoretical reconstruction, his own undertaking is argued to have contributed to division and, for later theorists, has served as its primary illustration. This suggests a flaw at the heart of the synthetic undertaking, but it is a flaw which has proven very difficult to bring to the centre of sociological self-consciousness. Because each synthetic attempt reproduces division it is easy for other theorists to criticize previous attempts for a failure fully to recognize the requirements of synthesis, or for a mistaken commitment to one side, or another, of a division. So, Parsons is variously (and, inconsistently, if we take them together) criticized for an 'idealist' over-emphasis upon common values and a neglect of power,[7] and criticized for a 'positivistic' over-emphasis upon 'structure' (or 'system') to the neglect of 'action'.[8] Little attention is paid to those aspects of his writings where he declares a concern to integrate values and power, structure and action within a single scheme of

31

theoretical categories. Where those aspects are addressed, the inconsistencies among the criticisms are 'resolved' by the claim that Parsons shifted his focus from an early 'action' perspective to a subsequent 'systems' perspective.[9] Why the shift occurs is unexplained. Thus, Dawe, for example, accepts that Parsons *began* with the initial premises of an action approach, but argues that his development of structural concepts has the consequence that, "in terms of its initial premises of subjectivity and historicity, action disappears ... [Parsons] subordinates action to system concepts in such a way as to remove the concept of action altogether".[10] Dawe's judgement is common and is mirrored in Giddens's claim that, "there is no action in Parsons' 'action frame of reference', only behaviour which is propelled by need dispositions or role expectations. The stage is set, but the actors only perform according to scripts which have already been written out for them."[11]

For the proponents of a 'synthetic' approach, the standard criticisms of Parsons serve to distinguish their undertakings from his. For them, the project of a general, synthetic social theory remains plausible, because it has yet to be properly pursued. Thus, Giddens claims that an approach which recognizes the mutal necessity, or 'duality', of structure and action, will overcome the problematic dualism of structure and action in the approach of Parsons (and others), while Habermas, as we have seen, offers a similar reconciliation of previously divided approaches, that of 'system' and that of the 'lifeworld' of actors, where Parsons is assigned to the 'system' approach.[12] It would seem from these arguments that merely seeking to achieve a synthetic theory is insufficient to guarantee its adequate realization. This is certainly so, but what is true of Parsons must also be a possibility for those who would criticize him. However, any failures of approach tend to be seen as contingent upon the idiosyncratic choices and decisions of a particular theorist. What is not called into question is the nature of the synthetic approach itself.

The standard criticisms of Parsons, then, are implicitly partisan and self-seeking in the sense that they serve to insulate the categories favoured by the critics from their implication in the deficiencies attributed to Parsons's scheme. What I shall suggest is that the problems of any particular version of synthetic, general theory are intrinsic to the categories common to all attempts. The failure to address seriously the reasons for Parsons's problems means that theorists who define their undertaking in a similar way are doomed to repeat them. The fate of Parsons's project is a lesson for all those who find its initial premises plausible and necessary.

It is true that some of the problems of interpretations of Parsons's approach are created by his own device for explicating his concerns – what he describes as the (Hobbesean) 'problem of order'. Since he subsequently comes to be criticized for an overemphasis upon stability, it is easy to imagine that he got there by beginning with order to the neglect of power and conflict. I shall examine this argument more fully in the next chapter, but it will become clear in this chapter that any idea that a concern with 'order' is to be set against issues of power and conflict would be at odds with Parsons's methodological claims in *TSofSA*. The very thrust of his approach is to provide a general, *inclusive* social theory, one which would be adequate to issues of consensus *and* conflict, stability *and* change (and, once again, a similar synthesis is what his critics propose).

Although Parsons's statements of his synthetic intentions are straightforward enough, the idea that he over-emphasizes the 'ideal' is a mistake that is also easy to make in terms of the particular sources and material that he discusses in *TSofSA*. For example, as well as considering the two traditions of 'positivism' and 'idealism', he also addresses the relation between 'economics' and 'sociology'. Very few commentators, until very recently, have attended to Parsons's arguments about 'economics'.[13] The logic of his argument identifies 'economics' as a distinct discipline concerned with material factors and instrumental, self-interested actions, while 'sociology' as a distinct discipline is associated with factors which emerge in 'economics' (especially, in 'institutional' economics), but lie outside its central categories, to some extent issues of power, but, more importantly, issues of norms and values.[14] In this way, 'sociology' is strongly associated with 'idealism', as against the 'materialism' of 'economics'. However, since Parsons is making a plea for the integration of these concerns within a general scheme, his idealist identification of 'sociology' is *far from being a commitment to an idealist scheme of general categories for social science*.

Indeed, for someone like Alexander, who is sympathetic to Parsons's undertaking and knowledgeable as to how it was constituted, the standard criticisms are self-evidently false. After all, he argues, Parsons was committed to a synthetic theory sensitive to different social influences upon conduct. According to Alexander, Parsons offers a 'multi-dimensional' approach; that is, an approach which recognizes the 'individual' and the 'collective', and their specification in terms of 'material' and 'ideal' factors, and 'power' and 'norms'.[15] For Alexander, then, it is the critics who are one-sided in their claims for an 'action' approach, set against a 'systems' approach, or a 'conflict' approach set against a 'consensus' approach. Moreover, since, according to Alexander, such one-sided approaches cannot be sustained, unsurprisingly, the critics move closer to Parsons's position as their own schemes are elaborated.[16] For Alexander, this convergence is evidence of the adequacy of Parsons's approach, rather than evidence of common problems across approaches.

Yet, Parsons's scheme *does fail to realise its aims*. Even Alexander suggests that his approach is by no means consistently realized. He hails Parsons's achievement in producing all the basic categories of an adequate, synthetic sociology, but allows that Parsons frequently 'falls' back from what he achieved and this is something of a riddle. "If we take Parsons at face value," Alexander writes, "he is often, in fact, the 'functionalist', the 'equilibrium theorist', the 'ideologist' that his critics portray. He can achieve each of these identities, moreover, while maintaining his generalised, presuppositional emphasis.

Parsons's critics, then, are correct; yet at the same time they are wrong."[17] What must be explained are precisely those features of Parsons's approach that seem to negate his own claims for 'multi-dimensionality' and which render the criticisms of him possible. Alexander accepts that, "it seems at first incredible that such contradictions could permeate the work of such a self-conscious thinker," only to offer the reassuring consideration that, "we should not really be surprised, for social theories are, in fact, rife with confusions and self-contradiction. None of Parsons's predecessors was entirely consistent".[18] This is an unconvincing account which trivializes the substance of the problem. At some level, Parsons's critics must be identifying real difficulties with his scheme, even if their criticisms are often serving merely to insulate their own arguments from their association with what they find problematic.

It is a measure of Parsons's integrity as a theorist that at the same time as he sets out his scheme he also offers the criteria by which it should be judged.[19] Thus, in *TSofSA*, Parsons argued that he was constructing his own theory out of the 'debris' of previous approaches. Different sociological approaches, he argued, had broken down and his own study was, to a large degree, an examination of the pieces. There were many contributors to the different positions, he suggested, and choosing one over some others was, perhaps, invidious. Nevertheless, "the best place to go to find the starting points of the breakdown of a system," he argued, "is to the ablest proponents of the system."[20] It is they who will recognize and address their problems, producing inconsistencies in the process. As a consequence, their work will appear 'difficult' and 'ambiguous', but it is precisely these 'difficulties' and 'ambiguities' which repay examination and enable a theoretical system to be opened out and reconstructed. In contrast, the lesser proponents of a system will dogmatically deny the difficulties and assert both the logical closure and theoretical adequacy of the scheme to which they are attached. Just as Marshall, Pareto, Durkheim and Weber served Parsons's purpose of demonstrating the breakdown of different systems of social theory, so Parsons provides the best illustration of the problems of any attempt at providing a synthetic framework of general categories for social scientific inquiries. Faced with the contradictions of his predecessors, Parsons argued that those contradictions were a sign of the breakdown of their theoretical systems. He did not regard the problematic features of their writings as contingent, but entailed, and what was required, he argued, was a fundamental reconstruction of their categories. We should pay Parsons the same compliment.

CONVERGENCE

What makes a discussion of Parsons so central to current issues in sociological theory, quite apart from his role as a 'foil' against which other theorists have defined their positions, is that the most systematic discussion of the requirements of any synthetic undertaking of general theory is to be found in his work.[21] In general outline, Parsons's representation of the two traditions of 'positivism' and 'idealism' (essentially, for Parsons, this is the tradition of German idealism after Kant), which are the objects of his criticism in *TSofSA*, is no different from other representations of the dualism at the heart of the sociological undertaking. He argues that approaches to social inquiry have become divided between 'positivists' who would promote a natural science of society and 'idealists' who, regarding such an approach as alienated and alienating, have emphasized, instead, the essentially moral issues of life in human communities. What divides them is their different conceptions of the nature of social objects and their different views on the appropriateness of the methods of the natural sciences to social inquiries. According to Parsons, the occurrence of two mutually exclusive epistemologies has deleterious consequences, undermining the coherence necessary to any rational social scientific undertaking.

Whatever their other differences, both sides agree that the objects and relations addressed by the natural sciences, such as physics, are external, unyielding and continuous. Natural objects, it is held, are independent of, and unaffected by, any inquiries made into them and the characteristics that they exhibit continue from the past into the present and will do so into the future. In recent years, this conception of natural science, which underpins both 'positivist' approaches to social science and the 'idealist' rejection of them, has been challenged, as we shall see in the course of this chapter. For the moment, however, this rather simplified account is sufficient to identify key themes in Parsons's view of the nature of general social theory, themes which he shares with many other theorists. The characteristic feature of the 'positivist' approach in social science is its emphasis upon external, conditional determinants of human conduct. As Parsons puts it, within positivism, "any attempt to explain . . . behaviour in terms of ends, purposes and ideals has been under suspicion as a form of 'teleology' which was thought to be incompatible with the methodological requirements of positive science. One must, on the contrary, explain in terms of 'causes' and 'conditions', not of ends".[22] Such a view finds its most extensive social scientific statement in the disciplines of economics and psychology (especially in 'behaviourism') and, in particular, in utilitarian assumptions about rational calculation and psychological motivation according to a pleasure-pain calculus. A further feature of the 'positivistic' approach, Parsons argues, is its emphasis upon mechanistic and empirically closed systems of theory.

In contrast, within 'idealism' it is argued that social objects, unlike natural objects, are internal, plastic and discontinuous. These characteristics, it is argued, arise from the fact that social objects have their origin in the actions of human subjects, who, at least to some degree, are responsible for those actions. Whether, or not, events from the past will continue into the future is a matter of decision, or choice, on the part of human agents. Those decisions may be informed by knowledge drawn from social inquiries so that, unlike natural objects and relations, social objects and relations are not independent of inquiries into them. According to the 'idealist' tradition, then, the human capacity for creativity, freedom and choice, introduces an irreducible contingency, or indeterminism, into any explanatory undertaking in the social sciences. In contrast to 'positivist' approaches, then, 'idealists' emphasize the independent role of internal, subjective factors and the wider context of cultural values in the organization of conduct. This tradition of thought is exemplified in what Parsons terms the Kantian predisposition, "to a certain 'particularistic' mode of treatment of human action, emphasizing the uniqueness of the particular human individual, and the freedom from determination by circumstances of his particular acts".[23]

According to Parsons there are considerable variations within the two traditions and it was part of his purpose in *TSofSA* to document the twists and turns of the different developments within each tradition (to the extent that he offers a typology of four forms of positivism, relevant to his study). For the moment, however, I want to concentrate upon the broader features of Parsons's argument for a synthetic general theory. The question that must arise in the light of any argument for a synthesis of opposed positions, is this: if each position can be separately developed, what determines their mutual necessity? After all, Parsons (and Habermas, Giddens, or anyone else committed to a synthetic approach, for that matter) argues that there are self-conscious proponents within each tradition – for example, those he calls 'dogmatists' – who believe that an adequate approach to social inquiry must be found entirely in the categories of one, or other, of the two positions. Why should the two approaches be connected? How could they be connected, if their categories are mutually exclusive?

Parsons's answer is offered in the first chapters of *TSofSA*, where he proposes a characterization of systems of scientific (including social scientific) theory and indicators of theoretical breakdown in those systems. He identifies two kinds of category relevant to any understanding of the dynamic processes of theory development. These are the *positive* categories of a theoretical system and its *negative, residual* categories. He writes that, "a theoretical system must always involve the positive definition of certain empirically identifiable variables or other general categories".[24] By *positive* definition Parsons means that they have a consistent definition *within* a theoretical system. However, he believes that there will also emerge categories which are *negatively* defined; for example, there are "facts known to exist, which are even more or less adequately described, but are defined theoretically by their *failure* to fit into the positively defined categories of the system".[25] Such residual categories are of fundamental importance. They are an indication of problems intrinsic to a theoretical system, reflecting 'facts' external to theory, but 'known' by virtue of its deficiencies. They are implicated in the positive categories of the theoretical system, but not consistently accounted for by them.

According to Parsons, the role of residual categories in theoretical development, "may be deduced from the inherent necessity of a system to become logically closed", in that, "the obviously unattainable, but asymptotically approached goal of the development of scientific theory . . . is the elimination of all residual categories from science in favour of positively defined empirically verifiable concepts".[26] This process of the elimination of residual categories will not occur by the accumulation of insights in a scheme in which new categories are simply added to the pre-existing, positive categories of a system. "Theoretical systems change. There is not merely a quantitative accumulation of 'knowledge of fact'," argues Parsons, "but a qualitative change in the structure of theoretical systems."[27] Development, then, involves the transformation of categories. Obviously the positive statement of previously residual categories transforms *their* meaning by placing them in a different network of theoretical relations, but the process also transforms the positively defined categories of previous statements of the theoretical system, as explanations are extended and new relationships postulated. Thus, Parsons writes that, "the process of the carving out of positive categories from residual categories is also a process by which the reconstruction of theoretical systems is accomplished as a result of which they may eventually be altered beyond all recognition. But this should be said: the original empirical insights associated with the positive categories of the system will be restated in different form, but unless they entirely fail to stand up to the combined criticism of theory and renewed empirical verification, they will not be eliminated".[28]

It follows from the preceding analysis that Parsons's claim is that each of the two broad theoretical systems of 'positivism' and 'idealism' will manifest a *common* structure of positively defined categories, alongside residual categories. This structure will also be found in any of the variations within a position and, indeed, the variations are to be explained by the way in which theorists have felt the need to grapple with the problems that an expanding domain of residual categories implies. Some try to excise the problematic categories altogether, looking to a more rigorous statement of the core categories; others attempt different solutions. But Parsons's basic point is that no adequate solution will be found unless the very core assumptions are critically addressed.

Once he has traced through the failures of all the variations within a position, Parsons's argument is that 'positivism' and 'idealism' occur as mirror images. Neither position is internally consistent and the positive categories of one emerge as the residual categories of the other. Thus, halfway through his survey of the two traditions, he offers the following description of his undertaking: "earlier in this study the attempt has been made . . . to bring out certain fundamental difficulties of a completely positivistic version of the theory of action, and to demonstrate to what extent the positivistic theory of action has itself become involved in these difficulties and in so doing has transcended the rigidly positivistic basis, developing at least partly in an idealistic direction. The task of the present section will be to follow the reverse process and show some of the inherent difficulties of a completely idealistic position and how positivistic elements have come into the idealistic tradition."[29]

37

A substantial part of *TSofSA* is given over to detailed demonstrations that the different traditions of sociological thought do, indeed, break down in the manner outlined. Parsons's analysis of Durkheim's theories, for example, is intended to show the instability of his position, moving between positivism and idealism, as Durkheim addresses the problems intrinsic to his categories and as residual categories emerge to undermine any coherence in his approach. Thus, Parsons suggests that in *The Division of Labour in Society* Durkheim proposes a form of positivism, albeit one that emphasizes 'collective' processes against the 'individualism' of standard utilitarian approaches.[30] When Durkheim locates the causes of the division of labour in external features of the social milieu – especially, environmental pressures of the 'struggle for existence' – Parsons suggests that he comes close to subscribing to an extreme form of positivism.[31] However, in *Suicide*, this extreme form is modified once again in that Durkheim there criticizes 'external' environmental explanations and moves to a conception of the social milieu in terms of normative elements which are internalized in personality.[32] This receives further elaboration in Durkheim's later writings which have a distinctly 'idealist' cast when compared to his earlier 'materialism'. However, even here, his 'new orientation' to the 'institutional aspect of action systems' is not wholly 'idealist' in character since it "has the effect of bringing utilitarian elements back into the picture in the form of 'interests' tending centrifugally to escape normative control".[33] Each of Durkheim's solutions reveals its inadequacy by the residual categories that are resorted to in the attempt to achieve theoretical closure. Ultimately, as he does with other theorists writing from different perspectives, Parsons traces Durkheim's problems to the inadequacy of his concepts to the relations between the 'individual' and the 'social' (issues which I shall address in the following chapter).[34]

For Parsons, the identification of distinct 'phases' in the different attempts at dealing with problems – for example, phases in the development of Durkheim's theories – is an interpretive device to indicate the instability of any particular solution. Undoubtedly, he overstates the distinctiveness of each phase and aspects assigned to any one are easily found in the other phases.[35] However, his purpose is also to discern the means by which a more adequate approach might be constructed. His identification of the shifts in theoretical emphasis characteristic of the work of each theorist is intended to point to the extent to which a more adequate approach must be synthetic, accepting the positive features of each tradition. When Parsons identifies a 'convergence' upon this position in the writings of his group of theorists he does not mean that this has been a self-conscious development. Thus, in setting out his own solution, he writes that his own scheme of categories, "does not contain only elements common to all the previous traditions. Though every one of its major groups of elements had some place in at least one of the other traditions as something more than part of a residual category, this is not true of the system as a whole ... The completed structure is at some vital point incompatible with each of these older systems."[36] Parsons offers his own 'completed structure' of social theory as a comprehensive scheme which has eliminated the residual categories characteristic of previous approaches and has transmuted them to the positive categories of a more comprehensive scheme.

A number of critics have taken issue with Parsons's theory of 'convergence', arguing that he misrepresents the different theorists he discusses and that they do not fit easily into the scheme he is proposing, frequently, even implying their hostility to it.[37] But this is precisely what Parsons accepts. The theorists he is discussing are more likely to be trying self-consciously to maintain one of the 'older systems', even as they reveal its limits and implicitly point to the new. It would be all too easy, but beside the point, to 'de-Parsonize' Weber or Durkheim, in the sense of, say, pointing out Weber's scepticism toward a framework of general categories and his hostility to what then passed for functional analysis, or pointing out Durkheim's hostility to the assumptions of a sociology of action. This merely re-describes the problem of antithetical conceptions of the sociological undertaking that Parsons is attempting to solve. Moreover, the true task of 'de-Parsonizing' his interpretations of the classics would be to demonstrate not only the different nature of the approach in question, but also its internal adequacy against the strictures of Parsons's criticisms of it. Parsons's critics, for the most part, have not attempted this and, as I have already observed, most attempts at finding a different way forward by selecting a different set of 'classics' have led back to Parsons's starting point. Certainly, we have been returned again and again to the ideas of 'two sociologies', each internally inconsistent, but whose different claims can be reconciled within a single scheme which will synthesize, or integrate, them.

What I want to suggest in the remainder of this chapter, however, is that there is something wrong with 'convergence' or, more properly, with the idea that the problem of divided approaches, or traditions, can be solved by a 'synthesis' of their categories within a general framework of social theory. Parsons's claim is that each of the two traditions contains negative, residual categories that correspond to the positive categories of the other, arguing, further, that an adequate approach can be constructed by combining the positive categories of each, leaving behind any problem of their antithetical, residual categories. But why should we believe that there could be a non-contradictory scheme that combines categories which, hitherto, have occurred in combinations which are contradictory? After all, the antithetical and mutually exclusive character of the categories is central to Parsons's conception of the breakdown of theoretical systems and his denial that progress could be made by any simple accumulation of insights. Were this not so, the expansion of residual categories, of itself, would be an approach to an adequate, 'synthetic' scheme. What, then, establishes that Parsons's approach is a *solution* to the problems he is identifying? *What protects it from being merely a phase in the process of theoretical breakdown*?

While the occurrence of residual categories in one approach which are the positively defined categories of another approach seems to open up an area of mutuality, or overlap, between approaches, this could be no guarantee of the adequacy of what they share. What *they* have converged upon, as Parsons himself demonstrates, is a *common problem*, where each is a mirror to the deficiencies of the other. In fact, Parsons's own ambivalence on these matters is evident in his claim for a non-contradictory, synthetic scheme. Having shown the emergence of antithetical idealist categories within positivist schemes, Parsons outlines his strategy of showing the emergence of antithetical positivist categories within idealism. He makes the following observation: "it will not, however, do merely to say that both the positivistic and the idealistic positions have certain justifications and there is a sphere in which each should be recognised. It is necessary, rather, to go beyond such eclecticism, to attempt at least in outline, an account of the specific modes of interrelation between the two. It is in this connection that the voluntaristic theory of action assumes a place of central importance. It provides a bridge between the apparently irreconcilable differences of the two traditions, making it possible, in a certain sense, to 'make the best of both worlds'."[38]

Parsons's notion that a 'bridge' could be built between them is weak when considered in the light of other of his arguments about the nature of theoretical systems. After all, he also writes of the need to *reconstruct* theoretical systems, where the consequence of reconstruction is that they 'may eventually be altered beyond all recognition'. Yet, in Parsons's synthetic action frame of reference, the categories are all too easily recognizable as the categories which he identifies as the positive substance of the previously antithetical schemes. To state the matter baldly, I shall suggest that all that Parsons succeeds in doing is to provide a highly generalized statement of the very contradictory divisions that confound the approaches he describes.

GENERAL THEORY AND SOCIAL EXPLANATION

Unsurprisingly, Parsons's arguments were initially strongly criticized by those committed to the then dominant positivistic and empiricist conception of theory construction.[39] For example, his emphasis upon the independent role of a system of theoretical categories in the organization of a domain of inquiry seemed to contradict both the empiricist view that scientific knowledge is, or should be, arrived at inductively from the systematic observation of 'facts', and the positivist view that scientific knowledge is organized in terms of universal laws. Subsequently, as the deficiencies of his scheme – in particular, concerning the problematic role of 'action' within it – became apparent, his arguments were held to be themselves a form of positivism.[40] Now, however, more sympathetic commentators have claimed on Parsons's behalf that his view of the role of general theory is a precursor to post-positivist developments in the philosophy of science and that he was misunderstood because he was 'ahead of his time'.[41]

Natural science, itself, has not been immune from the criticisms which have undermined the authority of positivistic conceptions of social science and parallel criticisms have occurred in the philosophy of science. These came to a head with the publication of Kuhn's *The Structure of Scientific Revolutions.*[42] Since then, 'post-positivist' philosophers of science, sometimes in criticism of Kuhn, sometimes developing and extending his views, have radically challenged the conception of natural science that has formed the backdrop to discussions of methodological issues in social science since the last century.[43] Positivism is not simply an inappropriate approach to social science, it is severely deficient as an account of natural science. However, any lessons for social science, that can be drawn from post-positivist accounts of science, in particular concerning the role of general theory, are not straightforward. A brief exposition of the central arguments of post-positivism, then, is necessary for a proper appreciation of Parsons's own claims about the nature of general theory in social science.

According to the once-standard, positivist view, scientific practices establish the truth, or law-like character, of general statements in terms of their *correspondence* to a world of external, empirical objects which can be represented independently of the explanatory claims of science. On this view, false statements are eliminated from the corpus of scientific statements as science accumulates its content of empirically verified statements. However, both the status of law-like generalizations and the independence of empirical observations from theoretical statements are challenged in post-positivist conceptions of science. The idea that scientific laws are built up from the painstaking observation of many cases, for example, fell foul of the problem of induction. No amount of confirming instances in the past of a general statement can guarantee that they will continue into the future. The belief that they will is dogmatic, justified by neither logic nor sense experience.

In the face of this difficulty, there were attempts to maintain a 'half-way' house. Popper, for example, suggested a solution to the problem of induction by reversing the argument. If no general statement could be said to be 'proved' by however many confirming instances, at least it could be *disproved* by *one* disconfirming instance. If scientific statements could not be shown to be 'true', at least they could be shown to be 'falsifiable'.[44] 'Testability', rather than 'verifiability', could be made the distinguishing criterion of scientific statements that demarcated them from non-scientific statements.

Popper's revision and the positivist view alike require that theoretical statements are independent of the empirical observations against which they are to be tested. However, post-positivist theories of science have shown the theory-dependent nature of 'facts'. There is no independent language of observation; at least, not without dogmatically presupposing the very truth of the theoretical categories to which they are supposed to be a guide.[45] If the language of observation is not theory-independent, then theories are potentially offering themselves for tests that are internal to them. As Quine argues, if observations are theory-dependent, it is always open for proponents of a theory to claim that any problem lies with the observations held to disconfirm it and not with the theory itself.[46] Theories, Quine argues, are *under-determined* by any 'facts' held to bear upon them and can always be maintained by some adjustment of terms.

Quine's argument seems to suggest that decisions to maintain or to discard theoretical statements are always, in some fundamental way, arbitrary. The implication is that a number of theories may be consistent with the 'same facts' which introduces an apparently irreducible indeterminacy into the evaluation of competing theories. This conclusion, however, is one which other philosophers of science, even those sympathetic to the arguments which underlie it, have sought to resist. Perhaps the most important and fruitful answer has been provided by Lakatos in his attempt to show that there are criteria by which 'Quinean adjustments' can be evaluated.[47] For Lakatos (and Kuhn, for that matter), scientific theories are not an aggregation of singular statements, but are made up of a network of interrelated statements, which constitute what he calls a 'research programme'. How 'anomalies', or apparently disconfirming instances, are addressed will, in part, depend upon the relative importance of the apparently 'disconfirmed' statement in the network; the 'hard core' of the programme generates a 'positive heuristic' of empirical implications, but is itself protected from disconfirmation by auxiliary theorems. Eventually, though, 'anomalies' will accumulate such that even the 'hard core' is called into question.

Thus, Lakatos answers Quine's claim that a theory can be maintained by an adjustment of its terms, by distinguishing between progressive adjustments, or 'problem shifts', which add to explanatory resources, and *ad hoc* modifications, or 'degenerate problem shifts', which merely re-describe problems and do not represent any explanatory advance. So, all 'readjustments' have consequences and, ultimately, can be evaluated in the light of those consequences.[48] Even so, any 'falsification' of 'hard core' assumptions will depend upon the emergence of another theory (with a different 'hard core') which solves the anomalies, at the same time as generating new explanatory resources. As Alexander puts it, glossing Lakatos, "fundamental shifts in scientific belief occur only when empirical changes are matched by the availability of alternative theoretical commitments."[49]

It is this which Alexander takes as one of the central planks of post-positivism implicit in Parsons's arguments about the status of general theory. It will be some time before we can properly evaluate the extent to which Parsons's arguments do pre-figure those of post-positivist philosophies of science. However, it is clear from the language with which Parsons approaches issues of theory – 'problems', 'breakdown', 'revision', 'positive' and 'residual' categories, and so on – that he does understand the elaboration and development of theoretical systems (together with their bodies of empirical knowledge) to be a dynamic and, to some extent, discontinuous process.

In setting out his methodological views, Parsons begins by attacking the dominant view of the nature of science, expressing his hostility to 'empiricist' accounts of scientific development where 'theoretical' terms are held to be otiose unless reducible to a language of observation or sense data. On an 'empiricist' view, as we have seen, scientific development is argued to take place through the accumulation of theoretical statements with increasing 'factual' content and by the elimination of theoretical statements which do not correspond to 'facts'. Such a view of science, Parsons suggests, neglects the 'independent' role of theory. According to Parsons, what is held to be a 'fact' depends upon its statement within some wider theoretical framework. In this way, he writes, "scientific 'theory' – most generally defined as a body of logically interrelated 'general concepts' of empirical reference – is not only a dependent but an independent variable in the development of science".[50] According to Parsons, 'empiricism' not only neglects the independent role of theory, but it is 'atomistic', turning attention away from the logical relations that exist between theoretical categories. Thus, for Parsons, theory is, "not only an independent variable in the development of science, but the body of theory in a given field at a given time constitutes to a greater or lesser degree an integrated 'system'".[51] Issues of coherence, and not just issues of correspondence, then, are relevant to the evaluation of any theoretical scheme. Moreover, once an 'empiricist' construal of theoretical terms has been rejected, 'correspondence' is complex, mediated by theoretical terms without a direct empirical reference.

It is clear that Parsons's concerns in *TSofSA* are meta-theoretical in the sense that the focus of his attention is the nature of theoretical categories and the logical relations among categories, both *within* and *between* different theoretical schemes. However, in setting out his opposition to 'empiricism', Parsons is anxious to stress that his concerns are, nevertheless, *empirical*. Thus, he writes that, "it would lead to the worst kind of dialectical sterility to treat the development of a system of theory without reference to the empirical problems in relation to which it has been built up".[52] However, it is the implications of empirical problems for general theoretical categories, rather than the *substance of the empirical examples in their own right and how they might be reconstructed*, that is Parsons's concern. So, he explains, in studying someone's empirical work, "the primary questions will, rather, be what theoretical reasons did he have for being interested in these particular problems rather than others, and what did the results of his investigations contribute to the solution of his theoretical problems? Then, in turn, what did the insights gained from investigations contribute to restatement of his theoretical problems and through this to the revision of his theoretical system?"[53] Nevertheless, it is Parsons's claim that the systematic examination of these theoretical issues will serve to illuminate and deepen empirical inquiry and, of course, his aim, ultimately, is to set out the scheme of categories that will be the basis of such inquiry.

Parsons's hostility to 'empiricist' accounts of science, then, is because they fail to recognize these theoretical processes and the role of theoretical reconstruction in the development of social (or natural) science. Borrowing a phrase from Whitehead, Parsons argues that their neglect of theoretical processes commits them to the 'fallacy of misplaced concreteness'. That is, to a situation where the immediate apprehension of 'facts' as 'real' neglects the issue of their theoretical constitution as either *positive* or *residual* categories. Thus, when Parsons discusses the various responses to the breakdown of theoretical systems, he argues that it is precisely the dominance of an empiricist methodology which encourages the view that the existence of residual categories will not entail any fundamental challenge to a theoretical approach. On an empiricist methodology, it must appear that any new 'facts' could be directly incorporated into a scheme by a simple process of accumulation. According to Parsons, however, this ignores the theoretical relations in which 'facts' are constituted. Ultimately, the simple acceptance of 'empirically observed facts' without regard to their relationship to the theoretical processes of a positively defined system leads to indeterminacy in the theory which is, according to Parsons, "a form of empirical inadequacy".[54]

Any claim that 'problems' exist outside theories is, on Parsons's analysis, a form of empiricism which fails to recognize how schemes are implicated in the very identification of the problems to which they are addressed. The development of a coherent theoretical scheme which solves these problems, then, will require a transformation of theoretical categories and relations, including those of the 'observations' associated with previous schemes. Parsons's fundamental insight is that it is the *failure*, or breakdown, of a scheme that produces both the appearance of problems beyond the scope of its positive categories *and* that any additional (for Parsons, residual) categories advanced in the *immediate apprehension* of those problems will be antithetical to the positive categories of the pre-existing scheme. Thus, the dualisms so evident in statements of the sociological undertaking are an artifact of explanatory failure, together with the implicit operation of an empiricist methodology.

On these arguments, we can see why any attempt at a general theory might appear to be 'positivistic' from the perspective of those committed to the 'idealist' tradition, who see in general theory a denial of the 'particularity' of subjective experience. However, according to Parsons, the identification of a 'particularism' of subjective meaning resistant to inclusion within a general scheme, is not, in itself, 'independent of a theoretical scheme', but is rather a consequence of indeterminacy in such a scheme. For example, Parsons criticizes Weber's conception of theoretical constructs as 'ideal types', or necessary fictions, as a form of 'idealist particularism'. Thus, Weber suggests that theoretical constructs can be necessary despite the fact that, in a concrete instance, the behaviours that they are designed to interpret, deviate from the processes established within the construct.[55] Weber accepts both the validity of the construct and the validity of the subjective meanings of actors which are at odds with it. For Weber, this is possible because actors have the capacity for freedom and may have 'chosen' to orient their activities in a manner different from that contained within the 'ideal type' initially offered in explanation of their behaviours. In this case, he argues, their different behaviours will require a different theoretical construct for their interpretation. However, since actors *could* equally well have chosen to act in conformity with the processes of the type initially proposed, *that* 'ideal type' remains necessary and valuable. The consequence of Weber's arguments is that because the different 'ideal types' are formed on the mutually exclusive principles informing the discrete meanings they express, the different behaviours they are designed to interpret cannot be represented within a single general scheme.[56]

According to Parsons, Weber's approach has the consequence of a 'type atomism' which cannot coherently (that is, theoretically) account for the 'facts' that it accepts.[57] That is, Weber breaks up the analysis of actions, which seem to be related concretely, between analytically distinct and theoretically unrelated types. What Parsons suggests is that the non-applicability of any type (or theoretical construct) *is* an issue of its validity and that a reconstruction of pre-existing theoretical constructs would be necessary to the adequate explanation – that is, their representation within a single scheme – of 'conforming' and seemingly 'non-conforming' behaviours.[58] His argument against idealist 'particularism' – a position in Parsons's time that corresponds with post-modernism in ours – is that it is a form of 'empiricism' of 'subjective meanings' (to prevent any misinterpretation of what is being argued, it should be stressed, once again, that what is being attributed to actors is not, in truth, *their* 'subjective' meanings, but the social scientist's *perception* of those meanings inferred from behaviours at odds with the 'objective' meanings represented within existing theoretical schemes).

As with other synthetic theorists, Parsons's claim is that what from the 'idealist' perspective seems to be the 'inhuman' character of general theory need not be the case and that it only appears to be the case because, hitherto, most attempts at general schemes have been self-consciously positivistic in character, seeking to exclude any conception of the human being as "essentially an active, creative, evaluating creature".[59] Parsons's claim is that such a conception can be adequately accounted for in a general scheme, once the limitations of a positivist conception of theoretical system are recognized. In other words, the idealist concern with the 'inhuman' character of a general scheme is not properly an issue of the logical requirements of a general theoretical system, but an issue of the particular categories of the positivistic version of such a system. Thus, Parsons is offering the possibility of an 'empirically closed' theoretical scheme which avoids the mechanistic character of positivist schemes. More fundamentally, he argues that it is *only by recognizing and accepting the active role of human beings that the positivist goal of empirical closure could be met*; that is, put the other way round, Parsons argues that the failure fully to accept the consequences of the active role of human beings is the cause of empirical indeterminacy in positivist schemes.

'Empiricism', or the 'fallacy of misplaced concreteness', then, is an issue from both sides of the positivism/idealism divide and part of the solution to the problematic division of approaches, Parsons argues, is to recognize a distinct, higher level of theoretical argument in which the correct identification of appropriate categories can be made. It is this latter argument which comes to dominate the development of Parsons's theoretical system. However, it is doubtful if it does overcome the very explanatory problems that he so powerfully and persuasively identifies.

Ultimately, what Parsons suggest is that the explanatory issues with which he is concerned can be dealt with by outlining a 'higher level' of 'analytical theory' in which the problems of relations among categories can be solved prior to their re-application to issues of empirical inquiry. The problems have emerged in the process of empirical inquiry – indeed, Parsons says that, "there is no possible explanation of this convergence into a single theoretical system which does not include the proposition that correct observation and interpretation of the facts themselves constitutes a major element"[60] – but the solution is not directly an empirical issue. In this way, Parsons seems to argue that, logically, the answer can be given in advance of any substantive inquiry in the form of putatively 'positive', general categories. Somewhat at odds with the implications of his other statements regarding the development of theory, then, he suggests that the synthetic scheme of these general categories, once given, is beyond further reconstruction. Thus Parsons argues that the scheme has what he calls 'phenomenological status', that is, "it involves no concrete data that can be 'thought away', that are subject to change. It is not a phenomenon in the empirical sense. It is the indispensable logical framework in which we describe and think about the phenomena of action".[61]

If we take Parsons's arguments seriously, concerning the 'empiricism' inherent in the immediate apprehension of 'residual' categories, the question can be asked whether there is not a similar problem in his acceptance of the 'reality' of the 'positive' categories. In other words, once there is an issue of mutually inconsistent categories – which is, for Parsons, the circumstance which obtains in the breakdown of a theoretical system – the 'reality' of *all categories* must be called into question. In the light of post-positivist strictures, all we can know is that there is a problem in our understanding, not where the problem lies and how it will be solved. In other words, the problem might be dealt with by a minor modification of categories or it may turn out that a more fundamental reconstruction of categories is necessary.

Admittedly, Parsons's epistemological arguments are inconsistent, or at least ambiguous, and the problems intrinsic to the claimed phenomenological status of general theory are more clearly expressed in Alexander's defence of the position. The latter offers an interpretation which, he suggests, places Parsons's epistemological arguments at the centre of current discussions in the philosophy of science. According to Alexander, the 'phenomenological' status of the action frame of reference is the substance of Parsons's meta-theoretical, 'synthetic achievement'. This form of theorizing, Alexander argues, establishes a non-relativistic set of truth criteria which will overcome the problems of a sociological undertaking divided by different and seemingly mutually exclusive epistemological claims. He sees a parallel between his own (and Parsons's) arguments for an independent 'theoretical logic' and post-positivist arguments in the philosophy of science. 'Theoretical logic' consists in 'presuppositions' which, according to Alexander, "refer to the most general assumptions sociologists make when they encounter reality. Every social theory and every empirical work take *a priori* positions that allow observers to organize in the most simple categorial terms the data that enter their minds via their senses."[62] For Alexander, then, the framework of general theory is a form of theorizing about *a priori* presuppositions, "without reference to particular empirical problems or domain".[63] Echoing Parsons, he writes that, in social theory, the presuppositions of 'action' and 'order' (or 'system'), "constitute the 'structural' properties of social theory. They are not, as such, the elements of any particular theory. They cannot be eliminated from one theory or another, nor are they subject to change depending on the historical circumstances."[64]

It seems that the framework of general theory is held to be necessary to any empirical inquiry, but it is not itself subject to revision as a consequence of such inquiries. Why should we regard past processes of theoretical elaboration as superseded in current practices, but current theoretical arguments as not similarly revisable? If, in the past, the more adequate address of empirical problems gave rise to the reconstruction of social theory, why will *our* empirical problems not require a similar transformation of our theoretical understandings? In fact, when Parsons himself addresses the role of empirical issues in the evaluation of theories, he sometimes appears to criticize any attribution of a 'phenomenological' status to a theoretical scheme. Thus, he writes that, "eliminating observation of the facts as an important element in the development of the theory of action really amounts to eliminating action itself, unless there be a purely fortuitous harmony between the outline of the theory and the facts to which it refers".[65]

Alexander is so anxious to establish the independence of 'theoretical logic' from any empirical consideration that he takes any contrary indication on Parsons's part as a sign of a 'latent positivism' – accusing him of a "positivist faith in the conjunction of theory and fact"[66] which retains its hold over him in *TSofSA*, despite his struggles to be free. Given the substance of what Parsons is actually saying, Alexander's charge is hardly credible. Indeed, Alexander frequently seems so anxious to avoid the 'fallacy of misplaced concreteness' that he is willing to dispense with the concrete altogether and to embrace what Parsons saw as a consequent 'dialectical sterility'. Nevertheless, the ambivalance toward his own project that Parsons here expresses does prefigure difficulties that will come to dominate the further elaboration of his theory.

We have seen that he is criticized by Giddens, Dawe and many others for an absence of 'action' in his action frame of reference. For his critics, as we shall see in the next chapter, this problem comes to be associated with his concept of the 'perfect integration' of systems of social interaction, a concept which comes to have a central place in his theoretical scheme. Yet, Parsons is drawn to this position despite having criticized an equivalent assumption of a 'natural harmony of social interests' in the writings of classical political economists.[67] Similarly, in the above statement about the nature of theoretical development, he criticizes an analogous idea of 'harmony' applied to the relation of 'theory' and 'empirical observation', at the same time as his statement of the phenomenological status of his scheme embodies precisely such an idea. His action frame of reference is designed to be adequate to 'action', and that must include the action of social scientists producing new understandings of the social world, yet, if it does have the phenomenological status he claims for it, once it is realized, it is itself beyond 'action'. Who, after Parsons, is to act?

Once again, we should regard this consequence as intrinsic to *any* claim to produce an *a priori* general, synthetic scheme, rather than as a peculiar feature of that of Parsons. Moreover, any claim for an *a priori*, general scheme is a form of 'foundationalism' that is at odds with the thrust of post-positivist philosophies of science. On a casual reading, there might seem to be a direct parallel between Parsons's phenomenological framework of action, or Alexander's 'presuppositions', and what Lakatos calls the 'hard-core' theoretical assumptions of a scientific research programme. Certainly, Alexander believes there to be a parallel. Nor is he alone in such an argument. Habermas and Giddens each justify their own projects of general theory by reference to post-positivist developments in the theory of science.[68] However, Lakatos's argument is that it is *precisely in terms of 'hard-core' assumptions that science manifests discontinuity*. After all, it is through change in the 'hard-core' assumptions that the *transformation* of research programmes (rather than the mere extension of their 'positive heuristic') takes place. In contrast to this view, Alexander (and, of course, Parsons in his own claim for the phenomenological status of general theory) is presenting the presuppositions of social theory as *transcendent* and beyond transformation.

Despite Alexander's claims, then, there is no simple convergence between post-positivist theories of science and his own account of Parsonsian 'theoretical logic'. The central thrust of the former is away from universalistic criteria for science. According to post-positivist theories of science, theoretical objects and categories are transformed in the process of substantive and located scientific activities of problem-solving. In contrast, Alexander is attempting to argue that 'theoretical logic' in social science is distinct from practical issues of social explanation. The categories of theoretical logic, he argues, are universal and *eternal*, without reference to empirical problems or domains. To see what is wrong with this conception from the perspective of post-positivist philosophy of science, we need merely contrast it with Lakatos's criteria for the replacement of one research programme by another which all refer to superior resources in explaining empirical problems significant within each programme.[69] Similarly, the Quinean idea of the 'underdetermination of theory by facts', which Alexander also draws on to establish the autonomy of theoretical logic, is a claim for the *plurality* of plausible theories.[70] It is a claim that there are 'different' theories which can be consistent with the 'same facts'. Alexander, for his part, is suggesting, that there is a *single* theoretical scheme with a unitary 'logic' which is independent of 'facts'.

Merely pointing out the difference between post-positivist theories of science and the claims made for a general frame of reference of social scientific categories is insufficient by itself to invalidate the latter project. However, I have suggested that there is a fundamental tension in Parsons's arguments. His criticisms of other writers and the identification of explanatory problems in their approaches – especially, for example, his criticisms of Weber's use of ideal types – are frequently cogent and powerful. As Alexander suggests, his arguments can be read as presuming some of the substance of post-positivist approaches to explanation. It is difficult to see that his claims for a general frame of reference can have this status, or, indeed, that such a framework will achieve what Parsons intended.

The implication of post-positivism is that where explanatory problems lie and how they are to be addressed is not (and could not be) given *a priori*, but must be worked out by attending to specific issues and problems of explanation. Parsons, himself, accepts that the theoretical issues with which he is concerned have a specific location within the particular explanations offered by the different theorists whose work he is addressing. Does it not seem likely that the answers will be found by addressing the substance of problematic explanations, rather than by retreating to a higher level of meta-theory? What I suggest is that Parsons's failure to address specific explanations means that his *general theory is merely the displacement, to a 'higher' level, of the explanatory problems which he has identified*. His scheme represents *the generalization of explanatory problems, rather than their general solution*.

For the moment, this is asserted rather than demonstrated. Ultimately, the case must rest upon an examination of the categories and their extended elaboration which is the topic of the next chapter. However, it is Parsons's great merit that, in the course of his criticism of others, he presents us with the criteria by which his own theory must be judged. Any theory, he argues, must be judged according to its internal consistency and empirical adequacy; that is, by its specification without resort to residual categories, including those of 'facts' or 'empirical observations', accepted, but without a positive statement within the theoretical system. In the next chapter, we shall see if his theory does, in fact, meet these requirements.

NOTES

1. See A. Dawe, 'The two sociologies', *British Journal of Sociology*, 21(2), 1970, pp. 207–18. For similar arguments, see D. Martindale, *The Nature and Types of Sociological Theory* (London, Routledge and Kegan Paul, 1961); N. DiTomaso, ' "Sociological reductionism" from Parsons to Althusser: linking action and structure in social theory', *American Sociological Review*, 47(1), 1982, pp. 14–28; S. James, *The Content of Social Explanation* (Cambridge, Cambridge University Press, 1984); B.H. Mayhew, 'Structuralism vs. individualism part I: shadow boxing in the dark',

Social Forces, 59(2), 1980, pp. 335–75 and 'Structuralism vs. individualism part II: ideological and other obfuscations', *Social Forces*, 59(3), 1981, pp. 627–48; and many, many more.

2. A. Giddens, 'Positivism and its critics', in *Studies in Social and Political Theory* (London, Hutchinson, 1977), p. 85.
3. J. Habermas, *The Theory of Communicative Action, Volume II: A Critique of Functionalist Reason* (Cambridge, Polity, 1987), p. 151.
4. Ibid., p. 151.
5. J.C. Alexander, 'The new theoretical movement', in N.J. Smelser (ed.), *Handbook of Sociology* (London, Sage, 1988).
6. T. Parsons, 'The place of ultimate values in sociological theory', in C. Camic (ed.), *Talcott Parsons: The Early Essays* (Chicago, University of Chicago Press, 1991), p. 232.
7. See, for example, R. Dahrendorf, 'Out of utopia', in *Essays in the Theory of Society* (London, Routledge and Kegan Paul, 1968); D. Lockwood, 'Social integration and system integration', in G. Zollschan and W. Hirsch (eds), *Explorations in Social Change* (London, Routledge and Kegan Paul, 1964); A. Giddens, ' "Power" in the recent writings of Talcott Parsons', *Sociology*, 2(2), 1968, pp. 257–72.
8. See, for example, the writers cited in note 1.
9. See, for example, J. Finley Scott, 'The changing foundation of the Parsonsian action scheme', *American Sociological Review*, 28(5), 1963, 716–35; D. Martindale, 'Talcott Parsons' theoretical metamorphosis from social behaviourism to macro-functionalism', in H. Turk and R.L. Simpson (eds), *Institutions and Exchange: The Sociologies of Talcott Parsons and George Caspar Homans* (New York, Bobbs-Merrill, 1971); K. Menzies, *Talcott Parsons and the Social Image of Man* (London, Routledge and Kegan Paul, 1977); H.J. Bershady, *Ideology and Social Knowledge* (Oxford, Basil Blackwell, 1973).
10. Dawe, 'The two sociologies', p. 211.
11. A. Giddens, *New Rules of Sociological Method* (London, Hutchinson, 1976), p. 16.
12. Giddens, *New Rules*; Habermas, *The Theory of Communicative Action, Volume II*.
13. Burrow's comment, for example, is typical; he writes that, "Parsons' chapter on Marshall in *The Structure of Social Action* is not essential to the development of his theme in the way that the chapters on Durkheim and Weber are". J.W. Burrow, *Evolution and Society* (Cambridge, Cambridge University Press, 1966), p. 260. This neglect of the background in 'institutional economics' of Parsons's early writings has recently been addressed by Wearne and Camic. See B. Wearne, *The Theory and Scholarship of Talcott Parsons to 1951: A Critical Commentary* (Cambridge, Cambridge University Press, 1989); C. Camic, 'The making of a method: a historical reinterpretation of the early Parsons', *American Sociological Review*, 52(4), 1987, pp. 421–39.
14. Habermas makes a similar claim for sociology, writing that, where economics and politics became disciplines restricted to questions of economic equilibrium and rational choice, "sociology emerged as a discipline responsible for the problems that politics and economics pushed to one side on their way to becoming specialised sciences. Its theme was the changes in social integration brought about within the structure of old-European societies by the rise of the modern system of national states and by the differentiation of a market-regulated economy." J. Habermas, *The Theory of Communicative Action, Volume I: Reason and the Rationalization of Society* (London, Heinemann, 1984), p. 4.

15. See J.C. Alexander, *Theoretical Logic in Sociology, Volume IV: The Modern Reconstruction of Classical Thought: Talcott Parsons* (London, Routledge and Kegan Paul, 1984).
16. See, for example, J.C. Alexander, *Theoretical Logic, Volume IV*, pp. 289ff. Bryan Turner makes a similar argument to Alexander, writing that, "any theory of society will have to attempt to resolve the relationships between agency and structure, order and change, conflict and consensus. The majority of social theories are typically partial in that they are addressed to a limited range of issues; they frequently focus on a narrow slice of issues in being, for example, theories of conflict or human agency or normative order. The merit of Parsons' sociology was that it attempted to be a general theory and the very breadth of Parsons' sociology means that most one-sided objections to Parsonian sociology are actually incorporated by his analysis or can be rendered compatible with it." See B.S. Turner, 'Parsons and his critics: on the ubiquity of functionalism', in R.J. Holton and B.S. Turner, *Talcott Parsons on Economy and Society* (London, Routledge and Kegan Paul, 1976), p. 206.
17. Alexander, *Theoretical Logic, Volume IV*, p. 211.
18. Ibid., p. 272.
19. Habermas, for example, argues that, "one need not share Parsons's conviction that convergence among the great theoretical traditions itself constitutes proof of the validity of his own approach to building theory". J. Habermas, 'Talcott Parsons: problems of theory construction', *Sociological Inquiry*, 51(3), 1981, p. 173. However, for Parsons, the 'proof' lay not in convergence *per se*, but in the arguments for theoretical adequacy set out in terms of his discussion of positive and residual categories. In any case, Habermas's comment is a little ironic, given his view of convergence upon the categories of his own scheme.
20. *TSofSA*, p. 18.
21. Not the least of the ironies in the present situation is the way in which the famous first line of *TSofSA* – where Parsons cites Brinton's remark, "Who now reads Spencer?" – has been 'wittily' applied to Parsons. See, for one example among many, C.G.A. Bryant, 'Who now reads Parsons?' *Sociological Review*, 31(2), 1983, pp. 337–49. However, Parsons was describing the leading figure of the 'positivist-utilitarian' tradition, arguing that the 'evolution' of science had moved beyond Spencer and the assumptions of that tradition. Those who adapt the phrase to dismiss Parsons do so in the name of a sociological undertaking which is *defined by precisely the same concerns as those of Parsons*.
22. Parsons, 'The place of ultimate values', p. 231.
23. *TSofSA*, p. 478.
24. *TSofSA*, p. 17.
25. *TSofSA*, p. 17.
26. *TSofSA*, p.19.
27. *TSofSA*, p. 19.
28. *TSofSA*, p. 19. Sica's interpretation of Parsons's argument is that it involves an "implicitly cautious claim for social science (that it must relinquish the great mass of phenomena to darkened 'residual categories' and accept the humble task of explaining minor portions of social reality)". A. Sica, *Weber, Irrationality and Social Order* (Berkeley and Los Angeles, University of California Press, 1988), p. 21. This is the reverse of what Parsons is arguing. Uniquely, Sica accuses Parsons of a "false theoretical humility before the empirical facts of social life" (ibid., p. 21)!

29. *TSofSA*, p. 486.
30. *TSofSA*, p. 306.
31. *TSofSA*, p. 322.
32. *TSofSA*, p. 327.
33. *TSofSA*, p. 710.
34. *TSofSA*, p. 337. Although most commentators see Weber as having engaged with Marx and re-stated the latter's insights in a more satisfactory form, Marx's (or modern Marxists') own attempts to deal with problems within his approach argued to produce the same instability and movement between 'positivism' and 'idealism' as Parsons attributes to Durkheim. See, for example, J.C. Alexander, *Theoretical Logic in Sociology, Volume II: the Antinomies of Classical Thought: Marx and Durkheim* (London, Routledge and Kegan Paul, 1982); Lockwood, *Solidarity and Schism: 'The Problem of Disorder' in Durkheimian and Marxist Sociology* (Oxford, Clarendon Press, 1992).
35. See, for example, J. Seigel, 'Autonomy and personality in Durkheim: an essay on content and method', *Journal of the History of Ideas*, XX(3), 1987. Parsons does not exaggerate the distinctness of the phases to quite the same extent as Alexander in the various volumes of his *Theoretical Logic in Sociology*. Moreover, the ambiguities and inconsistencies within phases are an important part of Parsons's argument for the inadequacy of the different positions.
36. *TSofSA*, p. 720.
37. See, for example, the series of articles concerned with 'de-Parsonizing' the classics; W. Pope, 'Classic on classic: Parsons's interpretations of Durkheim', *American Sociological Review,* 38(4) 1973, pp. 399–415; W. Pope, L. Hazelrigg and J. Cohen, 'On the theoretical divergence of Durkheim and Weber', *American Sociological Review*, 40(4), 1975, pp. 417–27; J. Cohen, 'DeParsonizing Weber', *American Sociological Review*, 40(2), 1975, pp. 229–41. This critique has even reached back to reconsider Parsons's representation of the 'utilitarian' dilemma, against which, or so he argued, his generation of theorists was writing. See C. Camic, 'The utilitarians revisited', *American Journal of Sociology*, 85(3), 1979, pp. 516–50.
38. *TSofSA*, p. 486.
39. See, especially, J. Finley Scott, 'The changing foundation'; G.C. Homans, 'Commentary' in H. Turk and R.L. Simpson, *Institutions and Exchange*.
40. See, for example, R. Keat and J. Urry, *Social Theory as Science* (London, Routledge and Kegan Paul, 1975); R.J. Bernstein, *The Restructuring of Social and Political Theory* (Oxford, Basil Blackwell, 1976); T. Johnson, C. Dandeker and C. Ashworth, *The Structure of Social Theory* (London, Macmillan, 1984).
41. See, for example, J.C. Alexander, *Theoretical Logic in Sociology, Volume IV*; P. Hamilton, *Talcott Parsons* (London, Tavistock, 1983). Camic has recently attacked these arguments for their anachronistic character. See Camic, 'The making of a method'. In turn, his argument has been criticised and Parsons's 'foresight' defended by Gould. See M. Gould, *'The Structure of Social Action*: sixty years ahead of its time', in R. Robertson and B.S. Turner, *Talcott Parsons: Theorist of Modernity* (London, Sage, 1991).
42. T.S. Kuhn, *The Structure of Scientific Revolutions* (Chicago, Chicago University Press, 1962).
43. For good general discussions, see A.F. Chalmers, *What is This Thing Called Science?* (St. Lucia, University of Queensland Press, 1976); D. Papineau, *Theory and*

Meaning (Oxford, Clarendon Press, 1979); M. Hesse, *Revolutions and Reconstructions in the Philosophy of Science* (Brighton, Harvester, 1980); W.H. Newton-Smith, *The Rationality of Science* (London, Routledge and Kegan Paul, 1981).

44. See K. Popper, *Conjectures and Refutations* (London, Routledge and Kegan Paul, 1963).

45. As Hesse observes, this means giving up the epistemological project of positivism "in favour of analyzing the ontology of theories as if current science is known to have arrived at or somewhere near the truth." *Revolutions and Reconstructions*, p. xiii.

46. W.v.O. Quine, 'Two dogmas of empiricism', in *From a Logical Point of View* (Cambridge, Harvard University Press, 1953). See also M. Hesse, *The Structure of Scientific Inference* (London, Macmillan, 1974).

47. See I. Lakatos, 'Falsification and the methodology of scientific research programmes', in I. Lakatos and A. Musgrove (eds), *Criticism and the Growth of Knowledge* (Cambridge, Cambridge University Press, 1970).

48. Ibid.

49. Alexander, *Theoretical Logic, Volume 1*, p. 32.

50. *TSofSA*, p. 6.

51. *TSofSA*, p. 7.

52. *TSofSA*, p. xxi.

53. *TSofSA*, p. 17.

54. *TSofSA*, p. 740.

55. Weber writes that, in contrast to theoretical constructs in the natural sciences, ideal types, "have no pretension at all to general validity ... [They] can function as hypotheses when employed for heuristic purposes. However, in contrast to hypotheses in the natural sciences to establish in a concrete case that an interpretation is not valid is irrelevant to the theoretical value of the interpretive scheme." M. Weber, *Roscher and Knies: The Logical Problems of Historical Economics* (New York, Free Press, 1975), p. 190. See J. Holmwood and A. Stewart, *Explanation and Social Theory* (London, Macmillan, 1991) for a detailed discussion of Weber's argument.

56. As we shall see in Chapter 4, the ultimate expression of these different principles, according to Parsons, is to be found in Weber's two pure types of rational action – 'value-rational' (*wertrational*) action and 'instrumentally-rational' (*zweckrational*) action. Where Weber assigns their elements to two mutually exclusive types, Parsons wishes to integrate them within a single scheme of action.

57. See *TSofSA*, pp. 593ff.

58. The tangle Weber gets into is apparent in the way in which he argues both that rationality can be an 'iron cage' and that any representation is 'fictional' and 'incomplete'. This is something which a number of commentators have pointed out. See, for example, P. Weiss 'On the irreversibility of Western rationalization and Max Weber's alleged fatalism', in S. Whimster and S. Lash (eds), *Max Weber, Rationality and Modernity* (London, Allen and Unwin, 1987); C. Campbell, *The Romantic Ethic and the Ethic of Consumerism* (Oxford, Blackwell, 1987); R. Schroeder, *Max Weber and the Sociology of Culture* (London, Sage, 1992). As Schroeder, puts it "we might ask whether, if we accept Weber's view of the charismatic origin of world-views, it necessarily follows that we must accept his pessimistic conclusion about their routinization?" (ibid.), p. 163. In one of his earliest essays (published in 1929),

Parsons writes that Weber hypostatizes ideal types, mistaking their partial representations for the totality of social reality, characterizing modern capitalism, for example, "in terms of one feature, the rational organization of labour, superimposed upon his capitalism in general. But this feature loses its original nature as a 'fictitious' ideal type and becomes identified with historical reality." See T. Parsons, ' "Capitalism" in recent German literature: Sombart and Weber', in C. Camic (ed.), *Talcott Parsons: The Early Essays* (Chicago, University of Chicago Press, 1991), p. 35.

59. Parsons, 'The place of ultimate values', p. 231.
60. *TSofSA*, pp. 723–4. Thus, Parsons does not present his own statement of 'meta-theory' in quite as disembodied a way, nor as disengaged from substantive, empirical inquiry, as does Alexander on his behalf. The latter, however, regards such arguments as evidence of a failure to have effected an appropriate separation of theoretical and empirical issues and, as such, as an indication of a 'latent empiricism' on the part of Parsons. See J.C. Alexander, *Theoretical Logic: Volume IV*, pp. 152ff.
61. *TSofSA*, p. 733.
62. J.C. Alexander, 'The new theoretical movement', in N.J. Smelser (ed.), *The Handbook of Sociology*, p. 84.
63. Ibid., p. 77.
64. *Theoretical Logic, Volume 1*, p. 115. Bryan Turner makes a very similar argument, writing that, "any social theory (whether in economics, psychology or demography) has to have an account of the structure of relations (a theory of 'systemness') and an account of the human agent (a theory of action). This is, so to speak, the grammar of social theory which provides the laws for the distribution of concepts within the *parole* of social sciences. Since, the grammar is logically universal, translation (or convertability) is always highly possible." See B.S. Turner, 'Parsons and his critics: on the ubiquity of functionalism', in R.J. Holton and B.S. Turner (eds), *Talcott Parsons on Economy and Society* (London, Routledge and Kegan Paul, 1986), p. 200.
65. *TSofSA*, p. 723.
66. J.C. Alexander, *Theoretical Logic in Sociology, Volume IV*, p. 154.
67. *TSofSA*, pp. 95ff.
68. See, for example, A. Giddens, 'Positivism and its critics', in *Studies in Social and Political Theory* (London, Hutchinson, 1977); J. Habermas, *The Theory of Communicative Action, Volume 1*.
69. Lakatos, for example, writes that scientific theory T is falsified when a new theory T^1 meets the following criteria, "(1) T^1 has excess empirical content over T: that is, it predicts novel facts, that is, facts improbable in the light of, or even forbidden by, T; (2) T^1 explains the previous success of T, that is, all the unrefuted content of T is included ... in the content of T^1; and (3) some of the excess content of T^1 is corroborated." See I. Lakatos, 'Falsification and the methodology of scientific research programmes', p. 116.
70. See Quine, 'Two dogmas of empiricism'.

4

THE ACTION FRAME OF
REFERENCE

It is Parsons's intention to produce a scheme of general categories which will form the necessary foundation of social scientific inquiries. These categories, he argues, must be adequate to the diverse influences upon social behaviour. They will have the form of a theoretical system, with logical relations among them, and they are to be evaluated according to criteria of coherence, generality and their non-reliance upon residual categories, including those of 'empirical' observations. In Chapter 3, I suggested that this project of general social theory is flawed and that any attempt to set up a scheme of general categories in advance of specific, located practices of explanation is mistaken. In this chapter, and the next, however, I shall take Parsons's own project at face value, judging it in its own terms, before I go on to suggest an alternative to it.

THE ELEMENTS OF ACTION

According to Parsons, any scheme of categories for the social sciences must take as its point of reference, human *action*. Hitherto, he argues, the dominant emphasis has been upon 'positivistic' schemes which seek to explain behaviour in terms of the 'external' influences upon it. Such approaches attempt to exclude reference to the 'internal', mental processes of actors, regarding these as 'subjective' and, therefore, illegitimate from the point of view of the theoretical requirements of a scientific scheme. In contrast, the alternative, 'idealist' approach emphasizes the subjective processes of action as necessary to any adequate understanding of human behaviour, but has a corresponding tendency to neglect a proper appreciation of the role of external conditions as facilities and constraints upon action. Neither 'positivism', nor 'idealism', then, provides a satisfactory account of the different elements of action. Nor can any one approach successfully expunge the issues raised by the other. In contrast to either approach, Parsons seeks to develop a scheme which will maintain a balance between both in their contribution to the explanation of behaviour.[1]

As a first step in setting out how each can be adequately combined in a single scheme, Parsons identifies what he calls the 'unit act' and its component elements. This 'unit act', however, should not be understood as referring to something which exists *concretely*. It does not have any immediate reference to the concrete individual acts of any person. Rather, Parsons is trying, by a process of logical abstraction, to identify the most basic elements of a wider scheme. Any issue of the concrete manifestation of action can only be addressed once that wider scheme has been fully elaborated. Thus, Parsons writes that, "the sense in which the unit act is here spoken of as an existent entity is not that of concrete spatiality or otherwise separate existence, but of conceivability as a unit in terms of a frame of reference".[2] Any confusion of the 'unit act' with concrete action would be a form of the empiricist 'fallacy of misplaced concreteness' which erroneously regards each 'analytical' distinction made in the elaboration of a theoretical scheme as necessitating a corresponding reference in empirical data. So, although 'empirical observations' outside the positive categories of a theoretical scheme are an indication of deficiencies, that does not mean, according to Parsons, that the converse is true; that is, "that all the analytical concepts of a theoretical system must correspond to units of concrete systems the independent existence of which is conceivable".[3] Of course, Parsons's identification of a *fallacy* of *misplaced* concreteness does not mean that his proposed scheme has no concrete reference. Its categories do not refer directly but, ultimately, the scheme will be used to generate processes with direct empirical implications. With the concept of the 'unit act' and its component elements, however, we are at some distance from being able to specify the implications of the wider theoretical scheme for the explanation of concrete actions.

The concept of the 'unit act' enables Parsons to identify different 'elements' with clear relationships to those occurring within what he describes as 'positivist' and 'idealist' approaches. He identifies four 'logical' elements of a 'unit act', of which the first three are: "(1) it implies an agent, an 'actor'. (2) For purposes of definition the act must have an 'end', a future state of affairs toward which the process of action is orientated. (3) It must be initiated in a 'situation' of which the trends of development differ in one or more important respects from the state of affairs to which the action is oriented, the end."[4] For Parsons, these distinctions represent the 'idealist' contribution to the scheme in that the 'ends' of action are independent of the 'situation' such that the agency of the actor is necessary to bring about 'a future state of affairs' different to that which would obtain without the intervention of the actor. However, in the realization of any ends, account must be taken of circumstances in their role as facilitating or constraining action. Parsons goes on to develop a further distinction applied to the 'situation' of action, writing that, "this situation is in turn analysable into two elements: those over which the actor has no control, that is which he cannot alter, or prevent from being altered, in conformity with his end, and those over which he has such control. The former may be termed the 'conditions' of action, the latter the 'means' ".[5] These are the elements which are emphasized in 'positivistic' schemes.

The final distinction that Parsons introduces is that, "(4) there is inherent in the conception of this unit, in its analytical uses, a certain mode of relationship between these elements. That is, in the choice of alternative means to the end, in so far as the situation allows alternatives, there is a 'normative' orientation of action."[6] Actors must select the appropriate means for the realization of their chosen ends and, so, must exercise judgements, which, implicitly or explicitly, depend upon evaluative 'standards'.

Given that Parsons comes to be criticized for an over-emphasis upon the 'normative', it would be all too easy to pounce upon this final element as the source of his difficulties in the sense that he unnecessarily associates the orientation of action with only one out of a number of possible orientations. For example, might action not also be orientated 'cognitively', rather than 'normatively'? Thus, critics of Parsons have taken the 'normative orientation of action' to imply a positive moral commitment to the substance of action, which they have contrasted with a 'pragmatic', or 'cognitive', orientation.[7] We must remember, however, the theoretical argument with which Parsons introduced his discussion of the 'unit act'. He distinguished between 'analytical' and 'concrete' points of reference, arguing that he was concerned with action, for the moment, from the point of view of drawing out the logical relations between elements within a theoretical system. The issue of the 'cognitive', as opposed to the 'normative', which his critics raise, would be an issue of the *concrete* orientation of action, where Parsons is using the term 'normative' to identify something *analytic* to action, per se; that is, *something which would be true of action however it was orientated concretely*. As Parsons explains, "what is essential to the concept of action is that there should be a normative orientation of action, not that this should be of any particular type".[8]

The standard criticism of Parsons implies that he committed the 'fallacy of misplaced concreteness', just when he was warning against the confusions that arise from failing to distinguish the 'analytic' from the 'concrete'. What Parsons is trying to show with these arguments is that *if* 'ends' are to some degree independent of 'conditions' and 'means', then, the actor must make decisions as to the appropriateness of the 'end' to be pursued. Action to realize an end entails the active intervention of the actor and, in some sense, the end must be deemed worthwhile or desirable by the actor for 'effort' to be expended in its pursuit.[9] The 'standards' by which this desirability are judged represent the 'normative orientation' of action. Indeed, this 'normative orientation' necessitates a 'cognitive' address of 'ends'. After all, Parsons defines 'ends' as 'future anticipated states of affairs'. Whatever is anticipated must be 'cognitively constructed'; that is, actors must formulate an idea of what they wish to bring about in the course of acting. Moreover, in realizing their ends, actors must also address 'cognitively' the means and conditions (and the consequences) of their realization.[10]

Parsons argues further that, "the term normative will be used as applicable to an aspect, part or element of a system of action if, and only in so far as it may be held to manifest or otherwise involve a sentiment attributable to one or more actors that something is an end in itself, regardless of its status as a means to any other end."[11] Once again, we must remember the claims of analytical theory. Parsons is trying to distinguish the normative as an *element* in order to place it systematically in relation to other elements within the theoretical system that is the action frame of reference. Thus, he is not arguing that an orientation to the 'normative' is one *type* of action, contrasted to another *type* orientated to the 'conditions and means' of action. This, for example, is what Weber proposes in his distinction between value-rational (*wertrational*) and instrumentally rational (*zweckrational*) types of action and, although Parsons is drawing upon Weber's treatment, he seeks to distinguish his own position from that of Weber, accusing the latter of a form of the fallacy of misplaced concreteness.

Thus, in instrumentally rational action, Weber argues that the actor takes into account, "the behaviour of objects in the environment and of other human beings; these expectations are used as 'conditions' or 'means' for the attainment of the actor's own rationally pursued and calculated ends".[12] In contrast, value-rational action, "always involves 'commands' or 'demands' which, in the actor's opinion, are binding on him. It is only in such cases where human action is motivated by the fulfilment of such unconditional demands that it will be called value-rational".[13] In his identification of instrumental-rational and value-rational action as distinct 'ideal types', Weber represents them as mutually exclusive and antithetical in their components, such that each, from the perspective of the other, appears 'irrational'. Weber writes that, "value-rational action may thus have various different relations to the instrumentally rational action. From the latter point of view, however, value-rationality is always irrational . . . The orientation of action wholly to the rational achievement of ends without relation to fundamental values is, to be sure, essentially only a limiting case".[14] It seems that, as with other 'ideal types', nowhere are these types of action found in their pure form. They are 'limiting cases' and most concrete actions represent some sort of combination of types.

If this is so, then, as Parsons suggests, we face something of a paradox. What apparently *typically exists* – and, therefore, is reproduced unproblematically – is to be understood *theoretically* in terms of constructs which represent their components as mutually exclusive and antithetical. Their *combination in practice* cannot be represented theoretically, only their mutually 'irrational' limiting cases. According to Parsons, with this sort of theoretical approach it is not surprising that Weber comes to give precedence in his explanations to the type whose specification contains a strong emphasis upon the practical conditions of the realization of action – that is, instrumentally rational action.[15] It is unlikely that Parsons sought merely to reverse Weber's emphasis and give precedence to value-rational action. According to Parsons, Weber's difficulties are an artifact of the dualism and particularism intrinsic to his methodological approach. What Parsons proposes is a *single* scheme of action in which the components that Weber assigns to the different types are recognized as mutually necessary elements.

Parsons's discussion of the 'unit act' and its component elements is accompanied by a detailed examination of different theories of action – at the point in *TSofSA* where the concept of the 'unit act' is introduced, mainly positivistic theories – and their limitations when contrasted with his own scheme. It is not necessary to deal in any detail with Parsons's classification of the different types of positivistic theory. However, it should be remembered that Parsons's purpose is not to judge these schemes 'externally'; against his own, better scheme, but to identify how they are inadequate in their own terms and generate residual categories which undermine them from within.

Given the way in which Parsons has represented the two traditions of 'positivism' and 'idealism', it is unsurprising that he sees the problems of positivism as consisting in the problematic role of the category of 'ends' within their schemes. For our purposes, we can understand Parsons's criticism by reference, once again, to Weber's ideal type of instrumentally rational action (since, ultimately, this is an ideal type of 'utilitarian' action). Within instrumental rational action, 'ends' are regarded as independent of means and conditions, but are considered as 'given' in the sense that how actors arrive at their preferences is not addressed, only the processes by which they are to be realised. Parsons's view is that to take ends as 'given' is to assign them a necessary status within the scheme, but to fail adequately to account for them. In so far as the category of 'ends' is given an independent role within positivism, the implication, Parsons suggests, is that ends vary, "at random relative to the means-end relationship and its central component, the actor's knowledge of his situation".[16]

The answer that Parsons is looking for will be found, he argues, by recognizing what Weber identifies, albeit in an unsatisfactory manner, in the ideal type of value-rational action; that is, the role of values in human conduct. This would involve 'stepping outside' the self-imposed limits of any positivistic scheme to accept the valid aspect of the opposed, 'idealist' approach. However, *within* the limits of positivism, an assumption of the 'randomness' of ends is also regarded as unsatisfactory (because of its implicit 'indeterminacy'), but the tendency is for theorists to move in the other direction to that suggested by Parsons. Thus, 'radical' positivists – for example, behavioural psychologists – attempt to deny the 'analytical independence' of 'ends', reducing them to the 'situation' of action; that is, they attempt to see action as entirely the product of determining stimuli located in the external environment. There is, then, what Parsons calls, a 'utilitarian dilemma' within positivism where, "either the active agency of the actor in the choice of ends is an independent factor in action, and the end element must be random; or the objectionable implication of the randomness of ends is denied, but then their independence disappears and they are assimilated to the conditions of the situation, that is to elements analysable in terms of nonsubjective categories, principally heredity and environment, in the analytical sense of biological theory".[17]

According to Parsons, part of the problem with positivistic schemes is their limited understanding of 'rationality'. Within positivism, what is rational in behaviour is judged by what accords with the standards of an external, scientific observer. Thus, as theorists respond to the problem of the randomness of ends within utilitarian schemes, action is presented as a rational adaptation to circumstances, where "the active role of the actor is reduced to one of the understanding of his situation and forecasting of its future course of development".[18] In so far as actual behaviours 'deviate' from this 'external', scientific understanding of what would be a rational adaptation, so theorists initially resort to the residual category of 'irrationality' (or 'ignorance' and 'error', as Parsons puts it) as the explanation of the active role of actors. For Parsons, this is a further indication both of the instability of their schemes and of the need for a definition of rationality which accords with the subjective meaning that actors attribute to their action. In contrast, radically positivistic schemes attempt to transmute seemingly 'irrational', but stable, behaviour to processes external to the actor, but meaningful (or, 'rational') in terms of external, environmental stimuli (for example, by reference to 'unconscious' biological drives).[19] Parsons, on the other hand, wishes to push in the other direction, where what apears to be 'irrational' from the point of view of a positivistic scheme, is to be accounted for by 'non-rational', rather than 'irrational' or external, criteria; that is, by criteria which are subjectively meaningful to the actors concerned.

Parsons's argument appears plausible. It has been reproduced in many other texts.[20] Once again, however, there is a weakness intrinsic to his claims. It should be recalled that Parsons argues that he is drawing out general implications from arguments which he allows have a specific explanatory substance. Moreover, he is not denying the role of positivistic elements in action, merely that they are exhaustive. Yet, when he addresses the *failure* of the positivistic scheme he argues that anomalous behaviours, which appear irrational on the basis of the strict application of the positivistic criteria, can be represented as 'non-rational', as explicable in terms of the 'subjective', rather than 'objective' components of a scheme. It should be clear that, in making this move, Parsons has in no way addressed the status of the putatively rational elements, themselves. They remain *untransformed*; they have merely been *added to*. In other words, the behaviours initially expected remain intrinsic to the statement of the rational, 'objective' criteria. It is simply the 'anomalous' behaviours that are re-described as being 'subjectively' meaningful to the actors concerned. On such a formulation, it must appear that the 'subjective' has the capacity to cancel the 'objective', while maintaining the integrity of each.

In order to see what is going on here we need merely consider the Marxist example, which I shall discuss in detail in Chapter 6. Within Marxist explanations, there is a problem that the behaviour of those designated as proletarian is at odds with what is anticipated on the basis of the Marxist theory of class. This failure of Marxist class theory produces the very effects that Parsons is addressing and incorporating into his general theoretical statement. For example, Marxist class theory appears 'positivistic' in its assertion of the priority of the explanatory processes intrinsic to its categories. Relevant behaviours deviate from those processes and, in consequence, it is frequently argued that 'action' must be addressed as a relatively autonomous category in any adequate account. However, the assertion of the independence of 'action' must be at the cost of the coherence of the initial statement and the 'action' intrinsic to it. Once again, the initial explanatory statement is not reconstructed by these measures, merely added to with 'additional' processes that are antithetical to the initial formulation.

Parsons's abstraction of his general argument from any particular explanatory issue, then, gives a spurious generality and plausibility to his claims. However, once what underlies his theoretical arguments is properly recognized, it is apparent that he has not, in fact, left behind the particular explanatory issues that have given rise to his general arguments. They are embodied in his framework of general theory. Thus, although Parsons – and others who embrace a similar conception of general theory – is proposing a theoretical framework of complementary elements, those elements also prescribe mutually exclusive behavioural possibilities. In particular, what the elements allow, at one and the same time, is the necessity of action to accommodate material constraint and the capacity of action to cancel material processes.

As I shall show, the antagonism intrinsic to the categories of Parsons's scheme does eventually come to the surface as an explicit contradiction. Notwithstanding any contradiction that his work ultimately contains, there can be little doubt that, in terms of any self-conscious elaboration, it is the *complementary* character of the different elements which Parsons stresses. The substance of his self-conscious claims about action, so far, can be summarized thus: Action is a process orientated to the realization of an end. It occurs in conditional circumstances that must be calculated upon and utilized by actors in the pursuit of their ends. However, 'ends' and 'conditions' (including 'means') are analytically distinct categories. This claim is important because it means that action cannot be understood as an emanation of cultural values as is the case with some forms of idealism: action is not free from determination by circumstances. Consequently, action involves effort to 'conform with norms' (which govern ends and the selection of their means of realization) since it must transform circumstances and, therefore, accommodate and calculate upon conditions if it is to be successful. Action, to be rational, must be adequate in terms of the knowledge necessary to the realization of ends. Thus, Parsons refers to the 'intrinsic rationality of the means-end relation' in terms of the necessary role of "valid knowledge as a guide to action".[21] However, action cannot be reduced to its conditions since an understanding of the agency of the actor and,

61

consequently, of the subjective meaning of an action is necessary in any adequate account. With conditions and means classified as technical in substance and, as such, external to any given actor, the 'subjective', voluntary aspect of action is associated with the actor's capacity to form ends. Instrumental rationality and value rationality, which were seen by Weber as the bases of distinct *types* of action, are seen by Parsons as analytically necessary elements of *all* action, that is as distinct *elements* of the 'unit act'.[22]

ACTION AND SYSTEM

We must remember that the discussion of 'unit acts' provides only the basic elements of an action frame of reference. According to Parsons, such a discussion "serves only to arrange the data in a certain order, not to subject them to the analysis necessary for their explanation".[23] Their 'explanation' requires a further step in the analysis, from 'unit acts' to their location within 'systems' of action. This step, "consists in generalising the conceptual scheme so as *to bring out the functional relations* in the facts already descriptively arranged".[24] This further generalization of the scheme will identify emergent properties of *systems* of action; that is, properties which appear in relation to any consideration of the co-ordination of actions and which are not reducible to analysis in terms of 'unit acts' alone. Thus, Parsons writes that, "action systems have properties that are emergent only on a certain level of complexity in the relations of unit acts to each other. These properties cannot be identified in any single unit act considered apart from its relation to others in the same system. *They cannot be derived by a process of direct generalization of the properties of the unit act*".[25] The concept of emergent properties, then, serves to identify the "elements of structure of a generalized system of action"[26] and these elements of *structure* are to be further analysed in terms of their *functional* relations; that is, in terms of the logical relations established within the theoretical system.

It is with this further step in the analysis of action that Parsons believes that the fallacy of misplaced concreteness can be overcome and a proper identification of the relation between theoretical system and the analysis and explanation of concrete action can be achieved. This is what underlies Parsons's use of an 'organic' analogy, where "the very definition of an organic whole is one within which *the relations determine the properties of its parts*. The properties of the whole are not simply a resultant of the latter".[27] The determining relations which general theory establishes are invariant. Thus, Parsons writes that, "analytical elements, once clearly defined, will be found to have certain uniform modes of relation to each other which hold independently of anyone particular set of their values".[28] These 'uniform modes of relationship' have the status of 'analytical laws' where "an analytical law ... states a uniform mode of relationship between the values of two or more analytical elements".[29] Concrete differences will be accounted for by differences in the 'values' (in the technical meaning of the content and levels of variables) of the elements which have been identified analytically. It is precisely the understanding of uniform modes of relationship between elements, which the analytical theory of action provides, that enables the prediction of changes in the 'values' of the variables of empirical systems consequent upon changes in the 'value' of some other variable in the system.

Weber seems to have regarded the sort of 'organic unity' of the components and processes of action that Parsons is proposing as a dangerous reification, with the implication of some sort of 'group mind'. For example, he writes that, "for sociological purposes there is no such thing as a collective personality which 'acts'. When reference is made in a sociological context to a state, a nation, a corporation . . . or similar collectivities, what is meant, on the contrary, is only a certain kind of development of actual or possible social actions of individual persons."[30] Although Weber's warnings are frequently applied to Parsons's analysis, in order to show the fundamental incompatibility between their respective approaches, Parsons does not, in fact, disagree with Weber on the specific point he is making about the dangers of 'reification' inherent in any concept of collectivity. What Parsons takes issue with is Weber's seemingly innocuous statement of the reducibility of such concepts to the 'actual or possible social actions of individual persons'. With his own analysis of 'unit acts' and the 'emergent properties' of systems of social action in mind, Parsons echoes Weber's own statement, but argues that, "there are no group properties that are not reducible to properties of *systems* of action and there is no analytical theory of groups which is not translatable into terms of the theory of action".[31] What Parsons is attacking is the methodological individualism of approaches, such as that of Weber, which imply that unit acts are 'real', while structural categories are mere 'fictions'.[32] On the contrary, Parsons argues that it is precisely the type of analysis associated with the isolation of the 'unit act' which is a form of abstraction involving, "the type of concept which is really and necessarily fictional, in the sense that Weber attributed to his ideal types".[33] This the core of Parsons's criticism of Weber's methodological arguments and the 'atomism' of his theoretical categories which is unable to constitute theoretically the relations among the elements that it isolates. This 'atomism' goes to the heart of Weber's substantive sociology and the fragmentation of sociological theory among discrete mutually incompatible theoretical constructs or ideal types.[34]

Contrary to nearly all of the secondary literature, then, from his earliest statement of the action frame of reference onwards, Parsons was concerned with the identification of 'unit acts' in order to locate their elements within wider systems. The discovery of a 'systems' approach was not a later development in which Parsons gave up an earlier attachment to 'action'.[35] Nor could it be regarded as a contingent choice, as Alexander suggests. The latter, for example, writes that, "[functional analysis] constituted an independent choice, for a wide range of different models would have been consistent with Parsons' presuppositional multidimensionality; among these he chose the 'functional system' ".[36] It may be that 'structural-functionalism' is regarded by most commentators as a distinct approach from that of a sociology of 'action', but there is in Parsons's own writings no justification for that claim. The wider action frame of reference, whose fundamental elements were introduced through the analysis of the 'unit act', is, according to Parsons, explicitly and necessarily, a 'structural', 'functional' approach to action. Moreover, in *TSofSA* 'structural-functionalism' is offered as the means of overcoming the false dualisms of social theory.

The idea of emergent properties of systems of social action is at the heart of what Parsons means by the 'problem of order'. Action occurs in systems and these systems have an orderly character. There are two issues of 'order', or integration, identified by Parsons. These are what we can term *personal* order and *interpersonal* order.[37] *Personal order* involves the recognition that any given act is, for the actor, one among a plurality of other chosen and possible actions with a variety of different ends in view with different requirements for their realization. *Interpersonal order* involves the recognition that actions occur in contexts which include, as Parsons puts it, "a plurality of actors".[38]

The emergent properties of personal order, according to Parsons, have received more attention in social theory (in particular, in economics), than those of interpersonal order. From the point of view of the analysis of the 'unit act', any relation of conditions (including means) to the realization of a given end is a purely 'technical' issue of the competent realization of the end in question. However, every action occurs in contexts produced by each individual's past actions which, in turn, affects the possibilities of their future action. Along with the requirement of a 'technical' efficacy of means, there is a requirement of consistency in the relation among purposes. Actions occur in what Parsons terms 'means-ends chains'. For any actor, there is a mutual dependency of acts as means and conditions of other acts. Where means are scarce relative to ends, actors will maximize outcomes by the most efficient selection of means and by placing their ends in a personal hierarchy of preferences. Actors' ends are determined by their preferences and values, but their 'cognitive' address to the means of the realization of their ends is also governed by what Parsons terms a 'normative standard', the 'norm of efficiency'. Thus, one of the emergent properties of personal order is 'economic rationality'.[39] As Parsons puts it, "economic rationality is thus an emergent property of action which can be observed only when a plurality of unit acts is treated together as constituting an integrated system".[40]

'Economic rationality', then, is analytical to action when considered as a *system*. Once again, this concept should not be confused with concrete actions. Such confusion is a form of 'empiricist' fallacy and it is committed both by those who would regard 'economic rationality' as a particular type of behaviour which occurs in, and is limited to, market economies and by those who regard market categories to have a general applicability.[41] In part, for Parsons, this is what explains Weber's problems with the distinction between value-rational and instrumentally rational action. As we have seen, Weber assigns any consideration of the calculation of the means and conditions of the realization of an end to the instrumentally rational type. However, even where a value is raised to an absolute standard, as Weber decribes the essence of the value rational type, there must be an issue of its effective realization and consequences and so an issue of its 'economic rationality'.[42] On the other hand, *'economic rationality' should not be confused with the totality of considerations relevant to action.* This is the error of utilitarian theorists – such as the contemporary proponents of 'rational-choice' theory – who seek what is, in effect, an 'economics of society'. Taken together, the two criticisms enable Parsons to challenge any sociological repudiation of economic theory, while retaining the basic insight that 'economic systems' vary and cannot be accounted for by a 'neo-classical' scheme of economic theory, but would require a sociological economics (that is, consideration in terms of a scheme which recognized the 'non-economic' aspects of action systems). Thus, Parsons writes that, "the assumptions necessary for a theory of economic *laissez-faire* cannot, for the general purposes of social science, be assumed to be constant features of all social systems, but such systems are found to vary in ways subject to analysis in terms of other, non-economic elements of the theory of action".[43]

Parsons drops the term 'economic rationality' in preference for the phrase, the 'intrinsic rationality of action in its means-end aspect'. He does so in order to propose an 'analytical law' of action systems that, in so far as there is a direction to action, it consists in the tendency to the maximization of rationality. Thus, he writes, "in any concrete system of action a process of change so far as it is at all explicable in terms of the intrinsic means-end relationship can proceed . . . only in the direction of increase in the value of the property rationality".[44] Ultimately, this is so because the maximization of rationality in personal systems is also the maximization of the actor's own interests (including their 'ultimate values').

For Parsons, much more fundamental and hitherto neglected issues of social theory arise when systems of social action involving a *plurality* of actors are the focus of attention. These are the issues of *interpersonal* order. He offers his analysis of emergent properties in terms of the increasing complexity of systems of action. Interpersonal systems are more complex than personal systems because, analytically, they presuppose the latter. Thus, what Parsons is concerned to identify are additional emergent properties of interpersonal order beyond those of personal order, but incorporating them. Such systems are *interpersonal systems of personal systems of action.* Interpersonal order concerns the coordination of systems of action where these systems include the activities of a number of actors. According to this conception, the actions of any given actor form the conditions and means of other actors in the system. Just as there is a mutual dependence of acts within the means-end chains of an actor's system of personal order, so there is a mutual dependence of acts and means-end chains among the interactions of a plurality of actors.

Parsons's basic argument is that a 'means' for an actor at one point in the system is an 'end' of another actor, differently located. According to Parsons, the nature of what he terms a 'total action system' is that actors must accommodate both a 'material environment' and a 'social environment' that consists in the actions of others. In choosing any particular end, with its rational requirement of the availability of the means and conditions of its realization, any given actor is dependent upon other actors who, though placed differently in the system, choose as *their* 'ends' those activities which are the 'means' of the specific ends of a given actor. Indeed, not only must the availability of means be addressed, but, in any complex system, the 'feedback' of particular ends into the system must also be considered. For example, means may be available to pursue a particular course of action, but if the consequence of pursuing that action is that other actors with whom the actor is in relationship withdraw their support because of its implications for them, then that too must be a part of the actor's rational consideration. A course of action may be regarded as personally beneficial or desirable when taken in isolation, but its consequences may be too costly for it to be practicable, or, at least, these consequences must enter into the actor's calculations.

It is these considerations which underlie the more directly 'sociological' aspects of the 'problem of order' which consists, as an analytical problem, in identifying the properties and processes of the system which maintain the commensurability of actions among the different actors in a system. Thus, Parsons argues there is a requirement of *consistency* in the coordination of an interpersonal system equivalent to that of any personal system. The implication is that just as there is an 'analytical law' of the 'maximization' of rationality in personal systems, so there is an equivalent 'analytical law' of interpersonal systems; facilities are 'maximized' in integrated systems.

In developing the properties of systems of social interaction, Parsons sets his own undertaking against individualistic approaches. His concern is to establish the importance of subjective meaning and the analytical independence of ends, but he is critical of, for example, Weber's restricted emphasis upon individual motivation and his failure fully to recognize the social and systemic aspects of meaning. Thus, Parsons argues that in Weber's formal approach to questions of subjective meaning (*Verstehen*) he fails to appreciate that there are two distinct issues. According to Parsons, Weber was concerned only with a form of *Verstehen* which, "meant essentially the accessibility of the subjective aspect of other people's action as a real process in time",[45] and he failed fully to appreciate the importance of 'atemporal complexes of meaning' which were drawn upon by actors in the formation of their motives.[46] According to Parsons, such 'complexes of meaning' – essentially cultural values and symbols – are of vital importance in patterning systems of social action as normative orders.

We have already seen that, in his analysis of 'unit acts', Parsons makes a distinction between conditions (including means) and ends. When considered from the perspective of 'unit act' analysis this distinction consists in the fact that objects in the situation of action are external to any given actor. However, when interpersonal *systems* of action are considered this distinction between conditions and ends is modified. There is a class of conditions which although external to any given actor is not external to action as such. As Parsons puts it, "what are to one actor non-normative means and conditions are explicable, in part, at least, only in terms of the normative elements of the action of others in the system".[47] Normative elements can be seen to 'interpenetrate' with any definition of the situation of action once the requirements of systems of social action are recognized. Interpersonal order is, in some fundamental sense, a *normative* order, involving atemporal complexes of meaning.

As Parsons develops his position in later writings – for example, in *The Social System* – he comes to stress the role of a common culture, both as the source of the standards governing interaction and internalized within personality as the basis of dispositions to act. However, he is far from arguing that the stability of systems of action depends only on the functioning of common value elements, as many of his critics suggest. Parsons's conception of normative order is more subtle than is usually allowed and he intends it to include a treatment of issues of power. Thus, in his hierarchical presentation of 'emergent properties', Parsons offers coercion as 'above' economic rationality, but 'below' common values. He writes, "where others are concerned coercion is a potential means to the desired control, which is not included in the economic concept as such. It also has a similar double aspect – the exercise of coercive power as a means and its acquisition as an immediate end."[48] However, according to Parsons, 'coercive power' does not *define* the system, in the sense that the system is founded upon it, as some radical conflict thereorists seem to suggest. Coercive power is a relation *within* the system. Thus, Parsons writes, "it cannot be a property of the *total* action system involving a plurality of individuals; it can only apply to some individuals or groups within a system *relative* to others. Coercion is an exercise of power over others."[49] The final emergent property of the total action system, then, is the requirement that, "in order that there may be a stable system of action involving a plurality of individuals there must be normative regulation of the power aspect of individuals within the system; in this sense, there must be a distributive order."[50] In other words, the distribution of resources, within the system and, therefore, the actions within which those resources are produced and reproduced, must be governed by some legitimating principles or norms.

Those critics of Parsons who accuse him of neglecting power might be on more secure ground were they themselves to be denying the role of normative order. This seems to be what is suggested by some conflict theorists, for example, in their emphasis upon the 'ubiquity of conflict' or the 'zero-sum' nature of power (which stresses the mutual exclusivity of interests in power relationships).[51] In Parsons's terms, such arguments over-emphasize the coercive aspects of power, seeing it purely in terms of a 'distributional struggle'.[52] In consequence, they fail to acknowledge the way in which 'legitimation' transforms interests to constitute them as 'collective'. However, most theorists who emphasize the coercive aspects of power against Parsons's supposed neglect, argue that to restrict analysis only to coercion would be unsatisfactory. Indeed, they usually suggest that, while Parsons's theories betray a one-sided emphasis upon normative order, an equivalent one-sidedness is not to be found in their own emphasis upon coercive power. Thus, Lockwood writes that, "when we talk of the stability or instability of a social system, we mean more than anything else the success or failure of the normative order in regulating conflicts of interest"[53], while Giddens proposes that, "a general theory of social systems must begin from the interdependency of norms and power"[54] and Habermas seeks to outline the "normative anchoring of power".[55] The pressing issue, according to these theorists, would seem to be to specify the relations between power and normative order. They make this argument in criticism of Parsons, but this is precisely what he was attempting in his general theory of action.

While Parsons's critics accept the importance of the normative regulation of systems of power, they suggest that his account is too simple and tends to assume that the existence of a normative order implies a positive moral commitment to it. Echoing Weber, it is suggested that legitimacy consists in 'claims' which may or may not be accepted in practice.[56] Giddens, for example, comments that, "it is an elementary mistake to suppose that the enactment of a moral obligation necessarily implies a moral commitment to it. Elementary though it may be, it is important to insist upon this point, because it is systematically ignored in that tradition of social thought linking Parsons and Durkheim."[57] Similarly, Habermas also argues that the orientation to norms, "does not, of course, rest solely on belief in their legitimacy by those affected. It is also based on fear of, and submission to, indirectly threatened sanctions, as well as on the simple compliance engendered by the individual's perception of his powerlessness and the lack of alternatives open to him."[58]

Once again, Parsons was there before his critics. Indeed, he devotes considerable attention to the possibility of an instrumental orientation toward norms, as we would expect given the role of the 'cognitive' in his general account of action, writing that it is necessary to distinguish, "between the fact of orientation to a legitimate order and the motives for acting in relation to it. The two elements of interest and legitimacy are interwoven in a complex way. The fact that an order is legitimate in the eyes of a large proportion of the community makes it ipso facto an element in the *Interessenlage* of any one individual, whether he himself holds it to be legitimate or not. Supposing he does not, his action, to be rational, must be none the less orientated to this order."[59] Nor is this a feature of Parsons's early writings which he subsequently comes to deny, since in his later writings he elaborates a complex argument concerning the mechanisms of sanctioning and their operation in a normative order.[60] At a minimum, it is difficult to see that Parsons could, at one and the same time, propose a theory of sanctions *and* neglect the possibility that they might play a role in securing compliance, that *empirically* conformity might consist in the desire to avoid sanctions rather than in a positive, moral commitment.

However, as his hierarchical presentation of emergent properties implies, Parsons does propose that normative order is logically – that is, analytically – prior. Thus, although sanctions are integral to systems of social action (indeed, embodied in the behaviours and responses of other actors), Parsons writes, "the primary source of constraint lies in the moral authority of a system of rules. Sanctions thus become a secondary mode of the enforcement of rules, because the sanctions are, in turn, dependent on moral authority."[61] The concrete norms of systems of social action reflect the primary form of integration, but they also form an aspect of a secondary form of integration, which consists in behaviour to avoid sanctions. Parsons writes, "a norm is a total description of the concrete course of action thus regarded as desirable, combined with an injunction to make certain future actions conform to this course".[62] Sanctions are processes of the system that can be called upon against potential deviants. The 'positive' form of sanctions are injunctions which stress either the material advantages of conformity (inducement) or membership in a moral community (persuasion). The 'negative' form threaten practical cost (coercion), or remind of past obligations (activation of commitments).[63]

Although their own approaches seem to be pushing in the same direction, most of Parsons's critics are uneasy about his conclusion that sanctions take their meaning from a normative order. They seem to want to maintain that 'power' and 'normative order' can be given an equivalent status, that neither need have priority within an action frame of reference. An example will help both to identify the claims of Parsons's critics and the difficulty in sustaining them. Giddens has criticized Parsons for his emphasis upon the role of 'trust' in cooperative relationships, suggesting that,"if the use of power rests upon 'trust' or confidence' as Parsons emphasises, it also frequently rests upon deceit and hypocrisy . . . any sociological theory which treats such phenomena as 'incidental', or as 'secondary and derived' and not as structurally intrinsic to power differentials, is blatantly inadequate."[64] However, 'trust' is a resource of cooperative relationships and so long as the activities that draw upon it are consistent with the conditions of trust, those resources will be reproduced and, with them, the possibilities for more extensive cooperation. It is certainly the case that the existence of trust offers the possibility of its deceitful use. However, actions which abuse trust must always run the risk of being 'found out', and so, 'deceit', in the long run, cannot be in a stable relationship with the reproduction of the resources that it requires. It is difficult to see that deceit could be 'structurally intrinsic' to resources. 'Trust' may be a poor analogy for complex systems of social action, but within the limits of the example Parsons's analysis is the superior.[65]

Parsons's analysis does not require that 'deceit' will necessarily be found out, merely that it *may*, and, therefore, that it is inherently unstable. Furthermore, on being 'found out' there is an immediate 'deflation' of the system in that the previously existing resources of cooperative action are no longer available. By analogy, then, an actor, or group of actors, may be concerned to pursue power 'for its own sake'. This project, however, will face the limitation that the appropriation of resources to pursue ends, other than those which are truly compatible with the system within which resources are produced, is limited by a possible systems deflation in their reproduction. This possibility has to be addressed in the calculations intrinsic to the construction of ends.[66] Similarly, an actor need not be positively committed to the substance of a relationship, but nevertheless, he or she may value the resources it contains for reasons strategic to his or her other ends. Such an orientation will require the correct calculation of the conditions of reproducing the resources it requires, albeit without a positive commitment to the relationship. Thus, an actor may be positively committed to the relationship, or have a purely instrumental attitude to it, but so long as he or she acts commensurately with the requirements of its reproduction, the relationship will be stable. Finally, while an 'instrumental' attitude necessarily involves a 'cognitive' orientation to the 'normative order' of trust, so, too, would any actions which involved a positive commitment. Actors must know what, say, friendship entails in order to express it, or cynically imitate it for other ends. That is, they must have a knowledge of the 'role expectations' which are a part of any concrete norm. As Parsons puts it, "the orientation to a normative order and the mutual interlocking of expectations and sanctions . . . is rooted, therefore, in the deepest fundamentals of the action frame of reference."[67] This is the substance of Parsons's claims that the 'cognitive' should not be opposed to the 'normative' as distinct types of action, but that each are necessary elements within a single scheme of analysis. Hence, Parsons's claim, which must otherwise strike his critics as distinctly odd and 'out of character', that, "the most elementary and fundamental 'orientational' category . . . seems to be the 'cognitive' which in its most general sense must be treated as the 'definition' of the relevant aspects of the 'situation' in their relevance to the actor's 'interests'."[68]

INTEGRATION AND THE 'DISPLACEMENT' OF ACTION

The identification of the requirements of a developed theory of action are not unique to Parsons – though he was the first to identify them – and similar conceptions are to be found in the arguments of even his most hostile critics. For example, Habermas writes, "every society has to face the basic problem of coordinating action: how does ego get alter to continue interaction in the desired way? How does he avoid conflicts that interrupt the sequence of action?"[69] Similarly, Giddens attacks Parsons's arguments only to suggest that there is a 'true' problem of order, apparently to be distinguished from Parsons's 'untrue' version, but, in fact, remarkably similar to it. For example, Giddens writes that, "the true locus of the 'problem of order' is the problem of how the duality of structure operates in social life: of how continuity of form is achieved in the day-to-day conduct of social activity".[70] He writes further that, "systems of social action, reproduced through the duality of structure in the context of bounded conditions of the rationalisation of action, are constituted through the interdependence of actors or groups".[71] Any problems attributed to 'structural-functionalism', including, for example, an apparent problem of agency, would seem to be intrinsic to the concept of action in any general frame of reference.

Although Parsons's analysis is more subtle than his critics usually allow, and, in some cases, is even the same as that which they offer as an alternative to it, it is far from adequate. We have reached the point where the problems intrinsic to the scheme are beginning to become evident. Parsons has defined voluntaristic action in terms of an actor's freedom to form and choose ends. However, if the voluntaristic aspect of action requires that an actor 'could do otherwise', the coherence of the system, upon which the rationality of particular choices depends, seems to derive from other actors not doing other than whatever is consistent with the realization of a given actor's ends. But what is true of other actors from the perspective of any given actor is true of that actor when his or her actions are considered from the perspective of other actors as means and conditions of the realization of their ends. In any stable system of interaction, the values, preferences, and other considerations which organize any individual actor's choice of ends must be consistent with those of other actors in the same system. The coherence of action, it seems, depends upon the predictability of purposes. Parsons began his analysis of 'unit acts' with a commitment to the 'openness' of human action, but this position cannot be maintained once the requirements of the 'total system of action' are addressed. Action is organized in relation to processes of the system where ends are mutually consistent. Thus, in systems which are integrated, the individual appears as the *expression of structures*, despite the initial perception that structures should be seen as a *product* of action.

Parsons's scheme fails in its own terms. He has come to define systems of interaction in terms of a theoretical construct of 'perfect integration' from which are deduced processes which tend to maintain it in the face of threats to its stability. However, this requires resort to 'disturbances' and 'strains' which are not produced by the 'system', but are accommodated to its processes. For example, in his discussion of sanctions, Parsons fails to account for the motives of deviants whose potential activities occasion the need to mobilize sanctions (or their threat). They are not located within the operation of the system, but are a statement of what obtains *empirically*; that is, that a complete consensus does not exist. In other words, Parsons has resort to residual categories which are not theoretically integrated with the positive categories of the scheme.

The consequence is the sort of construction which the critics take, albeit one-sidedly, as defining his approach. Thus, in *The Social System*, Parsons identifies two primary modes of the orientation of action, the internalization of a value-standard and expediency. Only the former is fully located in terms of theoretically specified (positively defined) processes of the system. As Parsons puts it, "there is a range of possible modes of orientation in the motivational sense to a value-standard. Perhaps, the most important distinction is between the attitude of expediency at one pole ... and at the other pole the introjection or internalisation of the standard ... the latter is to be treated as the basic type of motivation with a normative pattern structure of values."[72] Expediency, then, is a residual category in the sense that it is negatively defined, related to theoretical processes of the system in terms of concrete (theoretically unlocated or 'given') motives of potential deviance. Moreover, despite Parsons's stress that the 'cognitive' and the 'normative' should be integrated, it appears as if he is now offering them as two distinct types (though even here it should be said that what Parsons is really offering is one type in which cognitive and normative aspects are integrated – 'introjection' – alongside another – 'expediency' – in which they are not). Just as Parsons writes of Durkheim, so his own scheme, "has the effect of bringing utilitarian elements back into the picture in the form of 'interests' tending centrifugally to escape normative control."[73] In Parsons's own terms, the identification of an ever-present potential threat of deviance must be a form of 'randomness' attributed to 'ends'.

This position is one which Parsons sought to defend and maintain through his subsequent writings, but the question must be: how consistent is that defence in the light of the criteria and conditions that he had initially identified as the logical requirements of a system of theoretical categories? I shall examine Parsons's elaborations and subsequent defences of his theoretical scheme in the next chapter. For the present, I shall simply observe that his general claim for his frame of reference was that it would integrate a treatment of subjective meaning and motive with wider processes of social systems of interaction. As I have shown, however, Parsons's action frame of reference reproduces dualisms, where he had promised their resolution. First, there is a dualism of 'system' and 'environment'. What had been proposed was a *theoretical statement of action and its environment*. Second, there is a dualism of 'structure' and 'action'. What had been proposed was a *synthesis of structure and action*. These dualisms are evident in the way in which Parsons has resort to residual categories, necessary to the 'completeness' of the scheme, but outside the positive statement of its categories. Thus, there are 'facts' in the 'environment' of action systems which do not form part of the theoretical statement of those systems and these 'facts' include 'actions' (that is, concrete behaviours which correspond to the 'facts') outside the statement of 'structure' (the 'positive' categories of the theoretical system). Parsons argued that any theoretical sytem was to be judged by the internal consistency of its categories and their specification without resort to residual categories. His own action frame of reference fails on both counts.

NOTES

1. A word of clarification is necessary here. When Parsons (or Habermas and Giddens, for that matter) refers to the necessity of a social scientific scheme that is adequate to

subjective meanings, that scheme will always be, in some sense, the point of view of an external observer. Thus, Parsons in his concern to incorporate the 'subjective point of view' is not attempting to give an account of action as it is experienced subjectively by the actor. Schutz, for example, in drawing out this distinction, argues that Parsons's scheme is not properly grounded because it does not set out how that subjective experience is connected to the categories of a sociological scheme despite the subjective component of those categories. See A. Schutz, 'Parsons' theory of social action: a critical review by Alfred Schutz', in R. Grathoff (ed.), *The Theory of Social Action: The Correspondence of Alfred Schutz and Talcott Parsons* (Bloomington, Indiana University Press, 1978), p. 24.

Schutz is correct (it is an observation which he also directs against Weber), but I think that Parsons is also right to suggest that their different concerns are complementary, rather than contradictory. See T. Parsons, 'Letter, January 16, 1941'(ibid.). This is a point that Schutz appears to concede in his own comment that Parsons's system "begins where my own . . . ends." A. Schutz, 'Letter, March 17, 1941' (ibid.), p. 97. For example, Schutz is concerned to demonstrate that actors do not (except exceptionally) experience action in terms of the attribution of means and ends. For the most part, action is routinely taken-for-granted. It is only in relation to some discrepancy or problematic feature of interaction that actors step outside the 'natural attitude'. When they do so, however, they take the stance of a 'third party', reflecting upon their own behaviours and those of others. In so doing, they make assessments of the situation and attribute meanings and motives to actors, in a manner similar to what is represented in the rational constructions of social scientific schemes.

For Schutz, social scientists adopt a permanent and 'methodological' stance of the third party for whom actions are, as it were, 'routinely' problematic. Social scientific constructs, then, are different from the subjective experience of actors, without, by that token, being 'non-subjective', in Parsons's sense. Furthermore, they are rendered valid by the parallel between the circumstances in which actors become 'lay social scientists' and those of 'professional social scientists'. Schutz's arguments are intended to provide a phenomenological justification of an action frame of reference as a scheme of social scientific categories. In principle, his arguments are neutral as to the precise form of development within those categories.

Of course, Schutz's version of the implications of his scheme is not fully accepted, even by those who are strongly influenced by it. One strand in ethnomethodology, for example, takes the distinction between 'how action is experienced subjectively by actors' and the 'subjective point of view' as expressed within a social scientific scheme as the basis of rejecting the latter. See, for example, H. Garfinkel and H. Sacks, 'On the formal structures of practical action', in J.C. McKinney and E. Tiryakian (eds), *Theoretical Sociology: Perspectives and Developments* (New York, Appleton-Century Crofts, 1970).

2. *TSofSA*, pp. 43–4.
3. *TSofSA*, p. 609. Parsons's arguments are ambiguous in that he does suggest that the unit act concept may be used concretely in the *description* of action. However, as we shall see, Parsons immediately goes on to distinguish between *description* and *explanation*. He suggests that his interest in the unit act is 'analytical', concerned with the identification of 'elements', where 'further steps' and elaboration will be necessary in order to draw out the implications for concrete explanation. Parsons's

use of the term 'analytic' identifies his interest in the explanatory, rather than descriptive, use of the scheme.

4. *TSofSA*, p. 44.
5. *TSofSA*, p. 44.
6. *TSofSA*, p. 44.
7. See, especially, R.S. Warner, 'Toward a re-definition of action theory: paying the cognitive element its due', *American Journal of Sociology*, 83(6), 1978, pp. 1317–49; B.S. Barnes, *The Nature of Power* (Cambridge, Polity, 1988); J. Heritage, *Garfinkel and Ethnomethodology* (Cambridge, Polity, 1984).
8. *TSofSA*, p. 45.
9. Ironically, where Parsons's use of the term 'normative orientation' sees him accused of 'idealism', so his use of the term 'effort' in relation to action, sees him accused of 'positivism'. See J. Finley Scott, 'The changing foundation of the Parsonsian action scheme', *American Sociological Review*, 28(5), 1963, p. 716–35.
10. In keeping with his concern to develop a scheme in which the different elements are balanced, Parsons, for his part, is critical of approaches which over-emphasize the 'cognitive'. Such an over-emphasis, he argues, is typical of a positivist theory of action. See *TSofSA*, p. 61.
11. *TSofSA*, p. 323.
12. M. Weber, *Economy and Society, Volume I* (New York, Bedminster Press, 1968), p. 24.
13. Ibid., p. 25.
14. Ibid.,p. 26.
15. Thus, Parsons suggests that any 'iron cage' attributed to systems of action is an artifact of Weber's method.
16. *TSofSA*, p. 63.
17. *TSofSA*, p. 64.
18. *TSofSA*, p. 64.
19. Parsons suggests that, in the last analysis, there is no such thing as a radically positivistic theory of *action*. Were the reductions attempted by radical positivists to be successful – which, of course, Parsons denies – then, it would turn out that the categories identified within an action frame of reference, "can always be adequately stated in terms of a natural science system. In this sense a positivistic position always reduces the explanation of action to natural science terms". *TSofSA*, p. 762.
20. It is implicit, for example, in the writings of those who are seeking a synthetic theory of action. It is also the standard move by critics of rational-choice theory. See, for example, B. Hindess, *Choice, Rationality and Social theory* (London, Allen and Unwin, 1988).
21. *TSofSA*, p. 600. Giddens, for his part, writes of "the 'technical grounding' of the knowledge that is applied as 'means' in purposive acts to secure particular outcomes". A. Giddens, *New Rules of Sociological Method* (London, Hutchinson, 1976), p. 83.
22. As Alexander puts it, "in order for action to be conceived as multi-dimensional, for action to be seen as in part voluntary, in part determined, means and ends must be viewed as making independent contributions to any given act". See J.C. Alexander, *Theoretical Logic, Volume I: Positivism, Presuppositions and Current Controversies* (London, Routledge and Kegan Paul, 1982), p. 67. The substance of the point is clear, though reference to a 'given act' tends to elide Parsons's distinction between the 'analytic' and the 'concrete'.

23. *TSofSA*, p. 48.
24. *TSofSA*, p. 49.
25. *TSofSA*, p. 739.
26. *TSofSA*, p. 718.
27. *TSofSA*, p. 32.
28. *TSofSA*, p. 36.
29. *TSofSA*, p. 622.
30. See M. Weber, *Economy and Society*, p. 14.
31. *TSofSA*, p. 747.
32. *TSofSA*, pp. 579. ff.
33. *TSofSA*, p. 739. Critics of Parsons, especially those who seek to distinguish his later, supposedly 'structural-functionalist' approach, from his earlier 'action' approach, fail to grasp the nature of Parsons's argument in *TSofSA*. For example, Martindale argues that, "Parsons's conclusions are in all essentials identical with Weber's," enumerating these agreed-upon 'essentials' as follows: "(1) the act is the smallest unit of sociological analysis; (2) action appears in systems – hence system is the second structural concept; (3) systems may produce emergent properties which are not completely analysable into the individual acts; (4) systems of social action may, for convenience, be treated as structures, aggregates of persons; however (5) structures have only a fictitious reality; in principle every structure is analysable into unit acts, though this is slow and inefficient". See D. Martindale, 'Talcott Parsons's theoretical metamorphosis from social behaviourism to macro-funtionalism', in H. Turk and R.L. Simpson (eds), *Institutions and Social Exchange: the Sociologies of Talcott Parsons and George Casper Homans* (Indianapolis and New York, Bobbs-Merrill, 1971), pp. 168–9.
34. Parsons writes that, "limiting observation of the concrete phenomenon, then, to the properties that have a place in the unit act or other subsystem leads to indeterminacy in the theory when empirically applied to complex systems. This indeterminacy, a form of empirical inadequacy, is the fundamental difficulty of atomistic theories when applied to organic phenomena. They cannot do justice to properties such as economic rationality which are not properties of 'action as such', that is, of isolated unit acts or of atomistic systems, but only of organic systems of action beyond a certain degree of complexity." *TSofSA*, p. 740.
35. See, for example, J. Finley Scott, 'The changing foundation'; D. Martindale, 'Talcott Parsons's theoretical metamorphosis from social behaviourism to macro-functionalism' in H. Turk, R. L. Simpson (eds), *Institutions and Exchange: The Sociologies of Talcott Parsons and George Caspar Homans* (New York, Bobbs-Merrill, 1971); K. Menzies, *Talcott Parsons and the Social Image of Man* (London, Routledge and Kegan Paul, 1977). Even Turner and Beeghley, who have sought to challenge the 'folklore' inherent in much of the critical literature on Parsons, while arguing that action assumptions underlie Parsons's 'later' structural-functionalism fail to recognize the argument about systems intrinsic to *TSofSA*. Thus, they write, "Parsons appears to have become concerned with how unit acts are connected to each other and how this connectedness can be conceptually represented. Indeed, near the end of *The Structure of Social Action*, Parsons recognizes that 'any atomistic system that only deals with properties identifiable in the unit act . . . will of necessity fail to treat these latter elements adequately and be indeterminate as applied to complex systems,' (1937, pp. 748–9).

However, only the barest hints of what are to come are evident in the closing pages."
See J.H. Turner and L. Beeghley, 'Current folklore in the criticism of Parsonian action theory', *Sociological Inquiry*, 44(1), 1974, 49. Adriaansens is virtually the only commentator to recognise that Parsons's " 'action theory' is, by definition, a 'system theory' ". H.P.M. Adriaansens, *Talcott Parsons and the Conceptual Dilemma* (London, Routledge and Kegan Paul, 1980), p. 60.

36. J.C. Alexander, *Theoretical Logic in Sociology, Volume IV: The Modern Reconstruction of Classical Thought: Talcott Parsons* (London, Routledge and Kegan Paul, 1984), p. 47. Of course, if it were a matter of 'choice', this would mean that there would be a variety of mutually exclusive theoretical schemes compatible with 'theoretical logic' and Alexander would face the very 'relativism' that he claims that his own (and Parsons's) elaboration of general theory is designed to overcome.

37. See J.M. Holmwood and A. Stewart, *Explanation and Social Theory* (London, Macmillan, 1991).

38. *TSofSA*, p. 51.

39. See, especially, Parsons's discussion of Pareto. See *TSofSA*, pp. 228ff.

40. *TSofSA*, p. 740.

41. The background to Parsons's argument is the critique of neo-classical economics by the North American school of institutionalist economists, especially Clarence Ayres. See, C. Camic, 'The making of a method: a historical re-interpretation of the early Parsons', *American Sociological Review*, 52(4), 1987, pp. 421–39; B. Wearne, *The Theory and Scholarship of Talcott Parsons to 1951: A Critical Commentary* (Cambridge, Cambridge University Press, 1989). The way in which 'emergent properties' are implicit even in 'individualist' approaches which seek to deny them is apparent in Elster's discussion of 'functionalism'. See, J. Elster, "Marxism, functionalism and game theory: the case for methodological individualism', *Theory and Society*, 11(4), 1982, pp. 453–82. Elster regards functionalism as an illegitimate approach in the social sciences. However, he accepts that, as in economics, to the extent that functionalism "invokes teleonomy, as in the explanation of market behaviour through a natural-selection model of competition between firms, there can be no objection to it". Ibid., p. 455. Elster argues that there are numerous other cases where no such analogy exists and, therefore, that functionalism is deficient, but he fails to appreciate the extent to which Parsonian general theory is an attempt formally to extend the analogy, precisely to subsume cases other than those of market behaviour.

42. Indeed, although Weber sometimes writes of value-rational action as if it were beyond any issue of the consideration of its practical requirements and consequences, he also sometimes implies issues of the *practical realization* of fundamental values. For example, he writes, "examples of pure value-rational orientation would be the actions of persons who, regardless of possible cost to themselves, *act to put into practice their convictions* of what seem to them to be required by duty, honour, the pursuit of beauty, a religious call, personal loyalty, or the importance of some 'cause' no matter in what it consists". M. Weber, *Economy and Society, Volume 1*, p. 25.

43. *TSofSA*, p. 730.

44. *TSofSA*, p. 751. Giddens, for his part, writes that, "purposive conduct may be usefully thought of as the application of 'knowledge' to secure certain outcomes, events or qualities. To enquire into the rationalization of such conduct, I shall say, is

to enquire into (a) the logical connection between various forms of purposive acts, or projects, and (b) the 'technical grounding' of the knowledge that is applied as 'means' in purposive acts to secure particular outcomes." *New Rules*, p. 83.

45. *TSofSA*, p. 635.
46. *TSofSA*, p. 636. Parsons argues that Weber recognizes the importance of the distinction in his more substantive work – for example, where he identifies 'forms of legitimate domination' according to the meaning complexes which define their claims for legitimacy and distinguishes that from the subjective motives that specific individuals might have for compliance. See M. Weber, *Economy and Society, Volume 1*. However, Parsons argues, Weber fails to incorporate these insights into his formal statements of sociological categories.
47. *TSofSA*, p. 51.
48. *TSofSA*, pp. 239–40.
49. *TSofSA*, pp. 767–8.
50. *TSofSA*, p. 768.
51. See, for example, R. Daherendorf, 'Out of utopia', in *Essays in the Theory of Society* (London, Routledge and Kegan Paul, 1968).
52. Parsons's later criticism of 'zero-sum' conceptions of power is developed in 'Some reflections on the place of force in social process' and 'On the concept of political power', both reprinted in T. Parsons, *Sociological Theory and Modern Society* (New York, Free Press, 1967).
53. See D. Lockwood, 'Some remarks on *The Social System*', *British Journal of Sociology*, 7(1), 1956, p. 137.
54. See A. Giddens, ' "Power" in the recent writings of Talcott Parsons', *Sociology*, 2(2), 1968, p. 268.
55. See Habermas, *The Theory of Communicative Action, Volume 2*, p. 270.
56. For example, Weber writes, "naturally, the legitimacy of a system of domination may be treated sociologically only as the probability that to a relevant degree the appropriate attitudes will exist, and the corresponding conduct ensue. It is by no means true that every case of submissiveness to persons in power is primarily (or even at all) oriented to this belief. Loyalty may be hypocritically simulated by individuals or by whole groups on purely opportunistic grounds, or carried out in practice for reasons of material self-interest. Or people may submit from individual weakness and helplessness because there is no acceptable alternative. But these considerations are not decisive for the classification of types of domination. What is important is the fact that in a given case the particular claim to legitimacy is to a significant degree and according to its type treated as 'valid'; that this fact confirms the position of the persons claiming authority and that it helps determine the choice of means of its exercise." M. Weber, *Economy and Society, Volume I*, p. 214.
57. See Giddens, *New Rules*, p. 109.
58. See Habermas, *Legitimation Crisis* (London, Heinemann, 1976), page 96.
59. *TSofSA*, p. 652.
60. See especially, Parsons, 'Some reflections on the place of force'.
61. *TSofSA*, p. 463.
62. *TSofSA*, p. 75.
63. See Parsons, 'Some reflections on the place of force', pp. 269–70. For his part, despite his belief in the inadequacy of Parsons's scheme, Giddens presents Parsons's statement of sanctions as his own, writing that, "sanctions are easily classified, on

the abstract level, in terms of whether the resources which are mobilised to produce the sanction are 'internal': ie involve elements of the actor's personality, or 'external': ie draw upon features of the context of action. Each of these may be further categorised in terms of whether the resources the sanctioning agent is able to mobilise are 'positive' or 'negative' with regard to the wants of the actor who is the target of the sanction. Thus the actualisation of 'internal' sanctions may draw upon a positive moral commitment of the actor, or negatively upon anxiety, fear or guilt; the actualisation of 'external' sanctions may draw upon offers of reward or on the other hand may hold out the threat of force." *New Rules*, pp. 109–10. Since Giddens's scheme of sanctions is the same as that of Parsons, then whatever he claims for his own scheme should be there in Parsons, and any deficiencies of the latter's scheme will be reproduced in that of Giddens. See Holmwood and Stewart, *Explanation and Social Theory*.

64. See Giddens,' "Power in the recent writings of Talcott Parsons', p. 264.

65. Parsons's other analogy is between power and developed monetary systems. See T. Parsons, 'Some reflections on the place of force'. Habermas believes that what is wrong with this analogy is that it lacks a normative reference, that there is no structural analogy to 'legitimation' in monetary systems, while this is necessary in a system of power. See Habermas, *Theory of Communicative Action, Volume II*, p. 270. Habermas is wrong about what Parsons seeks to take from the analogy, but his criticism need not be pursued since for almost everyone else the problem is precisely Parsons's overemphasis upon legitimation, not his neglect. For a detailed criticism, see Holmwood and Stewart, *Explanation and Social Theory*, pp. 119ff.

66. Parsons writes that, "a deflationary influence is one that leads to a demand for a binding decision or exercise of power, to which the demander has some kind of right but which is out of line with the normal expectations of operation of the system". See Parsons, 'Some reflections on the place of force', p. 291.

67. Parsons, *The Social System* (London, Routledge and Kegan Paul, 1951), pp. 11–12.

68. Ibid., p. 7. Since most critics of Parsons believe that he offers only the 'internalization of norms', their representations of what he is arguing are wide of the mark (though widely accepted). Thus, Heritage writes that, "Parsons's actors are treated as broadly unreflexive with respect to the norms they have internalized. The result is that his actors can neither adopt a manipulative or game-like stance towards the norms, nor are they capable of the reflection necessary to make a moral choice." See J. Heritage, *Garfinkel and Ethnomethodology* (Cambridge, Polity, 1984), p. 111.

69. See J. Habermas, *The Theory of Communicative Action, Volume II: Lifeworld and System: A Critique of Functionalist Reason* (Cambridge, Polity, 1987), p. 179.

70. See A. Giddens, *Central Problems in Social Theory* (London, Macmillan, 1979), p. 216.

71. Ibid., p. 76. As we have seen, this is precisely where Parsons locates the 'problem of order'. For a detailed treatment of the convergence between Parsons, Giddens, and Habermas, see, Holmwood and Stewart, *Explanation and Social Theory*.

72. *The Social System*, p. 37.

73. *TSofSA*, p. 710.

5

STRUCTURAL-FUNCTIONALISM, THEORETICAL BREAKDOWN AND THE EMBRACE OF CONTRADICTION

At various points in this book, I have suggested that Parsons's difficulties derive from the fact that his theoretical framework generalizes, rather than transcends any specific explanatory problems that he identified in the course of his account of the breakdown of theoretical systems. In this chapter, I want to make good this claim. What I shall argue is that Parsons intended to produce a scheme of complementary categories, but he was unaware of how mutual antagonism was built into the component elements of his scheme because he paid insufficient attention to the circumstances of explanatory failure from which, even as he presented them, they took their meaning. For example, Parsons sought to reconcile the 'objective' and the 'subjective', as if these designations were unproblematic and self-evident. I have argued that their division – and the categories take their meaning from division – occurs whenever an explanation fails adequately to account for the observations of behaviours which it accepts. In these circumstances, what is 'objective' and what is 'subjective', what is 'structure' and what 'action', cannot be given in advance of addressing the particular explanatory problems that have given rise to the divisions. The consequence of Parsons's failure to recognize this is that he builds into his general categories the very inconsistencies and contradictory dualisms that occur in explanatory failure.

'PHASES' OF THEORETICAL DEVELOPMENT

The claim that Parsons's theory is deficient is not a novel one, but it is important that this is not a mere external judgement. The theory fails in its own terms. We can recall Parsons's own comments on the nature of the breakdown of theoretical systems and the responses that such breakdown elicits. The problems intrinsic to a theoretical system will be manifested in the instability of the

79

various positions that occur in its elaboration. Theoretical developments to address these problems will have the character of seemingly distinct 'phases'. These 'phases' are, however, soon revealed to be mutations. As one problem is 'solved' another occurs, thereby showing that, in truth, the initial problem was not solved, only displaced to pop up again elsewhere in the system in the form of residual categories. It is these processes which indicate that the problems of a theoretical system are fundamental and require a transformation of its categories, rather than merely further development within its categories.

According to Parsons, there are additional problems of interpretation which will be created by the advocates of any particular theoretical system. As Parsons puts it, although the 'ablest proponents' will address problems and, therefore, reveal them for inspection, in the case of 'mediocre proponents' the problems will be, "so vaguely stated as to be virtually meaningless . . . [while] . . . in the case of the dogmatists of the system their existence, or at least their importance for the system, may even be vehemently denied".[1] We can accept Parsons's account of the dynamics of theoretical advocacy, even if the issue of personal culpability is too strongly put. After all, no 'solution' to a theoretical problem will be proposed without at least some initial belief in its plausibility. So, where critics will be arguing that a theoretical system is fundamentally flawed, proponents will claim that there is a development of the theory in which the alleged deficiencies are not to be found and, therefore, that those deficiencies are not intrinsic to the system, but only to one of its 'phases' which has been left behind. Implicit in Parsons's argument, then, is the further problem that where theoretical breakdown involves different 'phases' of theoretical development some will be advocates of what they claim is a distinct position within a theoretical system, distinguishing it from the statements of position associated with other 'phases'. Precisely which 'phase' of theoretical development contains the 'true' core of the theory – and in what, precisely, that 'core' consists – will be a matter of controversy. Just as there have been disputes over the true substance of Marx's theoretical scheme – whether it lies in an 'early' humanist or Hegelian conception, or a 'mature' scientific position which effected an 'epistemological break' with the earlier position[2] – so there have been similar disputes over the 'phases' of Parsons's theoretical development.

At the same time, if we pursue the implications of Parsons's argument a little further, 'dogmatism' will be as much an issue among critics of a theoretical system as it is among its advocates. For example, as we have seen, some critics of Parsons argue that he switched from an early commitment to 'action' to an antithetical 'systems' perspective, where the purpose of the argument is to insulate the action assumptions from their entailment in what are accepted as deficiencies of the allegedly later 'systems' perspective.[3] On the other hand, others have accepted a similar distinction in order to argue their preference for the 'systems' perspective over any deficient, humanist – and, therefore, unscientific – 'action' assumptions.[4]

Recently, a third position has been added to these more conventional interpretations of Parsons. According to Adriaansens and Alexander, who are its major proponents, Parsons's theory evolved through (at least) three phases.[5] The first was a simple, but more or less consistent, initial phase – associated with *TSofSA* – in which the basic, logical requirements of a multidimensional theoretical system, including its grounding in action, are established. The second phase – associated with *The Social System* – is accepted as deficient, when judged both in terms of the theoretical requirements established in the earlier phase and those of conventional criticism. Adriaansens, for example, accepts that the 'middle phase' is characterized by the very failure adequately to integrate the analysis of subjective meaning and motive with the wider processes of social systems of interaction which I outlined in the previous chapter. However, Alexander and Adriaansens both argue that Parsons's theory went through a further development which solved the deficiencies of the 'middle phase' and realized the theoretical claims and ambitions set out in the first phase. Unfortunately, they argue, Parsons's critics did not keep up with this 'post-structural-functional' development of a 'new voluntaristic theory of action', which Parsons (writing with Smelser) first presented in *Economy and Society*.[6] In consequence, Parsons's critics continued to criticize him for deficiencies which had already been overcome.

I have already referred in a previous chapter to Alexander's claim that Parsons can be wrong, but is, in fact, right, while his critics can be right, but are, in fact, wrong – that, as Alexander says, "if we take Parsons at face value, he is often, in fact, the 'functionalist', the 'equilibrium theorist', the 'ideologist' that his critics portray. He can achieve each of these identities, moreover, while maintaining his generalized, presuppositional emphasis. Parsons's critics, then, are correct; yet at the same time they are wrong."[7] For Alexander, Parsons is 'right' in his first and last phases and 'wrong' in his middle phase. The errors of the middle phase are purely contingent and not entailed in either of the other two phases. The further paradox, according to Alexander, is that Parsons's critics frequently find themselves affirming the need to effect a synthesis of structure and action in a general frame of reference which is the substance of the Parsonsian first phase that is finally brought to mature fruition in the third phase. Now, argues Alexander, after a period of ideological rejection of Parsons's work in which the dangers of theoretical fragmentation have become so evident, sociological theory can once more, with a proper recognition of Parsons's theoretical achievement, be put back onto its proper, rational (or logical) course.

The idea that Parsons's critics failed to notice the third phase of his theoretical development, however, is not very plausible. After all, Alexander and Adriaansens each associate this phase with the so-called 'interchange theory' of the scheme of four functional imperatives. This is the period in Parsons's theoretical development in which everything is elaborated in terms of four-fold divisions, specifying discrete spheres with exchanges between them. Each space is divided by four and each quarter is open to further subdivision and so on. The diagrams representing the divisions and the exchanges between what has been subdivided become increasingly abstract and baroque. If some of Parsons's critics did not spend much time over this development, it is not because they failed to notice it, but because they regarded it as an accentuation of the position set out in *The Social System*, rather than an improvement upon it. In fact, when the arguments of Adriaansens and Alexander are examined more closely, even as they lay claim to the adequacy of Parsons's mature theory, so the criteria by which that theory is being judged are being modified. Put simply, the later phase of Parsons's theoretical development does not, in fact, confirm the criteria proposed in the first phase, even in the arguments of those seeking to maintain the adequacy of the later position. Ultimately, Alexander's claim is that the substance of Parsons's mature theory must be accepted *even where it breaches his early methodological requirements*; in effect, he comes to argue that the self-conscious criteria of 'theoretical logic' must be brought into line with the 'reality' of Parsons's theoretical development.

The problems of Parsons's approach, then, are reproduced, rather than transcended, in any development which his theory undergoes. His later arguments contradict the methodological claims made in *TSofSA*, but, as I have argued, that work is not itself free of the problems that confound his later arguments. The problems which the later positions reflect – whether in a middle phase or after – are instrinsic to the categories set out in *TSofSA*. For much of this study, I have restricted my analysis to Parsons's early work precisely because most critics are sympathetic to it, locating the problematic features of his work in later writings, with no appreciation of how they are contained in the earlier, less developed position. The later developments of Parsons's theory, however elaborate and extensive they might appear to be, also express the dualisms that his earliest work contains. In consequence, any return to Parsons's starting point is doomed to follow his journey. Yet, the very dualisms that occur in the development of his theory are the occasion for others to assign Parsons to one side of a dualism and to claim that what is necessary is a general frame of reference which synthesises 'structure' and 'action'. *This is precisely what returns anyone to his starting point. What we are witnessing in the work of Parsons is, at one and the same time, the constitution of the project of general theory in sociology and its breakdown.* The fact that some of Parsons's critics converge upon his position – whether in its first or later phases – is no indication of its validity, but an indication of our current theoretical dilemma.

Much of the critical debate over Parsons's work has concentrated upon his concept of the 'problem of order'. For many critics, it is this concept which explains his emphasis upon normative integration and the priority he gives to processes which maintain stability over any which might give rise to change. In the previous chapter, I suggested that this interpretation was too simple and that Parsons began with the intention of producing a theory which would be equally adept at addressing change as stability, and power as norms. Yet, as I have shown, in his account of systems of action Parsons does come to argue that questions of their stability and change and of the role of norms and power are best addressed by means of a concept of 'perfect integration'. In essence, the concept contains a statement of the rational requirements of systems (both personal and interpersonal), where action appears as an expression of systems. Although concrete systems are less than fully rational, there is no *theoretical* statement of their less than fully rational aspects and, in consequence, the only systematic processes which his theory can generate are processes of the system which manage concrete 'strains' and 'disturbances' in tendencies toward integration.

The analytical concept of 'perfect integration', and the integrative processes of concrete systems which are derived from it, has caused considerable difficulty for Parsons's critics and sympathizers alike. Critics – for example, conflict theorists – frequently mistook it for a claim about concrete states of systems suggesting that Parsons assumed that societies are characterized by harmony, rather than conflict.[8] On the face of it, this criticism is easily dismissed by apologists for Parsons. Thus, Johnson writes that, "Parsons never held, of course, that actors' orientations harmonize perfectly with the functional problems of action systems. If to some readers Parsons's theory gives an unrealistic image of social harmony . . . it can only be said that these readers must be approaching the theory with very stubborn misconceptions, able to resist many, many contrary indications."[9] Adriaansens makes a similar point, arguing that the 'structural analysis' propounded in *The Social System* takes, "a dominant value as starting-point . . . but the analysis aims to show why it is that this value is never fully-realized in practical reality".[10] 'Strains' and 'disturbances' are assigned to the contingencies of systems of interaction, and, ultimately, to the essential properties of action as creative and, therefore, indeterminate. A 'dominant value' is the starting point precisely because of the assumptions of an action frame of reference and, at the same time, 'action' is also the explanation of why it can have only a counterfactual status.

In developing the argument, Adriaansens pursues an analogy between Parsons's concept of 'perfect integration' and Newton's first law of inertia which, he argues, has a similar status as a theoretical assumption which takes its meaning from its location within a conceptual frame of reference – in Newton's case, that of classical mechanics. "Few natural scientists," Adriaansens comments ironically, "have made history by claiming that Newton's law obscured the view on movement and change of movement."[11] While Adriaansens's comment is apt, that any evaluation of a theoretical concept must first ascertain how it operates within a wider scheme, any irony is double-edged. Classical mechanics has given way, to be replaced by quantum mechanics. Moreover, it is precisely in attempting to come to terms with the meaning of the supercession of classical mechanics that philosophers of science have challenged positivist accounts of science.[12] In the process, they have developed post-positivist approaches to scientific development in which 'foundational' theory of the sort in which Parsons engaged has been called into question. After all, if even the Newtonian framework of classical mechanics can

83

be shown not to be 'foundational', or 'logically indispensable', might that not also be the case with Parsonian general theory in sociology? Moreover, classical mechanics was superseded in theoretical developments which directly addressed its explanatory problems and provided an increase in explanatory content.

In any case, even if we accept that Parsons's concept of perfect integration must be judged in terms of its role within a wider theory that would not guarantee its adequacy. Conflict theorists may misunderstand the relation between the concept of 'perfect integration' and concrete events, but, as we saw in the last chapter, the problem, from Parsons's perspective, is that it does not meet *his own* requirements of theoretical adequacy. So, where conflict theorists resist what are, as Johnson puts it, the 'many, many contraindications' to their interpretation which can be found in Parsons's work, Johnson (and others sympathetic to Parsons) resists those contrary indications which reside in Parsons's own methodological claims for theoretical adequacy. The empirical 'facts' of deviance, which occasion the integrative processes of social systems, are outside the *positive* statement of theoretical categories, since that statement is one of 'perfect integration'. The empirical 'facts' of deviance, are, then, 'residual categories' and it is Parsons, himself, who argues that 'residual categories' are a sign of the breakdown of a theoretical system.

Perhaps Parsons solved these problems as his theory developed. Certainly, this is what Adriaansens and Alexander believe and, they might argue, that, so far, I have made my case in terms of Parsons's arguments in *The Social System* which, it seems, they do allow are deficient. However, when one looks more closely at what they are proposing as an adequate position, it is, in fact, remarkably similar to the position that Parsons advances in *The Social System*. For example, Alexander promotes a 'neo-functionalist' approach which, he argues, "is concerned with integration as a possibility and with deviance and processes of social control as facts. Equilibrium is taken as a reference point for functionalist systems analysis, though not for participants in actual social systems as such."[13] Apparently this is an appropriate form of analysis and one which meets the logical requirements of 'multidimensional' theory. If it does, we would have to conclude that *those requirements allow residual categories.*[14]

Indeed, when Alexander refers to the two points of reference – that of the 'system' and that of 'participants'– we are reminded of Parsons's initial claim that they 'should correspond' and that what he sought was a 'satisfactory solution of their relations'. Now we are offered the 'system perspective' as an abstract possibility which does not exhaust the actual determination of concrete actions. The 'system (or structural) perspective' does not fully correspond to the 'action perspective'. It would seem that, whatever the rational requirements of structure and action as expressed in the positive categories of the developed action frame of reference they do not cover the contribution of 'action' to a full explanation of concrete events.

What Alexander accepts as an adequate neo-functionalist approach to social

84

issues, is precisely the position which Parsons began to espouse self-consciously in *The Social System*. In that work, Parsons distinguishes between the 'structural-functional' point of view and that of 'dynamic processes' of concrete systems. The distinction is similar to that of 'objective' and 'subjective' points of view offered in *TSofSA* with the difference that, now, doubt begins to enter. Having distinguished them, their relationship becomes problematic to the extent that the distinction is called into question, if only hesitantly. Thus, Parsons writes, "we simply are not in a position to 'catch' the uniformities of dynamic process in the social system except here and there. But in order to give those we can a setting and to be in the most advantageous position to extend our dynamic knowledge we must have a 'picture' of the system within which they fit, of the given relationships of its parts in a given state of the system, and, where changes take place, of what changes into what through what order of intermediate stages. The system of structural categories is the conceptual scheme which gives this setting for dynamic analysis. As dynamic analysis is extended the *independent* explanatory significance of structural categories evaporates. But their scientific function is nonetheless crucial."[15] What Parsons seems to be implying is that the 'structural-functional' point of view proposed in the development of his general theory might not have the 'phenomenological status' attributed to general theory, that it is not 'logically indispensable', merely 'pragmatically useful' and, therefore, potentially open to fundamental revision. This is an implicit recognition of the unsatisfactory nature of his theoretical development from his own perspective.

Nevertheless, Parsons's subsequent work is a robust – even dogmatic – defence of his categories against anyone else's attempt to have them evaporate. In this way, despite the misgivings expressed in *The Social System*, there is a strong tendency on the part of both Parsons and his sympathizers to promote as necessary and coherent the very formulations that were initially qualified by Parsons as inadequate. Is it not more likely that the confusion over the middle and later phases of Parsons's theoretical development is less a condition of his critics than of those who would rescue him from them? What we are witnessing is precisely that process which I identified in the introduction to this chapter where Parsons's early methodological claims are being modified and brought into line with the substance of his later theory, rather than any realization in the substance of the later theory of the early methodological claims.[16]

FROM 'INTEGRATION' TO 'DISINTEGRATION'

In the development of his general framework, especially in *The Social System*, and after, Parsons offers a distinction between different levels of analysis, namely personality, social system and culture (when he becomes fully conscious of a four-fold division in his categories, he adds a fourth level of 'organism', but this need not concern us here).[17] The levels correspond to the analytical distinctions made in the earlier statement of the action frame of reference. Thus, the level of personality corresponds to the individual actor viewed as a system. The level of culture refers to the symbols and meanings which are drawn upon by actors in the pursuit of their personal projects and their negotiation of social constraints and facilities. As Parsons says, the three key features of the cultural system are, "that culture is *transmitted*, it constitutes a heritage or a social tradition; secondly, that it is *learned*, it is not a manifestation, in particular content, of man's genetic constitution; and third, that it is *shared*. Culture, that is, is on the one hand the product of, on the other hand a determinant of, systems of human social interaction."[18] Finally, the 'social system' corresponds to that level of interaction among a 'plurality of actors' which was the primary focus of the analysis of the 'problem of order' in *TSofSA*. The 'social system' is a structure of positions and roles organized by normed expectations and maintained by sanctions.[19]

Parsons proposes that each of the 'levels' forms a system in its own right, where the characteristics of a system are relations of logical coherence among its parts. At the same time, each system functions in relation to the other systems and interpenetrates with them. In other words, *their interpenetration, or interdependence, also constitutes a 'system'*. This is what Parsons had previously referred to as the 'total action system'. There can be little doubt that Parsons's formal expressions of interdependence are at the core of his theory. They reflect his earlier concerns with personal and interpersonal order and are the substance of what his critics take issue with in their criticisms of *The Social System*. However, we have also seen that the 'perfect integration' of the total system does not 'exhaust' the statement of relevant considerations with regard to concrete systems. Concrete systems do not manifest 'perfect integration' and there must be some factors operating in addition to those derived from any statement of 'perfect integration'. In order to give these additional factors some meaning within his general scheme, Parsons suggests that the different levels of personality, social system and culture are defined by components which are *independent* at each level, as well as by components which are *interdependent*. It is Parsons's arguments about 'independence' which his sympathizers suggest that his critics have missed, proper recognition of which, they argue, must substantially modify the accepted version of his theory.

What Parsons tries to argue is that the independent aspects can define the separation and *integrity of each level*, despite the fact that, if this is so, what is independent must then contradict the very interdependence which defines the *integrity of the total system*, if the consequence of that 'independence' is to produce outcomes other than the full realization of the total system. Thus, Parsons proposes a formulation where 'higher' level possibilities of the cultural system are contradicted by 'lower' lever exigencies. He asks the question: "whether a completely pattern-consistent cultural system can be related to the exigencies both of personalities and of the social system in such a way that complete 'conformity' with its standards can be adequately motivated among all the individual actors in the social system".[20] His answer is both that it is a limiting case and, "that such a limiting case is *incompatible with the fundamental functional imperatives both of personalities and of social systems*".[21] Now, Parsons is not denying conformity with cultural principles in a diversity of individual experience, merely *complete* conformity. It is this relative freedom from cultural determination which, he argues, gives personality and social systems their meaning as distinct levels. It is what defines them 'functionally' as separate systems. Apparently, then, personality consists in culturally meaningful definitions of self and anti-cultural imperatives, while social system consists in culturally defined role expectations and anti-cultural activities.

At one and the same time, then, Parsons argues that there are imperatives of *interdependence*, specifying consistent relations among levels, and imperatives of *independence*, at odds with that consistency. On this formulation, interdependence must contradict any integrity of levels, while independence would contradict what they have in common. Interdependence defines the 'whole' (and, therefore, its 'parts'), while independence contributes an additional and antithetical substance to the statement of 'parts'. We are used to functionalism being described as a position where the 'whole is regarded as greater than the sum of its parts'. This is a position to which Parsons adhered when he elaborated the emergent properties of systems of action, arguing that, "the relations determine the properties of its parts. The properties of the whole are not simply a resultant of the latter."[22] What we are now being offered is a position where the 'whole' – interdependence – is *less than the sum of its parts*!

In so far as the levels of social system and personality contain both interdependent and independent elements, they must contain principles at odds with each other *within* each level. This feature of levels is evident in Parsons's further elaboration of his scheme in the third 'phase'. Thus, in his 'interchange theory', Parsons proposes four functional prerequisites, or imperatives, which are necessary to the constitution and operation of the social system. Two of the imperatives – pattern maintenance and integration – are concerned with normative issues and two – adaptation and goal attainment – are concerned with the non-normative. Similarly, two are concerned with cultural principles – integration and goal attainment – and two with issues of integrity in a potentially hostile lower-level environment – pattern-maintenance and adaptation. According to Alexander, these differentiated aspects of a social system are theoretically adequate and form the substance of Parsons's mature theoretical achievement. Together they supply the axes of the two-by-two tables that proliferate throughout Parsons's writings from *The Social System* onwards (including the four mechanisms of sanctioning discussed in the previous chapter). Given that Parsons's theoretical categories evolve around two dualisms, as we have seen, it is unsurprising that he comes to regard a four-fold division as their logical expression.[23]

Just as the contradictory requirements of interdependence and independence undermine the coherence of different levels and separate hierarchies, so functional prerequisites are similarly incoherent. Were they to be merely the categories of a descriptive approach to societies, then it might be argued that they could serve a heuristic purpose where the extent of their realisation in practice would be an 'empirical' issue. Even here, we would face Parsons's initial negative judgement concerning the acceptance of 'empirical' entities outside theoretical determination, though it would follow the lead suggested in *The Social System* concerning the reformulation of the scheme and the 'evaporation' of its categories. Indeed, Parsons suggests a 'heuristic' role to functional analysis when he claims that each function may operate independently of the others. For example, he argues that, "these four dimensions are conceived to be orthogonal; their values are independently variable in the sense that change of state with respect to any one cannot be interpreted to have an automatically given relation to change of state in any of the others (except so far as this relation comes to be known and formulated as a law of the system)".[24] At the same time, however, he also suggests that meeting all four (at least to some extent) is definitive of a society or social system. After all, Parsons calls them *prerequisites* and part of what is required is their interrelationship.

This latter position involves Parsons's initial claim that the general theory of action would establish 'uniform modes of relationship' between analytical elements, where these 'uniformities' contribute to the integration of a 'total action system'. Thus, Parsons writes that, "the concept 'integration' is a fundamental one in the theory of action. It is a mode of relation of the units of a system by virtue of which, on the one hand, they act so as collectively to avoid disrupting the system and making it impossible to maintain its stability, and, on the other hand, to 'co-operate' to promote its functioning as a unity."[25] However, as Parsons is at pains to point out, this is a conceptual, not an empirical claim. "A generalised social system," he writes, "is a conceptual scheme, not an empirical phenomenon. It is a logically integrated system of generalised concepts of empirical reference in terms of which an indefinite number of concretely differing empirical systems can be described and analysed."[26]

However, the *variance* of empirical systems in terms of the specific 'values' of their elements, as we have seen, was supposed to occur alongside *invariant relations* between their elements. The idea of the orthogonal status of dimensions – that is, that the 'values' of analytical elements are 'independently variable' – must, then, reflect the failure of Parsonsian general theory to realize what he claimed for it, that it would establish 'analytical laws'. This failure is not really disguised by Parsons's reference to the contingent possibility that 'analytical laws' may 'come to be known' in future developments of the theoretical system. The *phenomenological status* of the action frame of reference is precisely a claim to have established such laws. The frame of reference is a scheme of categories *and* their relations. Any statement of *interdependence* reflects the supposed operation of 'analytical laws', and *independence*, their denial. Each is argued to be a necessary assumption within the same theoretical system. At a minimum, this would be to accept empirical indeterminacy as a feature of the theoretical system, but, once again, it was Parsons, himself, who argued that empirical indeterminacy was a form of theoretical inadequacy.[27]

Neither the independence of orthogonal dimensions, nor the mutual necessity of functions can be established. That *both* are argued derives from the contradictory character of the principles or functions. As a consequence, Parsons comes to argue that each function, far from being either independent from, or in a relation of mutual necessity to, each of the others, *actually requires the negation of the others* for its full realization. Just as he argued that there were 'imperatives' of personality and social system that limit the complete realization of culture, so Parsons argues that there are imperatives of functions which are inconsistent with their mutual realization. He writes, "it is also true that maximization of all four, and probably of any two, is not possible in the same state of any given system."[28] According to Alexander, as we have seen, these are supposedly the categories of Parsons's most satisfactory treatment and are necessary to any adequate approach. Yet, Alexander argues that functionalism is predicated upon 'integration as a possibility', while here Parsons seems to be founding functionalism upon integration as an impossibility.

It is not necessary to follow Parsons through every further specification of his scheme, where, Russian doll-like, everything is divided by four and four again. The social system, for example, is further divided into subsystems defined by the priority accorded to one or other of the functional prerequisites in its organization (for example, the 'economy' subsystem defined by the 'adaptation' prerequisite; the 'polity' subsystem defined by the 'goal attainment' prerequisite; the 'societal community' subsystem defined by the 'integration' prerequisite; the 'socialisation' subsystem defined by the 'pattern-maintenance' prerequisite), but where each is also specified by the subordinate, but mutual operation of the other prerequisites. The diagrams of exchanges between systems and among subsystems within systems become increasingly complex, but they can never shake the contradictory dualisms that define them.

The relations of 'interdependence' among subsystems predominate in the way that Parsons develops his theory, as we would expect given the self-conscious constitution of his theoretical undertaking. He intended a scheme of complementary categories and mutually consistent relations among categories. He is very given to the diagrammatic representation of these categories and relations, and, certainly, any diagrams he offers *only express interdependence*. After all, the 'arrows' connecting the boxes are always presented as *mutual* exchanges of 'inputs' and 'outputs' and never of the negation of the substance of one box by the substance of another. For Alexander, this represents a continued, but unnecessary, 'idealist' over-emphasis upon orderly relationships. He suggests that, even in its final, 'adequate' phase, Parsons misunderstands the implications of his own theory, continually giving priority to 'interdependence', when, according to Alexander, from the perspective of the requirements of 'theoretical logic', no such priority need be assumed. Thus, Alexander writes, "the interchange model that Parsons develops in his later work is ineluctably multidimensional; his idealist deviation in no way affects the presuppositional nature of this formulation. It is rather when he applies or specifies the interchange model in social analysis that he tends towards an idealist reduction."[29] He writes further that Parsons, "demonstrates an alarming propensity to present 'adaptive' and 'goal attainment' institutions as facilitating the realization of norms and values, neglecting their functional capacity for antithesis and negation vis-à-vis normative ideals".[30] Alexander believes that the 'idealist reduction' is unnecessary because the 'independence' of principles offers the possibility that their relations are relations of denial, rather than mutuality (though he fails to see that, in reproducing Parsons's diagrams, he must also be reproducing what, for him, is the 'idealist reduction').

It would seem that, if Alexander is correct, 'multidimensional' theory allows the possibility that, at one and the same time, institutions can be founded upon functions which logically can either express mutual necessity or mutual antagonism. Apparently, functional analysis can be founded upon 'integration' as a 'possibility' and an 'impossibility'. If this interpretation goes beyond the standard accounts of Parsons's scheme, it would do so only to affirm that scheme in its incoherence. The priority which Parsons gives to 'interdependence' is no mystery, nor is it a form of 'reductionism'. Quite obviously, it reflects the formal role that the concept of 'perfect integration' has within his scheme. It is because this concept is continuous throughout his work that there is both a continuity to his problems and a continuity to the criticisms directed at his scheme. Ultimately, what Alexander calls Parsons's 'idealist reduction' derives from the fact that, although Parsons is brought to the contradictions that his theory contains, for the most part, he does not accept them as definitive of social inquiry, but struggles with them. The logical requirements of theoretical adequacy retain their force for him, even where he fails to achieve the coherence he was seeking. Throughout his work he holds to that which is apparently consistent, or coherent – interdependence – but he can never excise that which is contradictory. To embrace contradiction and call contradiction adequacy represents no answer. What it represents is the decadence of contemporary sociological argument.

NOTES

1. *TSofSA*, p. 18.
2. See, for example, L. Althusser, *For Marx* (London, New Left Books, 1969).
3. See, for example, H.J. Bershady, *Ideology and Social Knowledge* (Oxford, Basil Blackwell, 1973); A Giddens, *New Rules of Sociological Method* (London, Hutchinson, 1976); J. Habermas, *The Theory of Communicative Action, Volume II: Lifeworld and System; A Critique of Functionalist Reason* (Cambridge, Polity, 1987).
4. See, for example, J. Finley Scott, 'The changing foundation of the Parsonian action scheme', *American Sociological Review*, 28(5), 1963, pp. 716–35; S.P. Savage, *The Theories of Talcott Parsons: The Social Relations of Action* (London, Macmillan, 1981).

5. See H.P.M. Adriaansens, *Talcott Parsons and the Conceptual Dilemma* (London, Routledge and Kegan Paul, 1980); J.C. Alexander, *Theoretical Logic in Sociology, Volume IV: The Modern Reconstruction of Classical Thought: Talcott Parsons* (London, Routledge and Kegan Paul, 1984).
6. See T. Parsons and N.J Smelser, *Economy and Society* (London, Routledge and Kegan Paul, 1956). The phrases are from Adriaansens, *Talcott Parsons and the Conceptual Dilemma*.
7. Alexander, *Theoretical Logic, Volume IV*, p. 211. Adriaansens's equivalent fancy is to compare Parsons to a tightrope walker where, "the developments in Parsons's work which often appear so contradictory do not have their origins in inexplicable 'theoretical metamorphoses', but should rather be compared to the corrective movements of a rope dancer in danger of losing his balance". Adriaansens, *Talcott Parsons and the Conceptual Dilemma*, p. 97.
8. See especially, R. Dahrendorf, 'Out of utopia', in *Essays in the Theory of Society* (London, Routledge and Kegan Paul, 1968); D. Wrong, *Power: Its Form, Bases and Uses* (Oxford, Basil Blackwell, 1979); T. Burger, 'Talcott Parsons, the problem of order in society, and the program of an analytical sociology', *American Journal of Sociology*, 83(3), 1977, pp. 320–34.
9. H.M. Johnson, 'Talcott Parsons and the theory of action: editorial introduction', *Sociological Inquiry*, 51(3), 1981, p. iv.
10. Adriaansens, *Talcott Parsons and the Conceptual Dilemma*, p. 170.
11. Ibid.
12. See especially, I. Lakatos, 'Falsification and the methodology of scientific research programmes', in I. Lakatos and A. Musgrave (eds), *Criticism and the Growth of Knowledge* (Cambridge, Cambridge University Press, 1970).
13. J.C. Alexander, 'Introduction', in J.C. Alexander (ed.), *Neo-Functionalism* (London, Sage, 1985), p. 9. Despite his own concept of the 'duality' of structure and action, Giddens presents a similar 'dualism', arguing that what, from the point of view of 'structure', "appears as a normatively co-ordinated legitimate order" represents contingent claims from the point of view of 'strategic action'. See A. Giddens, *Central Problems in Social Theory: Action, Structure and Contradiction in Social Analysis* (London, Macmillan, 1979), p. 86. For a detailed criticism, see J.M. Holmwood and A. Stewart, *Explanation and Social Theory* (London, Macmillan, 1991).
14. Alexander often makes contradictory claims about the nature of the scheme he is proposing. As we have seen, he makes the comment that Parsons is frequently 'the functionalist' that his critics allege, implying that there is something deficient about a functionalist approach, even from the perspective of his 'multi-dimensional achievement'. Now, Alexander is affirming 'functionalism' as consistent with multi-dimensional theory.
15. T. Parsons, *The Social System* (London, Routledge and Kegan Paul, 1951), p. 21.
16. Bourricaud, for example, argues that "at bottom, the very concept of action is at stake when the term process is substituted for the term structure." See F. Bourricaud, *The Sociology of Talcott Parsons* (Chicago, University of Chicago Press, 1981), p. 94.
17. The following discussion of Parsons is taken from an article which sets out the parallel between his theoretical development and developments found in Giddens and Habermas. See J.M. Holmwood and A. Stewart, 'Synthesis and fragmentation in social theory: a progressive solution', *Sociological Theory*, 12(1), 1994, pp. 83–100.

18. Parsons, *The Social System*, p. 15.
19. Giddens and Habermas also offer a distinction of levels of structure (or culture), society and person. See Giddens, *New Rules*; Habermas, *Theory of Communicative Action, Volume II*. Habermas, for example, writes that, "the symbolic structures of the lifeworld are reproduced by way of the continuation of valid knowledge, stabilization of group solidarity, and the socialization of responsible actors ... Corresponding to these processes of cultural reproduction, social integration and socialization are the structural components of the lifeworld: culture, society and person". Ibid., pp. 137–8.
20. Parsons, *The Social System*, p. 16.
21. Ibid. Giddens, for his part, argues that, "the same structural characteristics participate in the subject (the actor) as in the object (society). Structure forms 'personality' and 'society' simultaneously – but in neither case exhaustively: because of the significance of unintended consequences of action, and because of unacknowledged conditions of action". See Giddens, *Central Problems*, p. 70.
22. *TSofSA*, p. 32.
23. Although, in fact, the origin of four-fold divisions that Parsons multiplies throughout his writings has puzzled commentators – after all, when he first outlines the pattern-variables, from which the functional imperatives are derived, he identifies five, not four, pairs. See, for example, Adriaansens, *Talcott Parsons and the Conceptual Dilemma*. For the latter, the four-fold division of the categories of Parsons's scheme represents the latter's conceptual achievement in finally integrating the specification of the different components and levels of his scheme.
24. T. Parsons, 'An approach to psychological theory in terms of the theory of action', in S. Koch (ed.), *Psychology: A Study of a Science* (New York, McGraw-Hill, 1959), p. 631.
25. 'An analytical approach to the theory of stratification', in T. Parsons (ed.), *Essays in Sociological Theory (Revised Edition)* (New York, Free Press, 1954), p. 71. Parsons refers the reader back to *TSofSA* for the detailed discussion of this argument.
26. Parsons, 'An analytical approach to the theory of stratification', p. 71.
27. Alexander regards these arguments by Parsons as a form of 'latent positivism'. See Alexander, *Theoretical Logic, Volume IV*.
28. Parsons, 'An approach to psychological theory', p. 631.
29. Alexander, *Theoretical Logic, Volume IV*, p. 231.
30. Alexander, *Theoretical Logic, Volume IV*, p. 231.

6

A MARXIST ALTERNATIVE?

It is little wonder that many sociologists turned their backs upon Parsons's approach once 'the incurable theorist', had succumbed to the temptations of its seemingly endless elaboration by division and sub-division. What is difficult to understand is why, now, Parsons's theory is being revived despite its contradictory categories, indeed, even in embrace of the contradiction internal to its categories. In part, it reflects the influence of postmodern conceptions of theory. More importantly, however, it can be explained by developments within the sociological approaches initially put forward as alternatives to Parsons's theory, but, which, in their elaboration, came to converge upon it.

In this chapter, I shall restrict myself to a consideration of one such approach, that of Marxism. I do so not because Marxist explanations have any special merits or demerits, but because they enable a clear illustration of how theorists, beginning with apparently very different assumptions to those of Parsons, come to share conceptions of approach with him. In this way, we get some insight into how Parsons, himself, might have come to his own understanding of the theoretical undertaking. After all, Parsons argued in *TSofSA* that he was addressing breakdown in theoretical systems and, in contemporary Marxism, we are witnessing precisely such a breakdown, or – at a minimum – explanatory crisis.

In fact, the recent reconstruction of issues of explanation in post-positivist philosophy of science has made the idea that Marxism has been falsified and should, therefore, be given up, seem almost too easy and deceptive. Burawoy for example, has drawn upon Lakatos's concept of a research programme in order to re-affirm Marxism's pretensions to scientific status in the face of what he sees as a predominant view of its unscientific character.[1] According to Burawoy, Marxism manifests the progressive problem-shifts that Lakatos associates with the productive phase of a research programme. It will be clear that my judgement is the opposite. Notwithstanding, the pathos of Burawoy's argument is that what Lakatos terms 'degeneracy' is a feature of any scientific research programme as it comes to exhaust its capacity for further development and begins to accumulate anomalies. The ultimate demonstration of Marxism's (or any other sociological research programme's) scientific status would be, for Lakatos, its theoretical breakdown and supercession.

Finally, I shall suggest that the Marxist critique of Parsonsian theory, at least initially, did identify deficiences in his scheme, but the failure to resolve these deficiences has contributed to our current impasse. Indeed, many current postmodern theorists began their intellectual careers as Marxists and their disillusion with the possibility of coherent social inquiry is bound up with the fate of contemporary Marxism.

THE MARXIST CRITICISM

In the previous chapter, I argued that 'interdependence' – or 'perfect integration' – is at the 'core' of Parsons's undertaking. Most fundamentally, the problem to which critics of his scheme initially drew attention was that processes of change could not be located *within* the 'core' assumptions of the theory. Once again, this does not mean that Parsons failed to address issues of change (even if critics sometimes made that charge). After all, 'integrative processes' take their meaning as an issue of sociological interest precisely from a perception of the reality of change. There could be no address of order without the perception that there is a *problem* of order. Parsons's difficulty is that he cannot get the issues of change into his scheme in a way that meets his own criteria of adequacy. He can give no explanatory processes with a similar analytical rigour to those which serve integration and, on his own arguments, this failure must compromise the integrity and coherence of those processes which he does identify.

In the end, what Parsons offers is a description of change, but no explanatory account. For example, the four-fold scheme of functions offers the possibility of describing societies in terms of the extent of their 'structural differentiation'. Thus, societies are classified according to the extent of institutional specialization around functions – for example, the extent to which political institutions are separated from economic institutions, or economic institutions separated from the household which then becomes specialized around functions of socialization (in passing, it can be noted that these arguments are not peculiar to Parsons. For example, Giddens also outlines four 'structural principles' – 'signification', 'legitimation' 'authorization' and 'allocation' – and argues that these can be used to generate the following sorts of analysis, "two aspects of . . . articulation can be distinguished . . . One is how far a society contains distinct spheres of 'specialism' in respect of institutional orders: differentiated forms of symbolic order (religion, science, etc.); a differentiated 'polity', 'economy' and 'legal/repressive apparatus'. The second is how modes of institutional articulation are organised in terms of overall properties of societal reproduction: that is to say, 'structural principles'."[2]).

94

The scheme of functional imperatives is supposed to apply to all societies. In which case, those societies with lesser specialization are no less 'adequate' than those with greater degrees of specialization. If the theory of 'interdependence' models 'integration as a possibility', it must be a 'possibility' whatever the extent of structural differentiation. There can be no 'internal' requirement of greater structural differentiation which might be the mechanism producing change. Of course, Parsons does describe more extensive differentiation as an improvement in 'adaptive upgrading',[3] and, in effect, this is to affirm the 'superiority' of more specialized systems over those which are less specialized. Moreover, the idea of 'superiority' does carry the implication of evolutionary change where better adapted forms are realized out of the deficiencies of 'lesser' forms. However, while it may explain why, once specialization occurs, a specific 'superior' adaptation becomes more widely diffused – much as Weber describes the pressure to adopt bureaucratic forms of organization more widely once bureaucratic forms exist – it could not explain why the 'superior' form was initiated.

Moreover, the way in which structural differentiation is understood to occur around four functions, each with its characteristic 'sub system', suggests an 'end' to the process of development – full institutional specialization in terms of each function. This is an 'end' which appears to coincide with the realization of the institutional structures of modern capitalism. Unsurprisingly, critics (and not only Marxist critics) accused Parsons of smuggling the specific content of modern capitalism into his avowedly contentless analytical categories. It seemed not so much the case that the scheme of general theory had a phenomenological character which contained no empirical content that could be 'thought away', but that it reflected a specific failure to 'think away' modern capitalism, or, rather, to think outside, or against, its categories.

For Marxist critics, both difficulties – that of identifying mechanisms of change and that of an uncritical attitude to modern capitalism – derive from a common problem, Parsons's failure to identify specific contradictions in social relationships and institutions (I shall return to this issue, but it is important to stress that, while Parsons's scheme is contradictory, that would not mean that it is thereby able to account for contradiction; the adequate address of contradictions is quite distinct from the embodiment of incoherence in the categories of a scheme).

Although not himself a self-conscious Marxist, Lockwood was the first to identify the issue of contradiction as important in the explanation of social change.[4] His argument marked the turn to Marxism in academic social science which took place in the 1960s and after. According to Lockwood, Parsons's failure to account for contradiction is shared with his conflict theory critics. Whatever their differences concerning the role attributed to power or values in social life, he argues, each is too concerned with immediate issues of overt action. In developing this criticism, Lockwood makes a distinction between issues of social integration and issues of system integration. The former, he suggests, concerns the immediate and self-conscious relationships between actors and the extent to which they are orderly or conflictual. Much of the old debate between conflict and consensus theorists, he believes, was a sterile one because it concentrated upon how best to characterize such relationships among *actors*, when the fundamental issue was to explain the underlying mechanisms of the *system* which served order or led to a re-organization of interests and a shift in the balance of power between groups (and which, in the latter case may, temporarily, not be manifested in conscious behaviours).

In order to explicate his argument, Lockwood drew on the Marxian example. Marx, he argues, "clearly differentiates social and system integration. The propensity to class antagonism (social integration aspect) is generally a function of the character of production relationships (e.g possibilities of intra-class identification and communication). But the dynamics of class antagonisms are clearly related to the progressively growing 'contradictions' of the economic system. One might almost say that the 'conflict' which in Marxian theory is decisive for change is not the *power* conflict arising from the relationships in the productive system, but the *system* conflict arising from 'contradictions' between 'property institutions' and the 'forces of production'."[5] As contradictions emerge they are addressed in actions designed to mitigate their negative consequences and, in the process, social practices are (or, more properly, may be) transformed. It should be stressed, however, that to recognize a contradiction is not the same as solving it and, until a contradiction is solved, it must be lived.

Lockwood poses the question, "does the Marxian view contain the elements of a more general sociological formulation?"[6] His own answer to the question is ambivalent about the status of Marxist sociological assumptions. Thus, the view that all societies are characterized by a contradiction between the forces and relations of production, he argues, is an unwarranted generalization of the specific role of the economic system under capitalism.[7] At the same time, the Weberian analysis of bureaucracy suggests that the Soviet-type of economic system might, in fact, be a more fundamental instance of the contradiction between the forces and relations of production which Marxists attribute to capitalism than is capitalism itself. More fundamentally, however, Lockwood suggests that the concepts of system integration and contradiction should not be made specific to the productive system of a society, nor should it be implied that societies should be classified according to their modes of production. Logically, he argues, there is no implication of the priority of class relations.

Nevertheless, Lockwood's choice of Marxism as an exemplar of the general argument is fateful. Although it caught the general mood of the times in the emerging opposition to Parsonian theory in the 1960s, the problem of the example is that it fails, even in the area of its apparent strength. In other words, *the Marxist contradiction is inadequate as an explanation even of capitalist developments*, quite apart from the issue of whether or not it can be generalized to other circumstances. As I observed in Chapter 2, the resort to Marxism in response to the perceived inadequacy of Parsons's theory to account for contradiction, conflict and change leads to a paradox. The specific changes anticipated on the basis of Marxist theory have failed to materialize and, so, the crucial issue, even from a Marxist perspective, comes to be how to explain the stability of capitalism. The pathos of post-Parsonsian social theory – especially its Marxist variants – is that it is brought back to the very problems of Parsons's own approach, and, in the process, theorists come to affirm what previously were regarded as the deficiencies of that approach.

MARXISM AND GENERAL THEORY

It is not necessary to enter into a very detailed discussion of the different versions of neo-Marxism that have been proposed. For my present purposes, I shall select just two – that of Habermas's 'critical theory' and that of the 'structuralist Marxism' of Althusser and Poulantzas.[8] The general characteristic of all attempts, however, is to argue *that capitalism is contradictory and, at the same time, that its contradiction need not be realized*. In essence, the strategy of modern Marxists is to take arguments made by Marx in the context of an integral relation between entities – say, the 'immediate' and 'fundamental' class interests of the proletariat – and to re-interpret them in the claim for their independent operation. Marx, for example, argued that 'bourgeois ideology', with its 'fetishization' of presumed natural 'economic' categories, gives rise to views of the 'fairness' of wages as an exchange for labour power contracted to a capitalist. Similarly, he wrote of a 'dominant ideology' which reflects the interests of a 'dominant class'. However, for Marx, there are processes whereby these ideological representations are dispelled. The basic thrust of Marx's analysis is the *instability* of ideology and its instability is part of the contradictory character of capitalism. In contrast, modern Marxists, where they stress the role of a 'dominant capitalist ideology', do so to identify its role in the *stabilization* of capitalism.

Habermas, for example, seeks to account for the failure of capitalism to develop in line with Marx's expectations by reference to limitations in Marx's own theory. In effect, he suggests that Marx concentrated upon material structures to the neglect of normative ones.[9] According to Habermas, Marx's work is characterized by the same sort of over-emphasis upon the 'systems paradigm' as is found among positivist writers, with a corresponding failure to accord proper recognition to the role of 'action' in social life. Habermas's 'solution' is to argue for the necessity of complementing Marx's 'systems' paradigm with insights taken from the paradigm of the 'lifeworld'. According to Habermas, there is a problem of 'action' in Marx's theory. However, the 'action' that apparently requires to be explained is 'action' which is consistent with the reproduction of capitalism. From the 'system' perspective, attributed to Marx, this is the very denial of that 'action' which would be in the proletariat's 'true' interests. The problem is not merely the absence of Marx's specific solution to the contradiction of capitalism, but the fact that the contradiction identified by

Marx appears not to be *lived* by the relevant actors in the absence of its solution. The 'normative', it appears, can cancel the operation of the 'material' in lived experience, but, Habermas argues, the 'material' is still to be characterized by contradiction and exploitation.[10]

As we saw in the previous chapter, Alexander suggests that the problem with Parsons's approach is that he has an 'alarming propensity' to 'present adaptive and goal attainment institutions as facilitating the realization of norms and values', rather than as having a capacity for antithesis and negation. Alexander is aware of the problem of change in Parsons's analysis and wishes to solve it by arguing that principles argued by Parsons to be mutually interdependent can be mutually contradictory. Habermas's problem is different. For him, the problem is to explain stability. Curiously, then, Habermas *is* presenting the capacity of norms and values to negate 'system' processes, but, in his analysis, their negation of system processes secures the reproduction of material structures which for Marx were exploitative and unstable. In the secondary discussions of Parsons's theory, his problems of change are frequently associated with problems of 'action'. What we see in Habermas's theory is that 'action' is embraced, but not to produce an account of change. As with Parsons, 'action' is linked to the maintenance of the (capitalist) 'system'. I shall return to this apparent paradox of 'action' serving stability, despite being seen as the producer of change, in the next chapter.

Similar features are evident in structuralist Marxism, despite the self-conscious hostility of its proponents to the 'humanism' of any emphasis upon 'action' and 'lifeworld'. Althusser, for his part, also identifies ideological conditions of social reproduction, as a neglected, or inadequately developed, aspect of Marx's theory, writing that, "the reproduction of labour power requires not only a reproduction of its skills, but also, at the same time, a reproduction of its submission to the rules of the established order, i.e. a reproduction of submission to the ruling ideology for the workers, and a reproduction of the ability to manipulate the ruling ideology correctly for the agents of exploitation and repression, so that they too, will provide for the domination of the ruling class 'in words'."[11] The 'relative autonomy' of this superstructure from the 'material base' allows it the possibility of acting to annul the tendencies within the mode of production to direct conflict over the relations of production.

Other Marxists have been critical of an over-reliance upon moral issues in neo-Marxist theories of ideology. Przeworski, for example, argues that, "consent is cognitive and behavioural".[12] He laments the way that the conception of ideology represents workers as the "perpetual dupe of ideological domination".[13] According to Przeworski, the problem derives from the lack of appreciation of the contingent role of politics in class formation. Hitherto, he argues, Marxists have made predictions about workers' behaviour in terms of their assignment to positions in the class structure and this accentuates the problem of behaviours at odds with theoretical expectations, where 'ideology' is made to fill the gap. However, according to Przeworski, "the structure of choices that results in class formation is an outcome of conflicts also in the realm of politics".[14]

For Przeworski, workers face a choice between improving their conditions under capitalism, or better conditions under socialism. However, to get to socialism they must traverse 'transitional valley' and their current conditions under capitalism are better than the conditions they must endure under that trek. In these circumstances, it can be demonstrated that the working class has *rationally* chosen capitalism. Reforms, then, are possible, but not a reformist strategy. Thus, he accepts that, "poverty and oppression are with us and will not be alleviated by the possibility of a better future", and writes further that, "the struggle for improving capitalism is as essential as ever before. But we should not confuse this struggle with the quest for socialism".[15] The pathos of his position is that the success of any such *struggle* within capitalism is the production of the conditions under which capitalism is rationally chosen. Przeworski's 'solution' to the problems of the conception of 'relative autonomy' of ideology is to argue for the 'relative autonomy' of politics. In this way, he believes that consent can be shown to have a material base, but, in either case, it is the stability of capitalism and the *consent* of wage-earners to relations which, it is held, exploit them, that is emphasized.

The very force of Lockwood's distinction between system integration and social integration is undermined in these developments of Marxist theory represented by Habermas and Althusser (and rational-choice Marxists such as Przeworski). The identification of contradiction is held to be consistent with conflict and change, *or* stability.[16] Indeed, structuralist Marxists come to argue that whatever will occur as an outcome is 'overdetermined', which is really to say that any outcome is 'indeterminate' (though it has to be said that they have reached this conclusion only because the outcome that Marx both expected and regarded as determinate has not occurred and is looking increasingly implausible as an occurrence even to those who continue to call themselves Marxists).[17]

In their further elaboration of the argument, Althusser and Poulantzas argue that it is necessary to distinguish clearly between the 'mode of production' and the 'social formation'. Poulantzas, for example, writes that, "the object of historical materialism is the study of different structures and practices (the economy, politics, ideology) which are connected and yet distinct, and whose combination constitutes a mode of production and a social formation".[18] Further, these different structures and practices, "present their own specificity, relative autonomy and particular effectiveness inside the unity of a mode of production and of a historically determined social formation".[19] At one and the same time, the structures and practices are 'united' and 'independent'. Poulantzas believes that an overemphasis upon 'unity' is an error of historicist, Hegelian Marxism (and of sociological functionalism, for that matter) which represents the totality of structures and practices as an 'expressive totality'. In contrast, it is the 'independent' operation, or 'relative autonomy', of the different principles which constitutes an 'over-determined' totality.

However, it is in terms of what is 'unitary' in the concept of mode of production that any directionality in history is claimed as a potentiality. After all, these are the relationships from which Marx can derive the determinate consequences of capitalism. The 'overdetermined', concrete course of history is *otherwise*, to be accounted for by the independent and countervailing operation of the other 'structures'. In this formulation, the 'independent' operation of structures and practices is the denial of the processes attributed to the 'unity' of the mode of production. At the same time, it is the inadequacy of those 'central' processes that gives rise to the claim for 'independence'.

This development within neo-Marxism is akin to Parsons's claims for 'interdependence' and 'independence' in the operation of the different levels of systems and subsystems. Yet, when Alexander confronts the Marxist version he is scathing. He writes, "every major revision of Marx's thought moves back and forth between the two equally unacceptable horns of the 'Marxian dilemma'. On the one hand, if it is to converge with the original theory, the revision must introduce determinism 'in the last instance'. This, of course, can only be achieved by partly neutralizing the revisions themselves. On the other hand, if the theorists will not neutralize their contributions, and if, at the same time, they wish to avoid the direct opposition to Marx's theory that would place them outside the Marxist tradition, there is only one option available, they must leave their revisions largely unspecified and, in the process, open up their theories to serious indeterminacy. A theoretical revision of Marx can only resolve this choice between indeterminacy and the last instance only if it takes neither option; to that degree it moves beyond the boundaries of Marxism itself".[20]

The implication of Alexander's argument is that beyond the boundaries of Marxism lies a more adequate approach. But when he presents the form of that approach, we find it has the very same characteristics as the position he is criticizing. Thus, when he outlines his own Parsonian, neo-functionalist approach, he argues that it, "models society as an intelligible system. It views society as composed of elements whose interaction forms a pattern that can be clearly differentiated from some surrounding environment. These parts are symbiotically connected to one another and interact without *a priori* direction from a governing force. This understanding of system and/or 'totality' must, as Althusser has forcefully argued, be sharply distinguished from the Hegelian, Marxist one. The Hegelian system resembles the functionalist, but it posits an 'expressive totality' in which all of a society's or culture's parts are seen as representing variations on some 'really' determining, fundamental system. Functionalism suggests, by contrast, open-ended and pluralistic rather than monocausal determinism".[21] It would seem that 'integration', or 'unity', is a possibility, to be set against the independent operation of factors which bring about practical deviations from that 'unity'. What Alexander elsewhere calls the 'Scylla of indeterminacy and the Charybdis of the last instance'[22], then, is intrinsic to the very approach to issues of social order which he wishes to take from Parsons.

The parallel between structuralist Marxism and Parsons's developed theory, or between Habermas's theory and either of the others, has been noticed by other writers. For some who claim sympathy to Marxism, it is the basis of arguing that Parsons was wrong to exclude Marx from his account of convergence upon the 'voluntaristic theory of action'.[23] The force of the claim, however, is the opposite of what is intended; it affirms the 'voluntaristic theory of action' as beyond Marxist criticism at the same time as that theory of action obliterates the force of Marx's account of contradiction.[24] According to Turner, and, by implication, Alexander too, the Parsonian version of the argument is to be preferred because it achieves greater generality than that of Althusser. As Turner puts it, this means that, "the corpus of Althusserian concepts can be rendered back into Parsonian system-theory with very little remainder".[25] And that is also Alexander's judgement about the relation between Parsons's theory and that of Habermas.[26] Which of the approaches is the more general is hardly the salient issue *when the generality upon which they have converged is contradictory*, such that *any outcome* can be argued to be consistent with general categories and no outcome will require us to revise them. In the neo-Marxist case, there is a claim for a specific contradiction, but an absence of its expected effects. In the Parsonian case, there is a general emphasis upon integrative processes alongside a recognition of specific instances of malintegration. What unites them, is the belief that specific explanatory problems can be absorbed by assigning them, either to a general potentiality for contradiction (and stability), or integration (and strain), with no specific requirement of instantiation.

We must remember that Lockwood invoked Marx's theory of capitalism as an example of the sort of sociological explanation which would be able to account for change. Notwithstanding the arguments of Alexander and Turner, the situation remains as Lockwood first described it. What could not be translated into Parsons's general categories (or those of neo-Marxism, for that matter) is Marx's initial version of capitalism's contradictory character. But that is not sufficient to establish the adequacy of Marx's specific account of capitalism as contradictory. For example, does it not seem that the Marxist contradiction does not obtain and that the absence of its effects is an indication of the absence of the mechanism held to produce them? Is this not more likely than any proposal that a contradiction can be real, but unrealized? The neo-Marxist 'general' statement, for example, merely generalizes the inadequacies of Marx's specific account. The real task would be to reconstruct the substantive, explanatory categories central to that account. In other words, we require to renew the theory of capitalism, rather than the theory of action.

The theoretical modifications of Marxism discussed above do not meet Lakatos's conditions of a progressive problem-shift. In contrast to what Burawoy claims, they indicate theoretical breakdown. This is something which Alexander is prepared to accept as applying to the Marxist case. But if the theoretical breakdown of the Marxist scheme produces concepts which can be 'rendered back' into Parsons's general theory, that would seem to suggest something other than the superior adequacy of that general theory. What it suggests is that the general frame of reference fails to transcend the explanatory problems to which it was supposed to be an answer. The conclusion must be that the scheme is merely the generalized form of explanatory failure.

Parsons was unaware of the contradiction at the heart of his scheme, but the development of his theory is, in large part, a working through of its implications. The categories with which he begins – essentially the division of the 'objective' and the 'subjective', of 'structure' and 'action' – take their meaning from explanatory failure. To specify these categories in terms of a general scheme is, quite simply, to generalize explanatory failure. In this way, the contradictions specific to particular instances of explanatory problems are given generalized expression, resulting in the contradictory frame of reference (the basic features of which have been outlined in the previous chapters). Parsons's project of general theory is not that different from other attempts, such as those of Habermas, Giddens and, of course, Alexander. Most of these other attempts are, like his, conducted at a very high level of abstraction. In the Marxist case, however, the relation between the general categories and particular explanations which is obscured by Parsons's manner of proceeding via meta-theoretical argument is more transparent.

On the face of it, Marxist writers are deeply hostile to the Parsonsian idea of general theory and have frequently expressed their rejection of it. Yet, as we saw, as they address the problems of Marx's specific explanation of capitalist development, all the features of Parsons's general theory are reproduced. The characteristic of the various neo-Marxist undertakings is that their proponents are looking for a way of rescuing the central core of Marxism, at the same time as they are addressing the problems of its explanatory adequacy. Whatever the 'radicalism' of the original position, their intentions are 'conservative'; they are seeking to insulate it from any requirement of a more fundamental reconstruction of its explanatory categories. The implication, then, is that Parsons's general theory has a similar 'conservative' role, serving to 'conserve' the categories which embody the very explanatory problems he has identified in the breakdown of other theoretical systems.

NOTES

1. M. Burawoy, 'Marxism as science: historical challenges and theoretical growth', *American Sociological Review,* 55(6), 1990, pp. 775–93.
2. A. Giddens, *A Contemporary Critique of Historical Materialism: Volume I, Power Property and the State* (London, Macmillan, 1981), pp. 47–8.
3. See, for example, T. Parsons, *Societies: Evolutionary and Comparative Perspectives* (Englewood Cliffs, Prentice-Hall, 1966).
4. See D. Lockwood, 'System integration and social integration', in G. Zollschan and W. Hirsch (eds), *Explorations in Social Change* (London, Routledge and Kegan Paul, 1964).
5. Ibid., pp. 249–50.

6. Lockwood, 'System integration and social integration', p. 250.
7. For an orthodox interpretation of the Marxist contradiction between the forces and relations of production, see G.A. Cohen, *Karl Marx's Theory of History: A Defence* (Oxford, Oxford University Press, 1978).
8. See especially J. Habermas, *Communication and the Evolution of Society* (London, Heinemann, 1979) and *Legitimation Crisis* (London, Heinemann, 1976); L. Althusser, *For Marx* (London, New Left Books, 1977); N. Poulantzas *Political Power and Social Classes* (London, New Left Books, 1973).
9. See Habermas, *Communication and the Evolution of Society*.
10. In fact, the implications of Habermas's 'two paradigms' are mutually contradictory (just as are the relations among Parsons's functional prerequisites). Thus, in his formal development of the paradigm of the 'lifeworld' (or communicative action), Habermas emphasizes consensual normative structures as the source of 'truth'. See Habermas, *The Theory of Communicative Action, Volume II*. However, when he confronts the problem that his own modifications of Marxism have led him to represent capitalism as reproduced in normative structures, he refers to any consensus achieved under capitalist conditions as 'false'. See Habermas, *Legitimation Crisis*.
11. L. Althusser, 'Ideology and ideological state apparatuses', in *Lenin and Philosophy and Other Essays* (London, New Left Books, 1971), pp. 127–8.
12. A. Przeworski, *Capitalism and Social Democracy* (Cambridge, Cambridge University Press, 1985), pp. 145–6. Przeworski's emphasis upon consent as 'cognitive' mirrors the criticisms that are made of Parsons's alleged emphasis upon positive moral commitment as the basis of conformity.
13. Ibid., p. 202.
14. Ibid., p. 96.
15. Ibid., p. 248.
16. In fact, the elements of this problem are there in Lockwood in his idea that contradictions can be 'latent' and not realized. Thus, he refers to problems of stability which occur only if contradictions are 'actualized'. See Lockwood, 'System integration and social integration', p. 252. For a discussion of this aspect of Lockwood's work, see J. Holmwood and A. Stewart, *Explanation and Social Theory* (London, Macmillan, 1991).
17. For example, Wright refers to Marx's concept of the polarisation of classes, commenting that, "given that it is no longer generally accepted that the class structure within capitalism is increasingly polarized, it has become more difficult to sidestep the theoretical problem of the gap between the abstract polarized concept of class relations and the complex concrete patterns of class formation and class struggle. It is no longer assumed that history will gradually eliminate the conceptual problem." E.O. Wright, *Classes* (London, Verso, 1985), p. 9.
18. N. Poulantzas, *Political Power and Social Classes* (London, New Left Books and Sheed and Ward, 1973), p. 12.
19. Ibid., p. 41.
20. J.C. Alexander, *Theoretical Logic in Sociology, Volume 2: The Antinomies of Classical Thought: Marx and Durkheim* (London, Routledge and Kegan Paul, 1982), p. 345.
21. J.C. Alexander, 'Introduction', in J.C. Alexander (ed), *Neofunctionalism* (London, Sage, 1985), p. 9.

22. J.C. Alexander, 'Habermas's new critical theory: its promise and problems', *American Journal of Sociology*, 91(2), p. 423.
23. See, for example, M. Gould, 'Parsons versus Marx: "an earnest warning ... " ', *Sociological Inquiry*, 51(3), 1981, pp. 197–218; T. Benton, *The Rise and Fall of Structuralist Marxism* (London, Macmillan, 1984).
24. In fact it brings Marxism into the terms of the standard debate between rational-choice theorists and advocates of a voluntaristic theory of action, as an alternative to neither. Thus, Gould and Benton defend Marx against Parsons's account of him as a utilitarian theorist, while Przeworski, in attacking the role of normative elements in neo-Marxist theories, seeks to present Marxism in terms of utilitarian, rational choice.
25. B.S. Turner, 'Parsons and his critics: on the ubiquity of functionalism', in R.J. Holton and B.S. Turner (eds), *Talcott Parsons on Economy and Society*, p. 195.
26. See Alexander, 'Habermas's new critical theory: its promise and problems'.

7

ACTION AND EXPLANATION

Any lessons that might be drawn from a consideration of Parsons's theoretical scheme must be negative. His theory fails in its own terms, but that failure also implicates other attempts to found a general theoretical frame of reference. This judgement must be distinguished from the postmodern critique of foundational, general theory. Postmodernism, in rejecting general theory, turns its back upon any positive explanatory undertaking in the social sciences. So, while explanation is displaced in the meta-theoretical projects of foundational, general theory, it fares no better under postmodern strictures. The postmodern 'turn' in contemporary social theory has encouraged the idea that contradictory theory is valid, even that contradiction is a condition of validity. This must render nugatory any explanatory undertaking.

I began this book with the impasse of abstract general social theory and the postmodern embrace of a contradictory particularism, suggesting that each position was connected and was the other side of a common flaw. The discussion of Parsons's general theory has shown the connection between the positions in the work of a single theorist. His attempt at general theory fails and its failure is evident in the incoherence of its categories. Where Parsons's initial claims for the necessity of general theory sought to establish a requirement of consistency, postmodern theorists merely accept the contradictions which general theory contains as expressing the 'truth' of any theoretical undertaking. In that sense, postmodernism is parasitic upon what it would deny. It requires the failure of foundational, general theory in order to establish its 'truth' of the necessity of contradictory theory. In a small way, we can see this in the manner in which some postmodern theorists have argued that Parsons's general theory is a form of totalitarian foundationalism,[1] and, therefore, have rejected it, while other theorists also sympathetic to postmodernism, have perceived the contradictions of general theory and embraced them.[2] I now want to suggest a way out of this evident impasse.

CONTRADICTION AND SOCIAL INQUIRY

At one time, the standard argument about the nature and consequences of contradiction would simply have been that the mere fact that Parsons's general theory (or any other theory, for that matter) is contradictory would be enough to render it valueless. This is what Popper, for example, implies when he argues that, "using valid rules of inference, we can infer from a couple of contradictory premises any conclusion we like".[3] Since any conclusion, apparently, can follow from contradictory premises, a contradictory theory is unfalsifiable, and, therefore, unscientific. However, this easy dismissal of contradictory theory runs up against the difficulties intrinsic to Popper's own conception of falsification as a criterion of science.

Although contradictions are, for Popper, akin to nonsense, for the most part (with the possible exception of postmodern theorists) they do not usually arise out of a self-conscious intention to produce them. Even apparently 'sensible' undertakings may be revealed as contradictory, while it is frequently the case that what appears 'nonsense' to those who are wedded to established theoretical approaches comes to be regarded as 'sensible' and resourceful by those who come after. Ultimately, Popper concedes that contradiction, of itself, is not a sufficient indicator of the unscientific character of a theory. He writes that a theory, "may be interesting in itself even though contradictory; secondly, it may give rise to corrections which make it consistent; and, ultimately, we may develop a method, even if it is an *ad hoc* method, which prevents us from obtaining the false conclusions which admittedly are logically entailed by the theory".[4]

In other words, we are dealing with processes of theoretical development in which success is not guaranteed in advance and where subsequent lines of inquiry may call into question what was previously accepted. Moreover, as Lakatos observes, and Popper seems to accept in the preceding statement, there is no 'instant' falsification.[5] The replacement of a theory requires the development of a better, more resourceful theory. Until that theory is produced we must live with the contradictions that existing theory contains. We cannot simply walk away from them. It is unlikely that contradiction drains all resources from a theory. Its positive categories will continue to yield those insights and practical resources which drew us to them in the first place. Indeed, as Lakatos observes, in his discussion of the role of a protective layer of auxiliary hypotheses, it is those positive categories that are subject to the *ad hoc* modifications, which, in Popper's terms, may serve to insulate them from their 'false conclusions'. However, as Lakatos argues, these *ad hoc* modifications cannot go on indefinitely without generating a crisis within the research programme. The problem is that the elaboration of any research programme will bring us to an understanding of its limits and inconsistencies. These will become increasingly pressing, in the sense that, ultimately, it will be recognized by at least some proponents that any new resources will require the reconstruction of categories which we had hitherto thought basic and necessary.

If contradiction – the generation of 'anomalies' and 'disconfirming instances' within a theoretical system – is to be regarded as part and parcel of scientific development, it does not follow that contradiction can be accepted as adequate in explanations. The fact that we have to live contradictions until we have solved them does not make contradiction acceptable, or render contradictory statements mutually valid. Indeed, if there is no falsification until the development of a better theory, we would need an account of why, in advance of falsification, some do the work necessary to produce the new scheme whose more resourceful character occasions falsification. The contradictions intrinsic to pre-existing theories must be part of that account. In other words, it is not the *fact of contradiction*, but the *belief that contradiction is acceptable*, which is nonsense in Popper's sense. Thus, he writes, "if we seriously intend to put up with it then nothing will make us search for a better theory; and also the other way round: if we look for a better theory, then we do so because we think the theory we have described is a bad one, *owing to the contradictions involved*. The acceptance of contradictions must lead here as everywhere to the end of criticism, and thus to the collapse of science."[6]

I have developed this argument at some length because, notwithstanding Popper's view that the acceptance of contradiction is the 'end of criticism', it is central to a number of avowedly 'critical' positions in social theory.[7] Postmodern theorists, as we have seen, in their criticism of 'positivistic' requirements of theoretical order, advance the view that contradictory theory is valid. This position has been reinforced by some feminist criticisms of scientific theory, where the apparently universalistic and context-free criteria of scientific adequacy initially advanced in 'positivistic' philosophies of science are now held to be patriarchal in nature. Indeed, the very concern with theoretical order is held to be oppressive, involving the denial of the 'difference', whose identification and expression, it is argued, should be the aim of feminist (and postmodern) theory. As Flax puts it, "if we do our work well, 'reality' will appear more unstable, complex and disorderly than it does now".[8]

But, if coherence is denied as a condition of theoretical adequacy, what determines that any supposed 'differences', or 'contradictory particularities', are appropriately expressed? Or is postmodern theory immune from mistakes such that, as Lyotard puts it, in 'alluding to the conceivable', anything goes? If 'disorder' is made the goal of theoretical activity, then we have the curious situation that the *worse* (from any standard perspective on conditions of adequacy) our social scientific explanations, the better they will achieve their postmodern aims. Indeed, the problem of distinguishing a real 'disorder' of the social world from the appearance of disorder created by the inadequacy of a theoretical scheme is evident, if only implicitly, in Harding's struggle with the confusions intrinsic to the postmodern conception of theory. She writes, "I am not suggesting that we should *try* to produce incoherent theories, but that we should try to fashion conceptual schemes that are more alert to the complex and often beneficial ways in which the modernist world is falling apart."[9]

Many postmodern theorists justify their claims by arguing that, under conditions of postmodernity, 'social reality', itself, has become 'fragmented', or disorderly.[10] Theories must be contradictory because social existence is contradictory. But how could we apprehend the 'true' nature of social existence independently of the social theories mobilized to account for it? Certainly, if social theory is 'falling apart', the world will appear to be 'falling apart'. But such 'disorder' will be an artifact of our theoretical confusion, not a feature of the world adequately expressed in a 'disorderly' theory. The 'observations' of 'disorder' are not independent of theory, merely because they cannot be accounted for by existing 'orders' of theory. The acceptance of 'deviant observations' as unproblematically reflecting the 'real' would be a form of 'empiricism'.

In arguing this, I am not denying 'difference'. Any elaborated scheme is necessarily a scheme of differentiated entities. The issue, then, is not one of the acceptance or denial of 'difference', but the coherence, or otherwise, of the scheme in which difference is expressed and accounted. The idea that a coherent, or inclusive, scheme would deny difference and is, therefore, 'oppressive' probably takes its force from those occasions on which there are attempts to uphold the adequacy of a theoretical scheme despite apparently 'disconfirming' instances; that is, from denials of any need to transform basic categories in the face of apparent inadequacies. In these circumstances, the attempt to assert the 'order' of pre-existing categories will, indeed, appear to suppress the 'differences' that the observations of behaviours at odds with that order seem to embody. For example, a standard claim within Marxist theory (and other mainstream class theories, for that matter) has been that 'gender' could be subsumed under class categories and that the theory did not, therefore, require fundamental revision in order to account for the 'anomalous' observations associated with gender. Yet, however justified is the feminist suspicion of a 'conservative' orientation among class theorists, this could not establish the validity of 'anomalous' observations in their immediate apprehension as the expression of 'differences'.[11]

For some there is a parallel between post-positivist theories of science and postmodernism. However, the acceptability of contradiction is not what distinguishes a post-positivist account of science from that of positivism as postmodern theorists might suppose. In Chapter 3, I argued that, according to post-positivist philosophies of science, mutual consistency among statements of objects and their relations remains a condition of adequacy. Lack of consistency constitutes a problem to be solved. Where post-positivist accounts of science diverge from standard positivist accounts is that they argue that the answer to problems is not given in advance, in a *method* which stands outside particular, located practices. Where problems lie and how they are to be solved produces no one correct strategy. Problem-solving is a creative activity of science, whereby what are transformed are not only categories and relations, but also methodological criteria. This is the sense in which post-positivist theories of science eschew prescriptive methodologies and can, thereby, be said to share an 'anti-foundationalism' with postmodernism, or, for that matter, with feminist criticisms of science. As I argued in Chapter 3, post-positivism would suggest that the project of general, *a priori* social theory is intrinsically flawed. Nevertheless, post-positivist theories of science continue to emphasize problem-solving as the creative practice of science, where postmodernism accepts the incoherence of the categories in which the problems are embodied as descriptively adequate to a disorderly world.[12]

Some of Parsons's most recent followers have adopted the postmodern position and, in their arguments, the force of Popper's criticism of the lack of sense entailed by the embrace of contradiction is clearly felt. For example, for Turner, the very discovery of 'contradictions' in the general theory is made the basis of claiming a new 'reading' of Parsons in which he is revealed as more sensitive to conflict and ambiguity and more flexible in the application of his theory to such issues.[13] As we saw in the last chapter, on this 'reading', the 'same' institutions, apparently, can serve integration and produce strains as part of their theoretical definition. In this way, all outcomes can be made to 'fit'. Thus, Turner applauds the 'generality' of Parsons's theory which allows mutually exclusive empirical outcomes as equally confirming its theoretical categories. At a minimum, such a general theory would be vacuous. So, while I have argued that a resourceful theory can be contradictory, the resources I have in mind belong to the *substantive categories* of a theory (or research programme) and *not* to the metatheoretical concepts of the general frame of reference under which the substantive categories are being organized.

Although Parsons is brought to the contradictions that his theory contains, it is to his considerable credit that, for the most part, he does not accept them as definitive of social inquiry as do postmodern theorists, but struggles with them. Indeed, it is quite evident that he believed coherence among theoretical objects and relations (including empirical observations) to be a condition of adequacy.[14] One reason why his treatment of issues – especially his criticisms of other writers, such as Weber – can be valuable despite the unsatisfactory character of his general theoretical framework, is precisely because of the commitment to coherence and empirical adequacy which was the initial thrust to the development of his general theory. He is able to identify problems in the work of others even where his own answers to those problems are unsatisfactory. In fact, Parsons's account of the 'breakdown' of theoretical systems in terms of the expansion of negative, residual categories, including 'observations' at odds with those expected on the basis of the positive processes of the theoretical system is an almost direct description of the constitution of postmodernist theoretical claims. However, where Parsons argued that the expansion of 'residual categories' indicates the need for a reconstruction of theoretical objects and relations (although, ultimately, failing adequately to specify the nature of that reconstruction), postmodernism accepts as 'real' the antithetical, residual categories of pre-existing theoretical schemes alongside their positive

109

processes.[15] Indeed, the best indication of the 'empiricism' of postmodernism is precisely the way in which, faced with the deficiencies of previous approaches, postmodern theorists do not seek a greater adequacy, but accept the deficiencies as descriptively adequate of an 'incoherent' world.

Notwithstanding the acuity of some aspects of Parsons's account of theoretical systems, his difficulties do derive from his attempt to solve *methodologically* what can only be solved *substantively* (or, to be more precise, what requires to be solved substantively before any implications – including their novel methodological insights – can be drawn for extension to other areas of inquiry). Even on his own account, previous social theories had failed in their substantive accounts of modern social relationships. Faced with the practical contradictions of previous approaches, Parsons argued that they could be solved by elaborating a general frame of reference which was not itself practical, but which would have a phenomenological status. This framework, he claimed, would be adequate to all empirical issues and all current and future empirical questions could be adequately stated within its theoretical categories. By implication, any problems would be 'mistakes' in the application of a scheme whose intrinsic adequacy to the issues at hand is given in advance as a logical condition of all inquiries. The general frame of reference would be beyond further transformation of its categories. At least initially, as we have seen, Parsons registered some reservations about this separation of empirical issues from questions of theoretical adequacy. To make such a separation, he implied, would be to neglect the role of 'action' in the development of science. With the arguments of post-positivist philosophers of science in mind, we can now be more precise and say that the 'action' which would be neglected is *problem-solving as the creative activity of science*. As we shall see in the next section, it is precisely this conception of 'action' which is missing from Parsons's action frame of reference more generally.

Alexander, for one, is worried about the consequences of abandoning the project of general theory in sociology, of denying the presuppositional status of theoretical categories. According to him, a general frame of reference is necessary in order to overcome the debilitating consequences of relativism and the fragmentation of social theory (so evident in postmodernism). At most, however, Alexander is describing a 'hope' which he has for general theory. He is certainly not describing what has been realized whether in his own writings or those of others committed to the same project.[16] Now, although post-positivist theories of science do deny that there could be a 'fixed point' to explanation, the conclusion need not be the relativistic position that there are simply different points of view and no criteria for distinguishing among them. We do not confront an 'either/or' dilemma – *either*, a general frame of reference, *or* hopeless relativism; *either* pluralistic, but fragmented social theory *or* a reified (and contradictory) general scheme. Standards of evaluation may, and indeed do, shift in the process of the development of explanations which transform theoretical objects and relations, but scientific judgements are 'indeterminate' only in the sense that there is no one, pre-given best way forward, not in the sense that judgements of superior adequacy cannot be made.[17]

Superior adequacy must be an issue of the greater inclusiveness, or resourcefulness, of one theoretical scheme over another. However, this does not mean that a 'totalizing', general scheme of categories is a *pre-condition* of social scientific inquiry, that a general framework is either necessary, or possible, in advance of any substantive inquiry. This is a position which postmodern theorists have rightly criticized. Social inquiries should be regarded as 'particular' – substantive might be the better term – in the sense of beginning from specific, located problems. However, the dynamic of inquiry is that of inference and extension to other 'particulars' and the general requirement of such inquiries, in social science as in natural science, is consistency among statements of objects and their relations. Lack of consistency constitutes a problem to be solved. The solution of problems is a creative task which involves the transformation of theoretical objects and relations, including the observations associated with the problems.

It might be objected that social inquiry differs from the natural sciences in that the practices we are seeking to explain may, themselves, be contradictory and that this means that the inferences we draw need not be consistent. For example, Marx argued that capitalist social relations were contradictory and, even if we argue that Marx was incorrect in his particular identification of the contradictory character of capitalism, this does not establish that contradiction, *per se*, is an irrelevant, or illegitimate, category with which to address social practices. This is indeed so. After all, inquiry is a social practice and I have been demonstrating the contradictions that it can embody. What is possible for the practices of social theory must be possible for other social practices. [18] Nevertheless, an adequate address of contradictions would imply a different sort of theoretical activity than that proposed by Parsons, or by any other proponent of general theory. There could be no *general theory* of contradictions. Contradictions must be particular, concerning specific social practices, or specific categories and their relations. Any social scientific account (and, by implication, solution) of contradictions must meet conditions of adequacy and consistency, but, once again, that does not mean that there is a general scheme available outside particular accounts, intrinsic to all accounts and known in advance of them. Either, a general theory of contradictions would imply a general solution of contradictions, and, ultimately, that must be a denial of contradiction. Or, it would imply the generality of contradiction which must deny any possibility of transcendence (as in postmodernism).

Equally, it is important to acknowledge that, to argue for the role of contradiction in social practices is not the equivalent of arguing that social life necessarily is contradictory, or that all social relationships are ambiguous and contradictory, as postmodern theorists suppose. Not all claims to have identified contradictory practices are justified. If social practices can be contradictory that possibility must include the practices of social inquiry. Adequacy of explanation

111

in social scientific inquiries could not be automatic. It cannot be guaranteed in advance. If there is something to be explained, there must be a risk of being wrong. The objects and relations we propose may not obtain.

For example, Marx's abstraction of the basic features and consequences of the capital-labour relation from the 'noise' of historically contingent and disturbing factors, which apparently contradicted them, as Burawoy suggests, might properly be regarded as an illustration of what Lakatos means by a progressive theoretical programme.[19] Thus, Marx offered a theory of capitalism and its developmental tendencies in circumstances where those tendencies were not fully realized and where actual circumstances might (and to other theorists did), in their immediacy, suggest alternative explanations. However, while progressive theoretical developments must have the character of appearing counter-intuitive, it does not follow that everything with the character of being counter-intuitive is progressive. Ultimately, explanation is a risky business and, however inventive a theoretical gambit, its mere inventiveness is not sufficient to guarantee its resourcefulness.

We do need inventive and resourceful social theory brought to bear upon our explanatory problems. We must risk failure in order to have the possibility of success. The world, or, more properly, certain practices within the world, *may* be contradictory, and we do need insight into contradictions wherever they exist. But where theories are contradictory, their contradictions cannot be the source of positive insights. Although, as I have argued, a resourceful theory may be contradictory, what should be clear is that *whatever is resourceful about a social theory could not reside in the contradictions it contains.* It is resourceful *despite* its contradictions, not *because* of them. The further expansion of resources would require those specific contradictions to be addressed and solved. An embrace of contradiction and its generalization, which, in the last analysis, is what general, synthetic theory and postmodern theory each entails, the one implicitly, the other self-consciously, represents the nadir of social inquiry.

PROBLEM-SOLVING AND ACTION

In the preceding section, I have demonstrated how explanatory failure, or contradiction, comes to be accepted *not as a challenge* for social theory, *but as defining the necessary limits of any theoretical undertaking.* The question must be: what are the obstacles to invention, or innovation, in social theory? Why are explanatory problems accepted as definitive, rather than as what must be solved? The answer, as I shall show, is found in widely held assumptions about the nature of social objects and their difference from the objects of natural science.[20] These assumptions are central to statements of an action frame of reference as the necessary form of general theory in sociology. Social objects, it is argued, are constituted in the actions of human beings and human beings have the capacity for freedom, choice and the creation of new meanings. I shall argue that following this position to its logical conclusion produces a paradox. In the name of human creativity, one group of human actors – social theorists – are denied their creativity. In what follows, then, I shall not be denying the substance of human creativity, but, rather, I shall seek to demonstrate that what many social theorists believe follows from its recognition, is itself its negation. Once again, the fate of Parsons's theory serves as an illustration.

I have been arguing throughout this book that the problems of Parsonian theory are typical, rather than idiosyncratic. In arguing for a synthetic, general theory, he attempts to organize its different categories within an action frame of reference. He accepts that these categories have previously occurred in the form of mutually exclusive and antithetical claims, but he believes that his general theory will provide consistency where previously there had been inconsistency. His general scheme of theoretical categories, he argues, will unite the perspective of the external 'observer' with that of the 'actor' (or, as Habermas puts it, the perspective of the 'system' and that of the 'lifeworld'). 'Action' is central to Parsons's undertaking, as it is to most other attempts at a general framework of social theory. Indeed, it is precisely in terms of 'action' that any additional component of the 'subjective' meanings of the actor, or the dimension of 'lifeworld', is introduced into social inquiries and which prevents social inquiry from being practised as a mere extension of natural science.

As we have seen, the common judgement of Parsons's theory is that expressed by Giddens, who comments that, "there is no action in Parsons's 'action frame of reference' ".[21] To the contrary, I shall argue that Parsons's problems are contained precisely in the very conception of action that is argued to be absent. Even on the face of it, Giddens's judgement seems odd. How could Parsons have denied the very substance of what he was seeking to affirm? If there is no 'action' in Parsons's scheme, how do we register its absence as an issue for him? How is 'action' brought to bear upon his scheme as a self-evident deficiency? Now, I have argued throughout this book that Parsons, himself, has an answer to these questions. For him, 'action' must emerge as a residual category, for it to be an indication of a deficiency in a scheme which was self-consciously defined in other terms. In other words, although the claim that there is no 'action' in Parsons's action frame of reference is intended by Giddens to identify a different set of assumptions forming social theory, in truth it brings us back to Parsons's starting point, the concern to overcome a dualism of 'structure' and 'action' by identifying their mutual consistency, or 'duality'. But if 'action' is Parsons's starting point, is it not likely that anyone seeking to 're-introduce' it will merely be setting out on the journey in which it comes ultimately to be denied. Once again, this perception is not novel. Dawe, for example, in his commentary upon the concept of 'action' in different sociological theories, suggests that hitherto this has, indeed, been its fate. The 'career' of the concept of action, he writes, "is the career of a paradox, whereby the *idée fixe* of social action has always and everywhere generated its own negation by culminating in the concept of a dominating and constraining social system."[22]

What requires to be explained is both, why 'action' is the *idée fixe* of sociological theory and why it has this paradoxical, or contradictory, character. Giddens's comment about the absence of action in Parsons's action frame of reference continues with the observation that, for Parsons, actors do not appear as, "skilled and knowledgeable agents, as at least to some extent masters of their own fate".[23] Yet, we have seen that Parsons began with these very assumptions about human agency. The situation is truly the opposite of that suggested by Giddens and other critics. The problems which they take as indicative of the absence of 'action' from Parsons's general theoretical scheme, occur *precisely because, like them, he assumes a generalized competence on the part of actors*. Moreover, that competence is tied to the integration and maintenance of systems of social action. Indeed, from the very way in which Parsons builds his theory – from the abstraction of unit acts and their component elements and their subsequent location in a wider statement of the properties of systems of action and interaction – it follows that *whatever is attributed to 'action' – its general rationality and adequacy – must also be attributed to the 'systems' which are held to be built upon 'action'*. Indeed, although the common criticism of Parsons is that he retains too much of what is unsatisfactory about Durkheim, we can see that the real problems of his scheme derive from what he (and others) take from Weber. It is the 'universal' categories of a theory of action which 'universalizes' anything built upon them. So, Parsons elaborates universal 'functional imperatives' (as does Giddens with his 'structural principles' and Habermas with his 'functional principles' of 'lifeworld' and 'system'[24]), in contrast to the historically specific functions identified by Durkheim.

The paradox of theories based upon rational action is that it is the rationality and adequacy of 'systems' that seems to exclude 'action'. It is this which seems to constitute 'systems' as 'iron cages' in which actors are 'trapped'. What I suggest is that there seems to be no 'escape' *because there are no problems intrinsic to systems whose solution would be the basis of reconstructing meanings, or identities and relationships*. We can see this feature of the general adequacy of systems in the way in which Alexander interprets the central core of Parsonsian theory – the statement of 'perfect integration' and its relations of 'interdependence'. As we have seen, Alexander suggests that Parsons is claiming no more than that integration is a 'possibility' and that deviance is a 'fact', arguing that such a conception is unproblematic. In effect, however, this is to argue that deviance does not call into question the integrity of the 'system'. As we have seen, Parsons's scheme is applied to circumstances of conflict and change (since he does not assume that concrete societies are perfectly integrated), but the only explanatory mechanisms he proposes are those which generate tendencies toward integration in circumstances of ever-present possibilities of deviance. In cooperative actions based on trust, for example, the existence of trust creates opportunities for deceit, but the answer to such 'deviance' is merely the re-statement of the advantages of cooperation and the obligations it imposes.

114

This is not to say that 'deviance' is not, in Parsons's sense of the term, 'structural'. For example, in any differentiated system of roles with different requirements and expectations, there is the possibility of 'strain' that derives from carrying the expectations from one setting into another and this, for Parsons's is a 'structural' issue. However, 'deviance' is not, in the sense that I am arguing here, an issue *intrinsic* to a particular structure. Thus, according to Parsons, 'strains' arise, even where the division between 'settings' is appropriate and an intelligible instance of 'structural differentiation'. For example, the professions are defined in terms of 'disinterestedness', but their corporate organization forms a monopoly of practice as well as creating the conditions for ethical self-regulation in terms of professional standards. There can arise 'strains' where individual practitioners may yield to the temptation of an expedient, self-interested orientation, which derives from the 'culturally appropriate' expectations of 'self-interested' behaviours in other settings (for example, those of business). However, while this is a form of 'deviance' which is ever-present, the only 'answer' is a strengthening and re-affirmation of the 'norms' of professional practice, rather than, say, a reconstruction of its corporate forms.[25]

For Parsons, then, the problem of 'deviance' always derives from a *mis*understanding, rather than being *intrinsic* to understandings. The 'system' is logical and coherent. In short, it is *possible* and its 'possibility' is the source of the resources mobilized to secure compliance. There are no problems to be solved which are integral to the 'system'. This is directly analogous to the 'phenomenological' role which he attributes to his general theory in the face of any empirical problems. What is missing in Parsons's account of 'science' as 'action', then, is also missing in his account of 'action' as 'science' (that is, as rational and competent). There is no room for contradiction as a substantive issue of social practices (including social inquiry) and, therefore, no appreciation of problem-solving as creative activity in his theory of action. *Integration could not be a possibility for a contradictory system.*[26] In the preceding section, I argued that there could be no general theory of contradiction, yet it is precisely an understanding of the role of contradiction which is necessary to locate the very creativity of action which the proponents of general theory are seeking to express in their foundational schemes.

If we pursue the analogy with 'science' as 'action', then we can see that, if, as I argued in the previous section, the solution of contradiction expands resources, so contradiction, in the absence of a solution, *must entail a statement of a specific incompetence*. In social life, generally, as in the more specific practices of science, contradictions are lived as the specific incompetence of problems (which, although they may be concentrated on particular groups and may be different in their effects for different groups, do not leave anyone immune from their processes). Once again, if we think of the Marxist example, and what Lockwood was suggesting might be drawn from it, we can see that Marx was describing contradictions as the subversion of competence and the

115

embodiment of practical alienation. By extension, then, the assumption of generalized competence – of actors as skilled and knowledgeable agents as a methodological principle of social inquiries that, according to many social theorists, must be built into the general framework of social theory[27] – is as misplaced as the idea of integration to which it is logically connected.

The question remains: why is the assumption of general competence on the part of actors believed to be necessary to any social inquiry? What I shall suggest is that it is tied to the very circumstances of explanatory failure from which the claims for a 'general frame of reference derive. This raises fundamental issues of social scientific practice.[28] At this point, my argument may be beginning to generate some unease, because it appears to go against the very ethos of social inquiry that has developed over the last decades, or so. After all, the idea of a general competence on the part of actors appears to be a sympathetic and 'democratic' idea. With this methodological assumption, for example, 'professional' social scientists seem not to be claiming any superiority over those that they study, treating them not as 'objects' of study, but as 'subjects' in their own right. Indeed, the standard criticism of the positivist conception of social science – a criticism which was also laid against Parsons – was precisely that it held to the superiority of the understandings of social scientists over those of the actors whose activities were the object of inquiry. Against this view, Gouldner, for example, argued for a 'reflexive' sociology where sociologists would recognize, "the depth of our kinship with those we study. They would no longer be viewable as alien others or as mere objects for our superior technique and insight; they could instead be seen as brother [sic] sociologists, each attempting with his varying degree of skill, energy, and talent to understand social reality."[29]

Gouldner's statement is ambivalent. The issue of incompetence is there, albeit faintly, in the idea that competence may be variable (though we might note that those with lesser 'skills, energies, and talents' are implicitly others). Nevertheless, the emphasis is clearly in the direction of 'equality'. In more formal, methodological statements of the principle of 'kinship', Gouldner's ambiguities are removed. Giddens, for example, writes that positivism involves the 'derogation of the lay actor'.[30] In contrast, he argues, social inquiry should recognize and be grounded in a symmetry between the practices of understanding and explanation engaged in by 'professional' social scientists and those engaged in by actors. On Giddens's version of symmetry – and it is reproduced in many other writers – actors' meanings are not corrigible, or criticizable, by 'professional' social scientists, but they are, rather, to be *understood and accepted* as the basis of social inquiries. Thus, Giddens writes that, "every (competent) member of society is a practical social theorist; in sustaining any sort of encounter he draws upon his knowledge and theories, normally in an unforced and routine way, and the use of these practical resources is precisely the condition of the encounter at all. Such resources (which I shall later call generically 'mutual knowledge') *as such* are *not corrigible* in the light of the theories of social scientists, but are routinely drawn upon *by them* in the course of any researches they may prosecute."[31]

Although Giddens directs the argument against Parsons's scheme, it is precisely the sort of claim that Giddens is making which is the source of Parsons's own difficulties. After all, the idea that the 'mutual knowledge' that sustains social interaction is not corrigible is not far removed from Parsons's own views on cultural values and meanings (as is evident in the way in which Giddens argues that, from the 'structural' point of view, 'mutual knowledge', "appears as a normatively co-ordinated legitimate order"[32] – in other words, from a 'structural point of view', integration is a possibility). However sympathetic the argument might initially appear to be, it is difficult to sustain. If actors are 'lay' social theorists, they would have to obey the requirements which are imposed upon 'professional' theorists. They would have to regard the 'mutual knowledge' that is a condition of their encounters as 'non-corrigible'. Since 'lay' social theorists show no inclination to obey this methodological rule, it is difficult to see why it should have a peculiar force for 'professional' social theorists! Clearly, social theorists seem to feel themselves constrained in a way that those they study are not constrained.

Why should the fact that actors are 'practical social theorists' place their 'theories' beyond criticism? The claim of symmetry between 'lay' and 'professional' social theorists would suggest that if 'lay' social theorists are beyond criticism, so too are 'professional' social theorists. Now, it may seem far-fetched to suggest that the 'professional' humility and equality implied by the injunction not to 'derogate' lay actors is, in truth, an injunction not to criticize, or transform professional social science, but, as we shall see, this is precisely what the argument implies.

I shall trace this peculiar sense of constraint to the very basic division between the point of view of the social theorist and the point of view of those whose activities are being studied – between what Parsons terms, the external 'observer' and the actor 'thought of as acting himself'. Parsons, in common with other social theorists, is seeking to bring the two points of view together, claiming that while 'they should correspond', that 'fact' was no reason why they 'should not be kept clearly distinct' in order to arrive at a 'satisfactory solution of their relations to each other'. But, why should they correspond? And, if they should correspond, how do they come to appear apart? Parsons (and Habermas, Giddens, and Alexander, too, for that matter) displays a remarkable lack of self-consciousness in allowing that they 'should correspond' without reflecting upon the circumstances of their separation. His own strictures on 'residual categories' should have forewarned him about the problematic status of anything which appeared as a mere 'fact'.

Indeed, it is the conception of 'action' and the limits it imposes upon social inquiry which explains a 'conservatism' of social science when compared with natural science. Natural scientists, when faced with problems of explanation, accept them as *internal* to their understandings and, therefore, as indicating that

117

those understandings might require fundamental reconstruction. In the social sciences, the orientation is quite different. In the extreme case of postmodernism, we have seen that any problems of understanding are argued to be *definitive* and consequent upon a 'chaotic' reality which cannot be represented by consistent theoretical categories. Notwithstanding any claims of 'difference', however, there is a direct connection between postmodernism and standard social scientific epistemology. Thus, it is a frequent defence of theoretical constructs in social science to claim their 'ideal typical' status.[33] On this basis, it is held that theories are not called into question by the deviation of circumstances from the processes internal to theoretical statements. On the contrary, theories are held to be valid as one-sided ideal types at the same time as the observations of behaviours at odds with them are accepted as descriptively adequate. Although Parsons, as we have seen, was aware of the deficiencies of Weber's conception of ideal types – in particular, identifying the fragmentation and hypostatization of reality that occurred as an artifact of the methodology of ideal types – he was insufficiently aware of how the separation of the 'objective' and the 'subjective', which he accepts, is a general form of the division which he attributes to ideal types. Despite his forceful criticism of the methodology of ideal types, then, he also builds its deficiencies into his own statement of general theory, with similar consequences. The 'particularism' of ideal types contains no alternative to the 'abstract generalities' of Parsonsian theory, and vice versa, because they are each versions of the same problem.

Elsewhere, the problems of standard social scientific epistemology have been examined at some length, where a fallacy specific to the social sciences has been identified.[34] This social scientific fallacy is the means by which social theorists *avoid* what natural scientists *accept*, the need to reconstruct failed explanations. The substance of this fallacy is the claim that behaviours which are inexplicable in the explanatory categories initially proposed can be apprehended and rendered intelligible without addressing the substance of the social scientist's constructions in which the behaviours have occurred as a problem. The justification of this claim is bound up with a distinction between natural and social science. Where the objects of the natural sciences merely reflect routine processes, it is argued, human beings intervene in the world and thereby can produce novel and discontinuous effects. In contrast to what holds for natural scientists, social scientists, apparently, may regard any apparent explanatory problem as reflecting the peculiar nature of their objects, that is, as deriving from their status as human subjects capable of freedom and choice. Conversely, any decision by actors to behave differently need not, it is believed, bear upon the theoretical adequacy of the construct previously held to obtain. Where the explanations that were initially proposed purported to identify contradictions in social practices, the claim is that the contradiction is a valid claim, despite the fact that it is not lived by the relevant actors. In this way, contradictions lose their substance as practical problems which must be lived unless they are solved. The 'subjective' it appears can cancel the effects of the 'objective' rendering it 'unnecessary', but not invalid. Whatever is organized within a construct could have been 'true' if it had been 'chosen'.

It is possible to argue that 'ideal types' *could* be used differently, that is as heuristic devices whose categories would be reconstructed in the process of the research that would be informed by them. Papineau, for example, has argued that 'ideal types' could be construed along the lines of Lakatos's account of research programmes.[35] However, as he observes, this is not how they have been used in the social sciences. Indeed, the epistemological arguments used to underpin the methodology of ideal types specifically argues against such an interpretation, since it is held that theoretical constructs can be valid despite their lack of application to the specific behaviours to which they are addressed.

The circumstances in which social scientists distinguish between the 'valid' and 'objective' criteria embodied in their theoretical constructs and the equally meaningful 'local' and 'subjective' criteria of meaning embodied in the 'deviant' behaviours of actors are circumstances in which, on the face of it, actors might be judged to be 'irrational' (according to the criteria of the social scientific construct). If social scientific constructs *were indeed valid*, might they not be regarded as superior to those of actors and the source of critical judgements about their 'subjective' meanings? That social scientists do not make this judgement is because actors, apparently, are able to maintain their behaviours, without the problems that would be expected on the basis of any supposedly 'superior' social scientific rationality. Were actors to experience problems reproducing their behaviours, then the 'superiority' of the social theorist's account would be confirmed. The point is that actors do not have the problems that would enable them to claim this. For example, in the Marxist case, actors appear not to be living the contradictions of capitalism, their 'subjective' meanings apparently 'cancel' them. Actors' lives reveal an unexpected 'order'. This is the paradox that undermines postmodern theory. Their claim for the essential 'disorderliness' of the world derives from their problems in negotiating their way around with their theories. But that perception of 'disorderliness' is predicated upon actors who do not experience the same difficulties!

Where actors reproduce their behaviours apparently unproblematically in circumstances where social theorists initially anticipate that they should have problems, it appears attractive to argue that there exist other, local or context-specific, equally rational (the term suggested by Parsons in *TSofSA*, and used extensively by others, thereafter, is 'non-rational') criteria which govern actors' behaviours. In this way, it seems that a negative, or 'residual' category, 'irrational' behaviour, is transformed into a positive category, 'non-rational' action, by a simple redefinition of terms. Yet, this cannot alter the fact that the apparently equally valid 'rational' criteria organized under 'sociologists' ' and 'actors' ' terms prescribe in contradiction to each other and that these contradictory 'possibilities' enter as a formal statement of the nature of social reality. In these circumstances, any claim that the two points of view 'should correspond', reflects an implicit awareness that their division is problematic, but no awareness of *why they could not correspond*, once the terms in which they are separated are accepted. Since they contain contradictory possibilities, these possibilities become generalized in the elaboration of any theory which accepts their 'basic', or 'presuppositional' terms.

The division in rational criteria is proposed as an appropriate humility on the part of social scientists toward the subjective meaning of actors. In truth, it is an unwarranted privileging of social scientific incompetence. Where the behaviours of actors deviate from the social theorist's expectations might not the problem lie with the theorist? Where social scientific judgements and those of actors diverge, might the situation not be one of somebody's irrationality, as first appears to be the case? There remains one actor whose actions seem never to get questioned and that is the social theorist making the judgements. Might it not be the social theorist whose behaviour is 'irrational' in asserting the 'validity' of his or her scheme despite its lack of practical efficacy? In which case, the division of 'rational' and 'non-rational' criteria and the claimed 'non-corrigibility' of the 'mutual knowledge' of actors seems designed not so much to protect actors from offensive judgements by social theorists, but to protect social theorists from the need to transform their theories.

Ultimately, as I argued in the previous section, the claim for the 'reality' of 'deviant behaviours' – the 'action' in any distinction between 'action' and 'structure' – alongside the validity of the schemes, or 'structure', in terms of which the deviant observations are made is a form of sociological 'empiricism'. This is a position which could not be sustained in the light of post-positivist theories of science and, therefore, is justified by features peculiar to the objects of social inquiry. A lack of integration of the 'theoretical' and the 'empirical' is regarded as definitive of social inquiry, rather than as an occasion for creative reformulation. It is argued that there need be no requirement in the social sciences of a reconstruction of theoretical objects and relations. On this view, it would seem that social science must be *ad hoc* and *ex post*, reacting to change and neither contributing to it, nor, apparently challenged by it.

It is a consequence of this form of argument, that by identifying human freedom with a contingency of human action which apparently lies outside social scientfic determination, any improvement in social scientific explanation, which must *reduce contingency*, would, by that token, reduce human freedom. In this light, it is perhaps not surprising that postmodern theorists represent the aim of explanatory coherence and adequacy as 'totalitarian' and 'offensive'. We might property conclude, however, that the problem lies with deficiencies in the particular conception of human freedom, rather than with any explanatory undertaking in social science. At a minimum, there is the paradox – or contradiction, given the claimed symmetry between 'lay' and 'professional' social theorists – that in the name of human creativity, social scientists are being denied *their* creativity. The 'freedom and creativity' of social scientists, it seems is set against the 'freedom and creativity' of those they study (even against those in whose name they study). However, where the consequence of the constructions is to attribute 'chaos' to the world, the only 'freedom' that actors could be offered is 'uncertainty' and 'unpredictability', at the same time as we are offered the possibility that the *worse* are social scientific explanations, the more actual behaviours will deviate from them and, therefore, the 'freer' actors will (appear to) be. Ultimately, the methodological assumption of general competence, removes creativity from actors and social scientists alike.

It is valuable and necessary to argue for the 'logical symmetry' between the undertakings of 'professional' and 'lay' social theorists, but it is important to recognise that symmetry would be maintained equally by an assumption that the practices of each might embody a specific incompetence, as by the assumption of general competence. Just as in the relation between scientific theories, where accounts diverge, there must be an issue of the superiority of one account over another. It is possible that each is inadequate, but what could not obtain is the adequacy of each (though, it is precisely this claim which forms the substance of standard social scientific epistemology). The fact that the issue will not always be resolved in favour of social theorists does not mean that it will never be, nor that our goal should not be the production of superior accounts. Indeed, what could anyone's interest in social theory be, if not the possibility of superior insight? What is evident is that when social theorists declare their unwillingness to derogate 'lay' actors, it coincides with those occasions when they would be unable to do so *precisely because their theories lack practical efficacy.* Conformity to an injunction not to derogate 'lay' actors is all too easy to accomplish in contemporary social theory! In these circumstances, the behaviours of actors at odds with what is expected on the basis of the schemes mobilized to account for them, should be taken seriously as the source of insight into what is 'invalid' in those schemes, not as something 'valid' in its own right, but without implication for the 'validity' of the social scientific scheme.

It is explanatory failure which produces the categories which form the 'synthetic' project of foundational theory and the 'contradictory particularism' of the postmodern rejection of foundationalism, alike. But this should not really surprise us. After all, in *TSofSA*, Parsons was quite explicit that the categories with which he was concerned were the product of the breakdown in theoretical systems. What now appears to be the case is that he failed to recognise the extent to which the categories, whose positive status he was extolling, were themselves bound up with the problems he had identified. The development of his own scheme of categories, then, reproduces the divisions which enable others to 'rediscover' his initial insights and to begin the cycle over again, or to capitulate in the face of the problem and declare the impossibility of coherent social theory.

In contrast to this unproductive cycle, or the postmodern embrace of incoherence, I suggest an alternative. We should return to the true starting point of Parsons's undertaking, the substantive problems of social theory, in order to engage with them and solve them *substantively.* This argument for a direct engagement with the substance of social explanations, is quite specifically an argument against the categories of meta-theoretical debate. The question is usually put: what then is *your* version of 'structure' and 'action'? How would *you* integrate, or synthesize them? To this question the answer can only be that, there is *no* answer, *once these categories have been accepted as appropriate and meaningful.* The problem of 'structure' and 'action' cannot be solved in advance of addressing the particular substance of the explanation in which the problem has emerged as an issue. Solving the particular explanatory problem will mean addressing substantive categories and their relations (for example, the categories and theories of class, bureaucracy, organization, gender, etc.). When these particular problems have been solved, 'structure' and 'action' as apparent issues will dissolve.

NOTES

1. See, for example, J–F. Lyotard, *The Postmodern Condition: A Report on Knowledge* (Minneapolis, University of Minnesota Press, 1984).
2. See, for example, B.S. Turner, 'Parsons and his critics: on the ubiquity of functionalism', in R.J. Holton and B.S. Turner (eds), *Talcott Parsons on Economy and Society* (London, Routledge and Kegan Paul, 1986).
3. K. Popper, 'What is dialectic?', in *Conjectures and Refutations: The Growth of Scientific Knowledge* (London, Routledge and Kegan Paul, 1963), p. 319.
4. Ibid., p. 321.
5. See I. Lakatos, 'Falsification and the methodology of scientific research programmes', in I. Lakatos and A. Musgrave (eds), *Criticism and the Growth of Knowledge* (Cambridge, Cambridge University Press, 1970).
6. Popper, 'What is dialectic?', pp. 321–2.
7. Popper, for example, suggests that Marxism involves an acceptance of contradictory theory. While some Marxists may have argued this and, as I argued in the previous chapter, Marxist theory is contradictory, for the most part, Marxist theorists are attempting to answer the problems intrinsic to Marx's scheme, rather than seeking to uphold it in its contradictions. In this sense, neo-Marxist theory exemplifies how processes of theoretical development ultimately reveal and expand residual categories.
8. J. Flax, 'Gender as a problem in and for feminist theory', *American Studies,* 1986, pp. 193–213.
9. S. Harding, *The Science Question in Feminism* (Milton Keynes, Open University Press, 1986), p. 164.
10. See, for example, S. Lash and J. Urry, *Disorganised Capitalism* (Cambridge, Polity Press, 1987); S. Crook, J. Pakulski and M. Waters *Postmodernization: Change in Advanced Society* (London, Sage, 1992).
11. Delphy, for example, expresses her suspicions of any inclusive theory because, she fears that, once again, gender will disappear under class. See C. Delphy, *Close to Home: A Materialist Analysis of Women's Oppression* (London, Hutchinson, 1984). But the necessary revision is to transform class theory to produce an inclusive account of inequality adequate to issues of gender.

12. Feminist criticisms of science apply primarily to a positivist conception of science which holds that scientific practices are concerned with the search for a set of 'eternal', timeless laws which are true universally. This conception is, however, denied in post-positivist theories of science which view science as an historically located activity. Recently, the feminist critique of science has been criticised from within feminism. See, for example, M. Hawkesworth, 'Knower, knowing, known: feminist theory and claims of truth', *Signs* 14(3), 1989, pp. 533–57; L.H. Nelson, *Who Knows: From Quine to a Feminist Empiricism* (Philadelphia, Temple University Press, 1990).

13. 'Parsons and his critics; on the ubiquity of functionalism' in R.J. Holton and B.S. Turner, *Talcott Parsons on Economy and Society* (London, Routledge, 1986).

14. This is a commitment by Parsons which has proven enough to have him cast as a 'latent positivist', even by those who profess sympathy for his project. See, for example, J.C. Alexander, 'The centrality of the classics', in A. Giddens and J. Turner (eds), *Social Theory Today* (Cambridge, Polity, 1987).

15. For example, as we have seen, postmodern theorists represent the postmodern phase of advanced societies as a stage of 'disorganized capitalism'. But, the only indication of 'disorganization' is the deviation of current circumstances from the 'order' expected on the basis of theories of 'organized capitalism'. The 'observations' of 'fragmentation' are not independent of theory, merely because they cannot be accounted for by existing theory. The postmodern position is to affirm the truth both of the pre-existing theories *and* of the practical deviations from them. In this way, current circumstances are described as defined by a 'dialectic' of orderly processes and their negation. Crook et al., for example, argue that the social differentiation characteristic of modernity produces its own reversal, social de-differentiation. They offer three theses on postmodernization, where, "first, its dynamic principles (differentiation, rationalization and commodification) are the same as those of modernization. Second, postmodernization is not simply an accentuation of modernization. The tension between these two theses generates the third: 'hyper' differentiation, rationalization or commodification produces outcomes which look very much like 'de' differentiation, rationalization or commodification." S. Crook, J. Pakulski and M. Waters, *Postmodernization: Change in Advanced Society* (London, Sage, 1992), p. 47.

16. For a detailed account of the triumph of hope over expectation, see S. Turner, 'The strange life and hard times of the concept of general theory in sociology: a short history of hope', in S. Seidman and D.G. Wagner (eds), *Postmodernism and Social Theory* (Oxford, Blackwell, 1992).

17. Although Feyerabend, for one, appears to be a post-positivist philosopher of science who is proposing a postmodern approach to science where 'anything goes', it should be noted that his basic argument is that no approach can be guaranteed (or ruled out) in advance, not that all approaches are equally successful. In other words, *there are criteria of success*, but we do not know where successful innovations will lie. In consequence, we should allow many different ways of dealing with issues, rather than attempt to prescribe a single, best way. See P.K. Feyerabend, *Against Method* (London, New Left Books, 1975).

18. This symmetry must also undermine the claims of writers like Winch, who suggests that the charge of 'contradiction' applied to the beliefs and practices of others is a 'category error', but is perfectly willing to identify the contradictory character of

much social inquiry. See P. Winch, *The Idea of a Social Science* (London, Routledge and Kegan Paul, 1958).

19. See M. Burawoy, 'Marxism as science: historical challenges and theoretical growth', *American Sociological Review*, 55(6), 1990, pp. 775–93.

20. For a detailed treatment of the issues which form this section, see J.M. Holmwood and A. Stewart, *Explanation and Social Theory* (London, Macmillan, 1991).

21. A Giddens, *New Rules of Sociological Method* (London, Hutchinson, 1976), p. 16.

22. A. Dawe, 'Theories of Social Action', in T. Bottomore and R. Nisbet (eds), *A History of Sociological Analysis* (London, Heinemann, 1978), p. 362. Dawe's own response is to retreat to the postmodern embrace of 'ambiguity' and 'contradiction' (though he was writing before the term, 'postmodern' became common currency); the 'paradox' is the 'real' condition of 'postmodern' humanity.

23. Giddens, *New Rules*, p. 16.

24. For Giddens's outline of 'structural principles', see A. Giddens, *A Contemporary Critique of Historical Materialism: Volume I, Power, Property and State* (London, Macmillan, 1981); *The Constitution of Society* (Cambridge, Polity, 1984). For Habermas's account of 'functional principles', see especially J. Habermas, *The Theory of Communicative Action, Volume II: Lifeworld and System; A Critique of Functionalist Reason* (Cambridge, Polity, 1987). For a detailed criticism, see J. Holmwood and A. Stewart, *Explanation and Social Theory* (London, Macmillan, 1991).

25. See T. Parsons, 'A sociologist looks at the legal profession', in *Essays in Sociological Theory* (New York, Free Press, 1954, revised edn). For a discussion of the reconstruction of the corporate forms of the professions, see J. Holmwood and J. Siltanen, 'Gender, the professions and employment citizenship', in T.P. Boje (ed.), *A Changing Europe: Trends in Welfare State and Labour Market* (New York, M.E. Sharpe, 1995).

26. As I showed in the last chapter, neo-Marxists have tried to argue that integration is a possibility for a contradictory system. However, the absence of the specific lived problems that the claimed contradiction would entail should rather be seen as the absence of the claimed contradiction.

27. See, for example, Giddens, *New Rules*.

28. For a detailed and extensive treatment of the issues discussed in the remainder of this section, see Holmwood and Stewart, *Explanation and Social Theory*.

29. A. Gouldner, *The Coming Crisis of Western Sociology* (London, Heinemann, 1970), p. 490.

30. See A. Giddens, *Central Problems in Social Theory: Action, Structure and Contradiction in Social Analysis* (London, Macmillan, 1979), p. 71.

31. Giddens, *New Rules*, p. 15. See also Barnes, who writes that, "the knowledge that constitutes society is self-referring ... Where knowledge is self-referring it must also be self-validating. A membership must learn it to become what it correctly describes." B. Barnes, *The Nature of Power* (Cambridge, Polity, 1988), p. 46.

32. Giddens, *Central Problems*, p. 86. For a detailed treatment of Giddens, see Holmwood and Stewart *Explanation and Social Theory* and J.M. Holmwood and A. Stewart, 'Synthesis and fragmentation in social theory: a progressive solution', *Sociological Theory*, 12(1), 1994, pp. 83–100.

33. See M. Weber, *The Methodology of the Social sciences* (New York, Free Press, 1949).

34. See Holmwood and Stewart, *Explanation and Social Theory*. There we identify two forms of the fallacy – the 'vertical' and the 'horizontal'. This distinction was made for expository purposes. Our argument is that each form tips over into the other, and so neither has a true 'integrity', and each contains elements of the other.
35. D. Papineau, 'Ideal types and empirical theories', *British Journal of the Philosophy of Science*, 27(2), 1976, pp. 137–46.

CONCLUSION

I have tried to keep issues of empirical enquiry central to my discussion of Parsons's general theory. Given the highly abstract and meta-theoretical nature of his arguments, this has not been easy. However, at various points, I have tried to show that Parsons, himself, regarded the ultimate justification of his theoretical endeavour to be the extent to which it deepened and extended empirical inquiry, even as his own theoretical undertaking seemed to take him away from that goal. Indeed, he describes *TSofSA* as an 'empirical' work and one of the reasons he gives for this description is that it is, "very much oriented to problems of the macroscopic developments in Western society, especially seen through the eyes of the four principal authors discussed in the study".[1] As well as providing the outline of a general framework of theory, then, Parsons intended to offer an interpretation of modern, Western society. In particular, he was concerned with the nature and consequences of the social structures of capitalism – what he called the 'individualism-socialism' dilemma – and the extent to which they gave rise to fundamental conflict as Marx had argued, or the extent to which they expressed an 'iron cage' of rationality as Weber proposed, rather than the solidaristic order suggested by Durkheim.

Despite Parsons's claims that the general position he was elaborating had arisen from an address to theoretical arguments which were practically engaged with empirical issues, any general conclusions on such issues are conspicuous by their absence. In *TSofSA*, his defence was that his concern with empirical issues was meta-theoretical and that he wanted to draw out the implications for a scheme of general theoretical categories, rather than to effect the direct reconstruction of the substantive problems at hand. But what was true of *TSofSA* proved to be the case for most of his major works in sociological theory and many of the essays, too. Most of Parsons's effort goes into lengthy exercises putting content into the empty theoretical boxes, or specifying the 'values' of the analytical elements of his general theory, despite the absence of a proper theoretical 'order' to their relationships. It is these exercises which are, perhaps, the dominant image that most sociologists have of Parsons's work and which contributes to that dismay – expressed by Seidman – over the detached and disengaged character of much sociological theory, which seems to define its issues internally, rather than by reference either to pressing problems shared with a wider public, or to a substantive programme of research.

Not all of Parsons's work has this meta-theoretical character and, in some of it, he addresses empirical problems with an explicit interest in reconstructing their substance. However, we do need to be careful with regard to how we interpret Parsons's more empirically orientated writings. As befits a self-acknowledged 'incurable theorist', none of his writings are free from their overlay of re-interpretation into a meta-theoretical framework. Moreover, Parsons's appetite for conceptual refinement and ever more elaborate developments of his scheme is not merely a personal idiosyncrasy. His failure to address empirical issues and illuminate them in any significant way is a consequence of the contradictory character of the very theoretical framework which he initially believed would facilitate empirical enquiry.

Parsons is not Weber. However perceptive Parsons's criticism of the latter's ideal type methodology, and however inadequate that methodology is to any reconstruction of a research programme, the consequence of Weber's more 'grounded' approach to sociological theory is that his work includes a large measure of substantive sociological argument. Parsons's contribution is meagre by comparison. The sad, but necessary, conclusion to be made about Parsons's sociological writings is that virtually his entire contribution stands or falls with his general theoretical framework. This is not the case for Weber. With him, it is possible to disentangle the positive substance of his sociological theories from what is negative about the meta-theoretical arguments with which he surrounds them. It is true that Weber's work currently finds favour because of what appears 'postmodern' in his conception of ideal types,[2] but it was once a commonplace of secondary interpretations that his substantive sociology was conducted in a way that could not be fully reconciled with his methodological prescriptions.[3] Indeed, this view of Weber's work has recently been promoted by Randall Collins, whose *Weberian Sociological Theory* is explicitly concerned with the reformulation and further development of a research programme using Weber's substantive sociological categories.[4]

Although I do not share Collins's confidence in the value of those categories (ultimately, Weber elaborates an unsatisfactory methodology in response to problems with his substantive categories), I do share his view that sociological theory must have this substantive and positive character. It would have been nice to conclude that there is a 'Parsonsian sociology' to be liberated from its unsatisfactory meta-theoretical glosses in the way that Collins proposes for Weber. Unfortunately, this is not the case which is the reason why – despite the inadequacies of ideal type methodology that Parsons had done so much to demonstrate – those who were concerned to develop substantive sociological theories rarely followed Parsons, but, for the most part retained a preference for Weber's approach.[5] Of course, this does not mean that Parsons's writings are without insight into empirical issues. However, for the most part, Parsons develops his theoretical categories at some distance from practical issues of explanation.

The problem of disentangling the positive from the negative is further compounded by the specific nature of what is one of Parsons's empirical strengths. I have argued that while 'contradictions' must be the focus of theoretical attention, the mere identification of a 'contradiction' is insufficient to ensure its validity. Much of the positive substance of Parsons's approach to empirical issues, is the demonstration that relationships which others have identified as contradictory do not contain the problems that have been attributed to them. This may seem to be a minor point, but it is very significant from the perspective of the current situation of sociological theory. The unsatisfactory legacy of the re-emergence of Marxist theory in the 1960s is that the description of social practices as 'contradictory' is now a routine and dulling feature of contemporary sociological argument.

There is something 'counter-intuitive' and, therefore, interesting, about the way in which Parsons 're-interprets' circumstances which others have claimed are contradictory. For example, he argues that the growth of the large-scale corporation, far from representing the concentration of economic power, as some argued, produces conditions for the dispersal of that power by a separation of ownership from the functions of control.[6] Parsons also takes issue with Weber's identification of an 'iron cage' of bureaucracy, arguing that the expansion of formal education and the growth of professional claims introduces a 'collegial' element which reduces the hierarchical aspects of formal organization.[7] Similarly, he criticizes those who argued that the professions are 'anomolous' within modern capitalist societies such that, as societies become progressively more commercialized, so the distinctive social structures of the professions will disappear.[8] In the same way, he took issue with those who saw a loss of functions of the family as indicative of a decline in its significance both socially and in the lives of individuals.[9]

This is what sociological argument should be about – claim and counter-claim, giving rise to further theoretical elaboration and research. Unfortunately, it proves all too easy for Parsons to assimilate these arguments to his general theory; that is, to a general argument about the progressive differentiation of social structures around specialized functions. Differentiation and functional specialization are argued to be integral to complex systems and their integration. At the same time, as each interchange in the complex contributes to the interdependence of the system, so there is the possibility of 'strain' at each nodal point. Very quickly, we are returned to the familiar and, as I have argued, empirically vacuous and contradictory terrain of Parsonian general theory. His 'empirical' work then, all too frequently begins well, only to degenerate into the elaboration of charts and figures expressing the 'formulae' derived from the general theory. In the end, there is something 'second-hand' about Parsons's empirical insights. For the most part, they can be found in Durkheim and found there without the unsatisfactory substance of Parsons's general theory.

This is, indeed, disappointing, because, as I observed in the first chapter of this book, Parsons had a very sharp awareness of changes in the social structures of modern societies which had effected a displacement of the categories of nineteenth-century social science and their associated 'ideologies'. In fact, he identified many of the features which later writers would associate with postmodernism and the displacement not merely of nineteenth-century conceptions of sociology, but the very possibility of sociology, itself. Clearly, Parsons's foundational, general theory has not survived the changes which he felt had brought it into being, but that does not mean, as I have argued throughout this book, that sociology as an explanatory undertaking must be given up.

EXPLANATION AND SOCIAL THEORY

In many ways, we are living the failure to bring about the very renewal of sociological theory which Parsons had felt to be necessary. Much recent debate has been given over to the examination of a new phase of modern societies, that of 'postmodernism', or 'postindustrialism'. As the concepts indicate, there is greater clarity about what the new phase is *not*, than about what it *is*. Block puts it neatly, writing that, "post-industrial society is the historical period that begins when the concept of industrial society ceases to provide an adequate account of actual social developments".[10] The same applies to the term, 'postmodern' society. The consequence, Block argues, is that our present times are a 'strange period' because, "people lack a shared understanding of the kind of society in which they live. For generations, the United States was understood as an industrial society, but that definition of reality is no longer compelling. Yet no convincing alternative has emerged in its absence."[11]

The task evidently is to produce a sociology of 'postmodernity' (or 'postindustrialism').[12] Yet, sociology cannot be so easily separated from those of its concepts which have failed. The implication is that sociology itself must be transformed in order to account for the transformation in society. What we require is a 'postmodern' sociology. But what sort of sociology is that? Most theorists of 'postmodernity' (whether committed to a 'sociology of postmodernity' or to a 'postmodern sociology') attempt to theorize *discontinuity*. In contrast, I suggest that the requirement is to theorize *continuity*. The sense that the present is a new phase of social development is, in part, a consequence of a misrepresentation of the trends of development in the previous phase. *An adequate theory of the present would, of necessity, reconstruct our understandings of the past in their relation to the present.*[13] This aim of reconstruction in sociological theory has to be set against an increasingly dominant theoretical sensibility that accepts theoretical disorder as an inevitable and realistic, existential condition of sociology. The issues are related. The acceptance of discontinuity between phases of social development, is accompanied by a representation of the present phase as 'fragmented', and, in turn, that it requires a 'fragmented' theory to represent it. Ultimately, as I have argued, the claims of postmodernism do not represent an answer to our current problems, but a capitulation in the face of them. The apparent displacement of sociology is merely our failure adequately to address our problems.

We can read Parsons's work with profit, but any lessons to be learnt are negative. If we understand why Parsons's theories take the form that they do, we can see that their problems are not peculiar to him, but are constitutive of a very common conception of sociological theory, shared by even his most vehement critics. By reading Parsons generously and sympathetically, we can come to understand how we share problems with him and, thereby, begin to revise our own thinking about sociological argument. In this way, meta-theory is a necessary adjunct of substantive sociological theorizing, but it could never be a substitute, or the direct means of developing substantive sociological theory. Moreover, as I have suggested, the current substance of meta-theoretical argument contributes to the present impasse in sociological theory because it offers no insight into how sociological theories can be reconstructed in the process of refining our explanations. The way out of our impasse will be found only by attending to our current explanatory problems.

Perhaps, there will seem to be nothing startling in this conclusion. After all, one of the first criticisms of Parsonsian general theory was that offered by Merton, who proposed that social theorists should concentrate instead on theories of the 'middle-range', an argument which has recently been reiterated by Mouzelis with regard to current attempts at general theory.[14] Merton had in mind a form of theorizing attached to specific programmes of research, a form of theorizing which, as he put it, "involves abstractions, of course, but they are close enough to observed data to be incorporated in propositions that permit empirical testing".[15] The problem with Merton's defence of substantive theory, however, is that it reproduces what it seeks to deny. For example, the very term 'middle-range' invokes practices to either extreme which are not being denied in principle. Merton merely suggests that, in the present state of the discipline, theories of the 'middle-range' are what we should anticipate as the best way of moving forward, in contrast to the *de novo* invention of a grand, overall scheme. Indeed, Merton has a positivistic view of the nature of the accumulation of social scientific knowledge and he suggests that from theories of the 'middle-range', social science might build toward the grand, inclusive scheme, though currently we are a long way off.[16] Merton's claims for 'middle-range' theory, then, are not as damaging to the idea of general theory as they might initially appear to be.

Alexander, for his part, has recently argued that Merton's proposals, and therefore any rejection of general theory in the name of substantively located undertakings, is a form of 'empiricism'.[17] While this may be a valid criticism of Merton, what I demonstrated in the previous chapter is that this could not be a criticism of substantive undertakings, *per se*. Alexander makes a false elision of 'empiricism' and 'empirical'. In fact, as I have shown, the very epistemological arguments underpinning the claims of general theory, themselves involve a form of empiricism. If Alexander, or any other proponent of meta-theory, is keen to eschew empiricism, they should address the empiricism that is intrinsic to their own claims for general theory.[18]

As Merton was aware, proposals for theories of the 'middle-range' seem unexciting and unchallenging. However, once the positivistic assumptions which underpin his arguments are discarded, the claim that social theories should be substantive takes on a different light. On a post-positivist understanding of the nature of research programmes, the address of explanatory problems, as we have seen, will be challenging and exciting. The successful solution of explanatory problems and the progressive development of social theory will involve the transformation and reconstruction of categories. Progressive social science will be creative social science. Moreover, the term 'middle-range' is inappropriate precisely because there will be no painstaking ascent toward a final adequacy, but a continued imaginative address to our problems which reconstructs what we had previously felt to be secure and necessary.

The concept of 'middle-range' theory is also unsatisfactory, precisely because it fails to identify the circumstances in which the claims of a meta-theoretical general framework arise. This failure is shared with Mouzelis's recent attempt to re-direct sociological theory toward substantive issues.[19] He argues that the major problem of contemporary theory is the reduction of social theory to philosophy. Where the classical sociologists left philosophical anthropology behind to develop a substantive sociology, Mouzelis argues, contemporary sociology shows the opposite tendency with the consequence of an ever-widening gap between theory and research. As should be apparent, I have every sympathy for Mouzelis's concerns, but there could be no simple return to earlier positions. After all, current arguments were a response to the problems of earlier positions and those problems remain, whatever the deficiencies of current arguments. What Mouzelis and Merton each fails to address is: why sociological theory took the form each so vehemently criticises. Without an answer to that question, we are likely to repeat the errors.

As I have shown, the idea of general theory is not an outside import into the practices of social inquiry. It emerges within those practices as an apparent answer to the limitations of specific explanations. Thus, the epistemological arguments which have had such a debilitating effect upon social inquiry are there at all 'levels'; there is nothing magical about substantive inquiry that means that the false claims of meta-theory will not frequently seem to be plausible. Those engaged in substantive inquiry must face the issue of the possible inadequacies of their account. What could be more seductive than the claim that those inadequacies are not specific to the particular scheme, but define the limits of what anyone could achieve? So, the unsatisfactory features of meta-theory, which I have set out, are found as frequently among those conducting empirical research as they are among 'grand theorists'.[20]

SOCIAL SCIENCE AND SOCIAL CRITICISM

The task of recovering relevance, which Seidman sets out so eloquently, is one that does currently confront sociological theory. However, it is not the case that we need to address, *either* publicly meaningful debates, *or* ground our theoretical activities in a programme of substantive research. The two are necessarily connected. It is unlikely that sociology could contribute to public debates in a positive way without something novel to say about the circumstances of those debates; that is, *without some substantive transformation of the categories of the debate*. What is so troublesome about contemporary meta-theoretical arguments is that both aspects of a possible contribution are undermined. Thus, much current meta-theoretical argument seems to deny the possibility of social explanation, claiming that a commitment to explanation is 'positivistic', or 'empiricist'. As I have shown, this claim has 'conservative' consequences because, by denying that consistency need be a criterion of adequacy, it appears that sociological theories need not be reconstructed to solve what appears inconsistent. In this way, it is guaranteed that sociological arguments cannot contribute to public debate. All that anyone could see in current sociological arguments is a mirror in which problems are 'reflected' back as intrinsic to the lives we now live.

In the process, and with all the appearance of democratic humility, social theorists argue against any 'authority' being vested in sociological insights. Although it is argued that 'lay' actors must not be derogated, as we saw in the last chapter, this is frequently accompanied by a complete derogation of the 'professional' claims of social science. Rather, 'authority' is to be vested with those we study. There are many versions of the argument, but some of the difficulties can be illustrated by reference to its radical version. In the case of radical theorists, it is argued that we must take the 'standpoint' of the 'oppressed' among those we study.

Social inquiries might be identified with all those who are 'oppressed' and 'subjugated', but how is that identification to be secured? For example, actors' own understandings may be a guide to their predicaments, but, at least in part, they will also reflect the operation of processes which are outside the immediate consciousness of actors, despite their negative consequences for them. Once this is accepted, however, the authenticity of the experiences of the 'oppressed' must be called into question, at the same time as there must be an issue of the explanatory adequacy of any 'representations' of the wider processes in which actors' understandings are being located. As I argued in the previous chapter, the identification of the 'subjective' meanings of actors could not be unproblematic.

132

In claims – radical, or otherwise – that we must accept actors' meanings, it is frequently forgotten that we have no direct, unmediated access to those meanings. The substance of those meanings is inferred from the social theorist's negotiation of actor's behaviours in their contexts. Any 'meanings' attributed to actors are inextricably bound up with the 'meanings' of theorists. Much emphasis is currently given to claiming the 'reflexivity' of action, but little attention, it seems, is given to the 'reflexivity' of the action of social theorists.

Even if we were to accept that the ultimate 'judges' of the validity of an argument must be the actors whose behaviours are being addressed, whose judgements would we need? The issue is not merely that actors may disagree with social theorists, they may disagree between themselves. For example, in identifications of the capital-labour relation as exploitative, who must accept that characterization, workers, or both workers and capitalists? After all, ideologies which extol capitalism do not do so on the basis of *affirming* exploitation, but by *denying* it. This is not a trivial issue. The difficulties are clear in Habermas's statement of conditions of authenticity. He believes that a proper answer can be arrived at by asking how members would have acted, "if they could and would have decided on organisation of social intercourse through discursive will-formation, with adequate knowledge of the limiting conditions and functional imperatives of their society".[21] Yet, what Habermas would regard as the 'false' ideology of capitalism – indeed, even seeming to regard it as 'false' against the apparent acceptance of it by the members he is addressing – itself lays claim to an adequate knowledge of the 'limiting conditions' and 'functional imperatives' of *any* system of production. However, the question of validity is broached, it seems that we are returned to the issue of finding some way of distinguishing between competing *explanatory* claims. Moreover, once again we see the paradox where the 'lay' members of a community apparently can make these decisions, where their 'professional' colleagues declare themselves unable.

The arguments I have been discussing are an unnecessary legacy of the criticisms directed at Parsons. However, as I have tried to show, his own work is implicated in the problems that beset current debates. We will not find the criteria for deciding between competing explanatory claims within a general foundational theory. The idea that there could be an agreement on fundamental categories, prior to any problems about particular cases, is deeply flawed. It does not really matter whether the foundational theory has the rather 'conservative' cast of that of Parsons, or the more radical appearance of a 'critical theory of society'. How could answers be given in advance? For example, why, *in principle*, should we be critical of society? That would seem to be to accept alienation as the necessary condition of the life of the social theorist. How could we be critical, *in principle*? Any critical judgements must be about specific social relationships and circumstances. They cannot be issues of general methodological principle, but must arise in relation to *specific* claims about the nature of particular social arrangements. Criticism, then, is consequent upon substantive sociological research and argument, not an *a priori* attitude which can inform it regardless of the substantive content of research findings. In this way, the explanatory undertakings of sociology must be at the very heart of any critical contribution it can make to public debates.

The fact that the audience for sociological argument is not unified need not undermine our undertakings. We do not need a consensus to ground our undertakings, whether they be the practices of social inquiry or wider social life. We contribute best through disagreement, among ourselves and (implicitly) between ourselves and those we study. This does not mean that we should agree to disagree. It is not the case that there are simply different points of view each of which have to be accepted. As I have tried to show, there are issues of superior adequacy, whenever there are issues of different points of view. This does not mean that we can simply assert the superiority of one view over another, or that we could decide in advance which view is superior (or even that it would be enough that one view was the superior and that that was an end to it). The point is that we need to engage with differences as a *problem of understanding and explanation*, and ultimately, as a problem common to our lives. If the critical task in sociology is to take the problematic understandings of others as something to address, then that requires us to be similarly rigorous in any address to the deficiencies of our own views. There is no criticism without self-criticism. All criticism is an occasion of a difference in views, where the superiority of the position from which criticism is being made is claimed over that which is the object of criticism. If this is so, any occasion of difference must be a situation where it is possible that it is the other view which is more adequate – or, if neither is satisfactory, that the adequate criticism of other views will require the simultaneous reformulation of one's own.

My aim in this book has been to dispel the sense of resignation that hangs over much contemporary social theory. Talcott Parsons's attempt to found a general frame of reference is merely one side of the problem. As I have shown, it soon reproduces the deficiencies that gave rise to it. Contemporary theoretical approaches merely differ over the extent to which they remain attached to the dream of at last finding the adequate general framework, or whether they are given over to the embrace of incoherence. Each response entails the displacement of explanation from the centre of social inquiry. There is an impasse in contemporary social theory, but it is not the necessary postmodern condition of any social inquiry. It is an unnecessary artifact of flawed methodological arguments deriving from unresolved explanatory problems. What I have tried to show is that these problems can be answered – or, at least, it cannot be shown in principle that they could not – but that to answer them requires us to accept that explanation is central to social inquiry as a creative undertaking.

NOTES

1. *TSofSA*, p. vii. One of the other reasons given by Parsons is the rather fanciful one

that it is an empirical study in the analysis of social thought, where, "the writings treated are as truly documents as are manorial rolls of the Middle Ages". *Ibid.*, p. vii. Certainly, if *TSofSA* is 'empirical' in this sense, it would fail to meet the standards of inquiry established by those who have researched manorial roles. For example, Parsons's 'presentism' – or neglect of the details of the historical context in which his selected authors were writing – is defensible only because he was engaged in an exercise in the development of contemporary theory. On the 'historicist controversy' and the critique of 'presentism', see the symposium (including contributions by Jones, Seidman, Warner and Turner in *Sociological Theory*, 3(1), 1985).

2. See, for example, S. Crook, J. Pakulski and M. Waters, *Postmodernization: Change in Advanced Society* (London, Sage, 1992).

3. See, for example, H.H. Gerth and C.W. Mills, 'Editor's introduction' to M. Weber, *From Max Weber* (London, Routledge and Kegan Paul, 1948); J.E.T. Eldridge, *Sociology and Industrial Life* (London, Michael Joseph, 1971); B.S. Turner, *For Weber: Essays on the Sociology of Fate* (London, Routledge and Kegan Paul, 1981).

4. See R. Collins, *Weberian Sociological Theory* (Cambridge, Cambridge University Press, 1986).

5. See, for example, T. Burger, 'Talcott Parsons, the problem of order in society, and the problem of analytical sociology', *American Journal of Sociology*, 83(3), 1977, pp. 320–34. However, as Burger is well-aware, Weber's statements of the methodology of 'ideal types' do not constitute an adequate approach. See T. Burger, *Max Weber's Theory of Concept Formation: History, Laws and Ideal Types* (Durham, North Carolina, Duke University Press, 1976).

6. See, for example, T. Parsons and N.J. Smelser, *Economy and Society* (London, Routledge and Kegan Paul, 1956).

7. See, for example, T. Parsons, 'Some considerations on the growth of the American system of higher education and research', in *Action Theory and the Human Condition* (New York, Free Press, 1978).

8. See, for example, T. Parsons, 'The professions and the social structure', in *Essays in Sociological Theory* (New York, Free Press, 1954).

9. See, for example, T. Parsons, 'The American family: its relations to personality and to the social structure', in T. Parsons and R.F. Bales, *Family, Socialization and Interaction Process* (London, Routledge and Kegan Paul, 1956).

10. F. Block, *Postindustrial Possibilities: a Critique of Economic Discourse* (Berkeley, University of California Press, 1990), p. 11.

11. *Ibid.*, p. 1.

12. See, for example, M. Featherstone, 'In pursuit of the postmodern', *Theory, Culture and Society*, 5(2), 1988, pp. 195–215; Z. Bauman, 'Sociology and postmodernity', *Sociological Review*, 36(4), 1988, pp. 790–813.

13. A 'sociology of postmodernity', then, does not necessarily imply 'business as usual', as postmodern theorists imply. See B. Smart, 'Modernity, postmodernity and the present', in B.S. Turner, *Theories of Modernity and Postmodernity* (London, Sage, 1990).

14. See R.K. Merton, 'On sociological theories of the middle range', in R.K. Merton, *Social Theory and Social Structure* (enlarged edition) (New York, Free Press, 1968); N.P. Mouzelis, *Back to Sociological Theory* (London, Macmillan, 1991). Merton, for his part, was rather circumspect concerning the extent to which it was Parsons who was the primary object of his criticism. Nevertheless, the essay was read in that way.

15. Ibid., p. 39.
16. Thus, Merton writes that, "some sociologists still write as though they expect, here and now, formulation of *the* general sociological theory broad enough to encompass the vast ranges of precisely observed details of social behaviour, organization and change and fruitful enough to direct the attention of research workers to a flow of problems for empirical research. This I take to be a premature and apocalyptic belief. We are not ready. Not enough preparatory work has been done." Ibid., p. 45. Ironically, Merton registers with approval Parsons's shift in *The Social System* toward the representation of his categories as contingently useful, rather than phenomenologically necessary, but he fails to notice the problems intrinsic to the categories which gave rise to that shift of emphasis.
17. See J.C. Alexander, 'The centrality of the classics', in A. Giddens and J.H. Turner (eds), *Social Theory Today* (Cambridge, Polity, 1987).
18. See, for example, the essays collected in G. Ritzer (ed.), *Metatheorizing* (London, Sage, 1992), where Lemert refers to those who are unpersuaded by the project of general theory as its 'cultured despisers', wedded to an outmoded view of science. See Lemert, 'Sociological metatheory and its cultured despisers', ibid.
19. See Mouzelis, *Back to Sociological Theory*.
20. After all, as thoroughgoing a scourge of fashionable fads in sociology as Goldthorpe betrays a similar flight of fancy to those of any postmodern theorist. For example, he concludes an essay on British debates on the working class with the comment that, "it is possible to view with considerable satisfaction the refusal of the British working class to become peaceably integrated into capitalist society, *or* to perpetuate organicism, *or* to make a Marxist revolution: in other words, its refusal to fit in with any of the attempts at historicist, or crypto-historicist, pattern-making that intellectuals have sought to impose upon it. For the latter, the recalcitrance of the working class is evidently the cause of much disillusion and disappointment. It is rather for those of us who would always wish to see such pattern-making discredited in practice as well as in principle that the working class appears as a resolute and effective ally." See J.H. Goldthorpe, 'Intellectuals and the working class in modern Britain', in D. Rose (ed.), *Social Stratification and Economic Change* (London, Hutchinson, 1988), p. 54. There is no claim that working-class 'recalcitrance' serves *their* interests and no argument to establish that this 'recalcitrance' is a self-conscious, 'resolute' position! Just as postmodern theorists invoke the 'narrative' of the 'end of narrative', so Goldthorpe invokes a form of 'historicism' to declare the 'end of historicism'. But what is most odd about the statement is his declaration of enmity toward 'patterns'. Just how would an empirical undertaking that denied 'patterns' be conducted?
21. See J. Habermas, *Legitimation Crisis* (London, Heinemann, 1976), p. 113.

INDEX

action
  cognitive and normative orientations, 57–8, 70, 72
  criticisms of Parsons' analyses of, 31–2, 47–8, 71–2, 113, 114
  idealist approaches to, 55
  Marxist example of, 60–1, 97–8
  Parsons' concept of 'unit act', 56–7, 62, 63, 64, 66–7
  Parsons' perceived shift to systems approach from, 31–2, 63, 80
  Parsons' theory of, 61–2
  personal and interpersonal systems of, 64–7
  phenomenological status of Parsons' frame of, 46, 48, 88
  positivist approaches to, 55, 59–60
  power in systems of, 67–70
  social and natural science explanations of, 117–19
  in sociological theory, 112–14
  systems of, 62–5, 83, 114
  value-rational and instrumentally rational, 58–9, 65
actors, competence of, 114
  and social scientific explanations of behaviour, 115–21, 132–3
Adriaansens, H.P.M., 81, 83, 84
Alexander, J.C.
  crisis and future of sociology, 18–19

criticisms of Marxism, 100, 101
  and criticisms of Parsons, 33–4, 81–2, 89–90, 98
  and general theory, 19, 47, 110, 130–1
  neo-functionalism and revival of Parsons' work, vii, 84–5, 100
  and Parsons' interchange theory, 87, 89–90
  and structural functionalism, 63–4
  and theoretical logic, 46–7, 48–9
Althusser, L., 98, 99, 101

Baudrillard, J., 22–3
Bell, D., 3, 23
Block, F., 129
Burawoy, M., 93, 101, 112

capitalism
  Marxist theory and stability of, 21, 97–9
  Marxist view of contradiction in, 96–8, 99, 101, 111, 115–16
  in Parsons' theory, 95
change
  and Marxist criticisms of Parsons' theory, 95–7
  in Parsons' theory, 94–5
classical sociology
  end of, 3–4
  reformulations of, 20–2, 39

137

and power, 68
and social action and actors, 70,
97–8, 133
Harding, S., 107
humanist approach in sociology, 7

ideal types, 44–5, 58, 118–19, 127
idealist position in sociology
analysis of human action, 55
and criticisms of Parsons, 31, 33,
89–90
Parsons' view of, 30, 35–6, 37–8, 40
perceptions of general theory, 44–5
ideological age, end of, 3–5
and postmodernism, 23
independence in Parsons' theory, 86–7,
88–90
instrumentally rational action, 58, 59, 65
integration, 47, 71, 83–4, 86, 88, 94,
95, 114
interchange theory, 81, 87–90
interdependence in Parsons' theory,
86–7, 88–90, 94, 95
interpersonal order, 64, 65–6, 67

Johnson, H.M., 83, 84

Kuhn, T.S., 17–18, 41

Lakatos, I., 42, 48, 93–4, 106
Lockwood, D., 68, 95–6, 99, 101, 115
Lyotard, J-F., 23

Marxism
and contradictory nature of
capitalism, 96–8, 99, 101, 111,
115–16
criticisms of Parsons, 95
demise of Marxist sociology, 10–11
and explanation, 112
and general theory, 97–102
interpretations of, 21, 22
parallels with Parsons' theory, 100–1
Parsons' view of Marx, 20
'phases' of, 80
scientific status of, 93–4
social action and actors, 60–1, 97–8,
119

social and system integration, 95–6
and stability of capitalism, 21, 97–9
Merton, R.K., 6, 130–1
Mouzelis, N.P., 131

natural science
explanation in, 117–19
Kuhn's theory of, 17–18
post-positivist challenges to, 41
Nisbet, R., 1–2
normative order and power, 67–70, 82–3
normative orientation of action, 57–8,
70, 72

object, and subject in sociological
analysis, 30, 31, 117–19
order see social order

Papineau, D., 119
Parsons, T.
commitment to coherence, 90, 109, 110
contradictions in theory, 61, 90, 95,
102, 109, 110
criticisms of action frame of
reference of, 47–8, 57, 68, 69,
113, 114
criticisms and misunderstandings of,
1, 40, 68, 69
criticisms of synthetic theory of,
31–4, 39
dualisms in theory, 79, 82
inadequacy of theory and
reproduction of problems, 81–2,
83–4, 85, 121
parallels with Marxism, 100–1
perceived shift from action to
systems approach, 31–2, 63, 80
reconstruction of classics, 20, 22, 39
revival and interpretation of, vii, 1,
11, 21, 80–1, 93, 109
theoretical orientation of, 126–9
views of empiricist accounts of
science, 42–4
particularism, of subjective meaning,
44–5
personal order, 64–5, 66
personality, and Parsons' levels of
analysis, 86–7

crisis in, 1–3, 7, 18
critique of positivism and rise of
humanist approach, 6–7
cycles of criticism and renewal in,
20–2
development of, 1–2, 3–4
dualisms in, 30–1, 32, 35
end of classical and emergence of
scientific, 3–4
Merton's 'middle-range' theories and
future of, 130–1
postmodernism and future of, 22–5,
129–30
as profession, 3, 4–5, 8
reflexivity in, 10, 116, 133
role in public debate, 132
and social change, 8–10
synthesis and fragmentation of,
viii–ix, 17–20, 31
structural differentiation, 94–5, 115,
128
structural-functionalism, 6, 64, 85
Structure of Social Action, The
(TSofSA), 20, 30, 31, 126
subject, and object in sociological
analysis, 30, 31, 117–19
system integration, and Marxism, 95–6
systems approach
and action approach, 31–2, 84–5
of Marxism, 97
Parsons' consideration of deviance,
114–15
Parsons' fourfold divisions of
subsystems, 81–2, 87–9
Parsons' perceived shift from action
to, 31–2, 63, 80
Parsons' total action system, 66–7,
86–7, 88
see also action

theoretical systems
adequacy of, 110–11
development and contradiction in,
106–8
explanatory problems in social and
natural science and adequacy of,
117–19
Parsons' positive and
negative/residual categories of,
36–40, 44, 46, 71–2, 84, 109–10
Parsons' views of empirical inquiry
and, 43–4
'phases' in breakdown of, 79–85
social scientific explanations of
behaviour and adequacy of,
115–21
see also general theory; Parsons
total action system, 66–7, 86–7, 88
TSofSA see Structure of Social Action,
The
Turner, B.S., vii, 101, 109
Turner, J., 8
Turner, S.P., 2

'unit act', 56–7, 62, 63, 64, 66–7

value-rational action, 58, 59, 65

Wardell, M.L., 2
Weber, M.
and general theory, 24
and ideal types, 44–5, 58, 118, 127
interpretations of, 21–2, 127
and subjective meaning, 44–5, 66
and theory of action, 58–9, 63, 65
welfare state, 10
Whitehead, A.N., 7

Zeitlin, I.M., 19